The Pocket Guide to Victorian Artists and Their Models

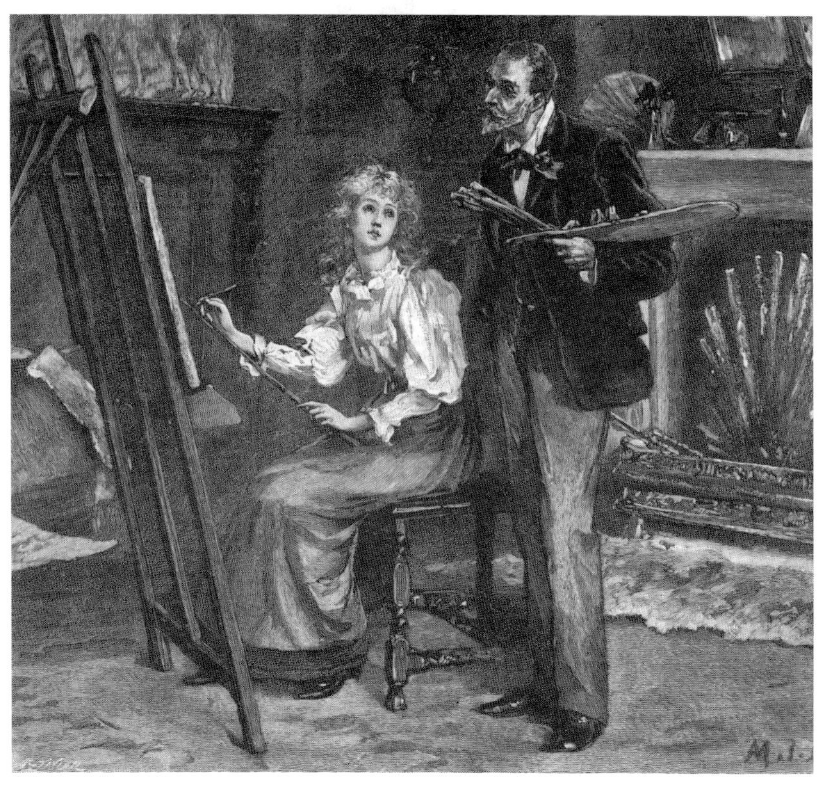

The ideal student, from a male point of view

The Pocket Guide to Victorian Artists and Their Models

Russell James

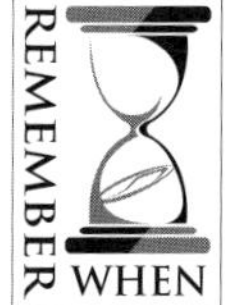

First published in Great Britain in 2011 by
REMEMBER WHEN
An imprint of
Pen & Sword Books Ltd
47 Church Street
Barnsley
South Yorkshire
S70 2AS

ISBN 978 1 84468 095 5

A CIP catalogue record for this book is available from the British Library.

Typeset by Phoenix Typesetting, Auldgirth, Dumfriesshire
Printed and bound by CPI UK

Pen & Sword Books Ltd incorporates the imprints of Pen & Sword Aviation, Pen & Sword Maritime, Pen & Sword Military, Wharncliffe Local History, Pen & Sword Select, Pen & Sword Military Classics, Leo Cooper, Remember When, Seaforth Publishing and Frontline Publishing.

For a complete list of Pen & Sword titles please contact
PEN & SWORD BOOKS LIMITED
47 Church Street, Barnsley, South Yorkshire, S70 2AS, England
E-mail: enquiries@pen-and-sword.co.uk
Website: www.pen-and-sword.co.uk

Contents

Introduction

Long before Victoria died the nation's top artists, like modern pop stars, were fabulously rich, lived in mansions, and surrounded themselves with luxury. They were household names. Outside the top bracket, artists struggled or starved; some drank themselves to death, some overdosed on drugs, others died lonely and disillusioned. The pop world again. Some had tangled love affairs, a few of which were played out and lapped up by the public. And most artists, for all their dilettante lifestyle, worked far harder at their craft than they let on; many were more commercial than they let on; they had managers, agents, supporters and promoters, and they displayed their talents in prestigious venues. They were in the entertainment business.

In this guide we look at some 400 artists, from the famous to the long forgotten, from the classical to the advanced – and we look as much at the artists' lives as at their canvases. Who were they? How did they live? Why do so many of us today warm to nineteenth-century art, liking it more than we like art from any other century, including our own? Is it just nostalgia or is it that the pictures Victorians produced were, to put it simply, very, very good?

Art books tend to ignore artists' models, despite their being close, often intimately close, to the artists who painted them. But in this book models are brought into the light and have a chapter to themselves. They and all the artists, famous and obscure, are listed in the index, though in the book I have arranged artists by the type of work they produced. Many – indeed, most artists – cannot be classified into one single category; artists experiment, they change. Though most, at some time, painted portraits, I have put into the Portraits section only those best known for portraiture. Similarly with the other sections. Was Landseer a Landscape or an Animal Life painter? Though Holman Hunt was a Pre-Raphaelite, shouldn't he be seen also under Religion and Foreign Climes? Several artists I've called Fairy Painters might be surprised, even disappointed, to see themselves listed in that chapter; wasn't Fairy painting an incidental part of their art? Not, I suggest, if it is for Fairy painting that they are best known today.

Though every one is in the index, I hope you'll turn to certain chapters first: the chapters that interest you, and where you'll discover, perhaps, that if you like the works of Alma-Tadema, you might want to look for Ernest Normand. And have you met Normand's wife?

Chapter One

THE PRE-RAPHAELITES
Back to the Future

Stephen Spender, in his article 'The Pre-Raphaelite Painters' (1945), called Pre-Raphaelitism 'the greatest artistic movement in England during the 19th century'. Few can disagree that, in Britain at least, it was the most influential. How did it begin, and what did it achieve?

In the late 1840s, at London's Royal Academy Schools, the brightest star – he'd entered as a child prodigy – was John Everett Millais, the youngest ever student and one from whom much was anticipated. Millais had befriended a fellow student, Holman Hunt, as had another student, Gabriel Rossetti. Less conscientious and already a rebel to the Academy, Rossetti had quit to become an awkward pupil to the slightly older (and equally rebellious) Ford Madox Brown. Hunt and Millais were already bosom friends when, in August 1848, Rossetti met with them in Millais's comfortable Gower Street house (where he lived with his parents) and, while looking at a book of engraved early Italian frescoes, the three young men talked up the idea of an art student rebellion, in which they would reject the stuffy dictates of the Academy but, rather than carve a new niche as students like to do, they would rediscover the sharp and sincere simplicity of medieval painting before what they saw as its corruption through the stultifying polish of Raphael. They would emulate early masters; they would throw out contemporary rules and conventions and, instead of producing 'studio' pictures applauded by the Academy, would work directly from nature to reveal truth.

Rossetti, ever impulsive, invited what can only be called a motley band to join them: a budding sculptor, Thomas Woolner; an art student, James Collinson; one of Hunt's students, F G Stephens; and Rossetti's brother William – who had never made any great claim to be an artist. The group drafted a Pre-Raphaelite manifesto (which in retrospect seems remarkably tame):

1. *To have genuine ideas to express*
2. *To study Nature attentively, so as to know how to express them*
3. *To sympathise with what is direct and serious and heartfelt in*

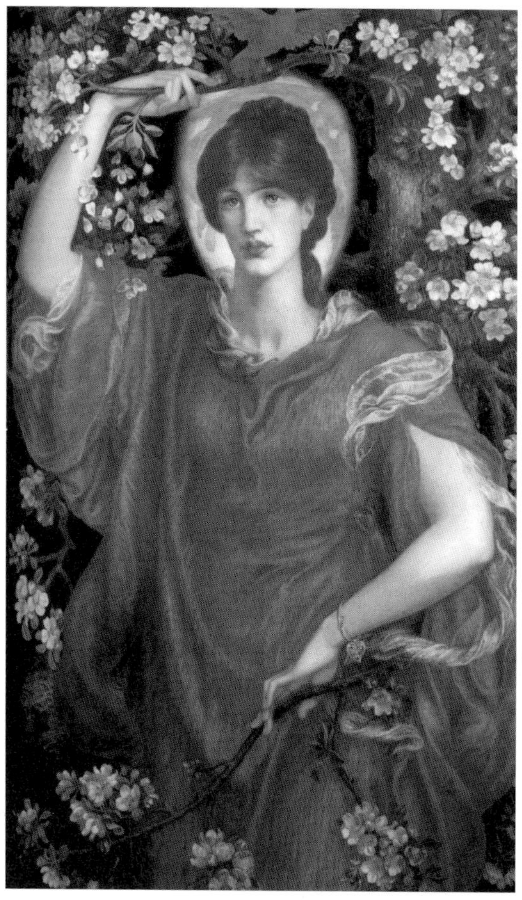

Laus Veneris by Burne-Jones (1873–8)

previous art, to the exclusion of what is conventional and self-parading and learned by rote

4. *And most indispensable of all, to produce thoroughly good pictures and statues.*

They would declare their intentions at the following year's RA Exhibition, they decided, with works to astound the world. So far, so very student rebellion. Not for them still-lifes or unpopulated landscapes. For the 1849 Exhibition Millais prepared *Isabella*, a scene from Keats, Rossetti *The Girlhood of Mary Virgin* and Hunt a scene from a Bulwer-Lytton novel

(*Rienzi*, in which Rossetti and Millais were his models). Each painting would bear the initials PRB (Pre-Raphaelite Brotherhood). Rossetti, true to form, pulled out, and displayed his picture instead at the Free Exhibition in a minor gallery in Hyde Park. But the world was not astounded. Though the pictures were decently received, they created no sensation. No one noticed the meaningful initials.

The following year the still-unknown Brotherhood launched a putative student magazine, *The Germ*, which limped through four editions before closing with unpaid bills. Rossetti (a lifetime avoider of exhibitions) chose the Free again, while the others chose the Royal Academy. Rossetti, true to form again, spiced things up a second time by letting slip what the letters PRB stood for. And it was that which brought sensation.

It's hard for us today to see why those three letters should cause offence. Why did the students call themselves a Brotherhood, people asked? Did they presume to challenge Raphael, the greatest painter of all time? What lay behind those gaudy paintings with Romanish imagery; were they Catholic propaganda, mounting a challenge to the Church? (The British Church was at the time fiercely split on issues of dogma: High Church, Low Church, the 39 Articles, Tractarianism, Newman, Pusey and the Catholic threat were all contentious issues.) The Press rose up, and the young men's paintings were duly vilified. Today's critics are milksops compared to the usually anonymous critics of that time.

Collinson's entry, *The Renunciation of Queen Elizabeth of Hungary*, was harmless, but Hunt submitted a flagrantly Pre-Raphaelite painting, *A Converted British Family Sheltering a Christian Priest from the Persecution of the Druids*. (They liked long titles.) Millais entered three paintings: a portrait, a Shakespearian if Pre-Raphaelite *Ferdinand and Ariel*, and the one that would create the biggest brouhaha, *Christ in the House of His Parents*. This 'sacrilegious' and 'offensive' painting whipped up a critical storm. To be fair to the critics, it was unlike any 'Bible picture' seen before, but their criticism extended to each of the Pre-Raphaelite artists, in part because they were new, in part because they'd dared establish a 'secret sect'.

The Brotherhood was shaken. Rossetti, under fire for having caused or provoked the storm, vowed to shun further public exhibition. Collinson resigned from the PRB. Woolner lay low. Millais was badly shaken, and had to be persuaded to stay in the group. But the volatile Hunt took umbrage and railed against the old men of the Academy – a loathing he never lost: even at the height of his fame he never joined. He now became leader of the Pre-Raphaelites. Never one to flinch from a fight, he encouraged Millais to fight on – and Millais, the one Brother from a well-off family, stood by his impoverished friend, finding him money and small commissions. Among the Brotherhood, Millais was the only one with any kind of reputation, a reputation based on his pre-Pre-Raphaelite years.

At the next year's RA Exhibition (1851) Millais showed another three paintings: *The Return of the Dove*, *The Woodman's Daughter* and *Mariana*. Hunt chose a different literary scene, *Valentine Rescuing Sylvia* (from Shakespeare's *Two Gentlemen of Verona*). And the press tore into them again. *The Times* set the tone, berating 'that strange disorder of the mind or the eyes which continues to rage with unabated absurdity among a class of juvenile artists who style themselves PRB'. It was shrewd enough

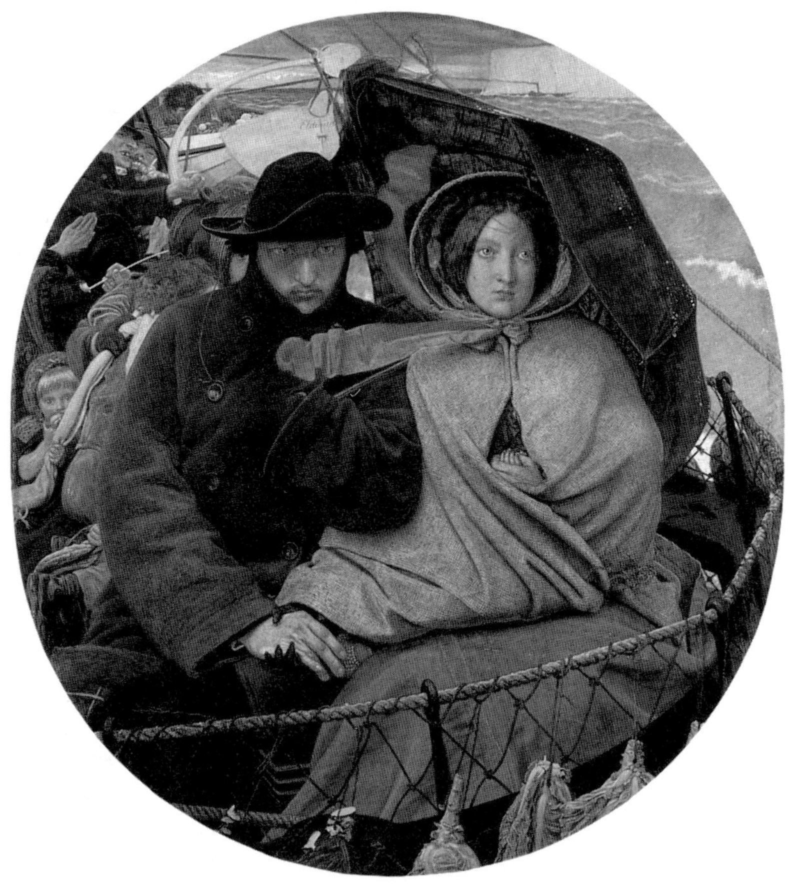

The Last of England by Ford Madox Brown

to rope two non-members into what it called the 'Pre-Raphael-brethren': the artists Charles Collins, who had entered *Convent Thoughts*, and Ford Madox Brown, who had entered a painting he'd worked on for several years, the shortened title for which was *Chaucer Reading the Legend of Custance*.

This time Millais began the fight-back. He was the one best placed to do so; already acknowledged as an up-and-coming artist and young man to watch, Millais had influence. He spoke to his friend Coventry Patmore, a respected poet who held a post of some importance at the British Museum. Patmore knew John Ruskin who, in his early thirties, was the leading critic of the day; his *Modern Painters* had been an unqualified success, and 1851 saw the publication of his blockbusting *Stones of Venice*. For Ruskin to write against the tide, as he did, in *defence* of the Pre-Raphaelites was as unexpected as if Brian Sewell had praised the early works of Damien Hirst. Fellow critics withdrew their daggers and, by August, Hunt's *Sylvia* had been judged Best In Show at the Liverpool Academy. Millais became the youngest man ever elected an Associate of the Royal Academy. Their pictures began to sell.

In the following year's RA Exhibition Hunt and Millais were adjudged its stars. Even Rossetti, who still would not show his work there, was taken up by Ruskin. Rossetti's brother and F G Stephens switched from practising art to become critics. Woolner emigrated to Australia. It seemed the end of his career, but it was his departure that inspired Madox Brown's *The Last of England*. Woolner failed as an emigrant and returned to England a few years later – to find success.

Life around them carried on. In 1854 Britain embarked on the disastrous Crimean War but, at the RA Exhibition where the war was largely ignored and where the climate was more welcoming to the Pre-Raphaelites, Millais exhibited nothing, presumably because he'd become embroiled in a painful marital tangle between himself and Mr and Mrs Ruskin. Stephens had his second and final exhibition (a painting of his mother) and Collinson showed his *Thoughts of Bethlehem*. But it was Hunt who created headlines: he was applauded for his religious picture, *The Light of the World*, destined, as no one yet realised, to become the most reproduced painting of the century. Yet at the same time he provoked controversy and a deal of genuine bemusement with his other work, *The Awakened Conscience*. Critics were divided: it was '. . . very great . . . perfectly represented', exclaimed the *Literary Gazette*; 'absolutely disagreeable', grumbled the *Morning Chronicle*, and 'repulsive', concurred the *Athenaeum*. Again Ruskin came to its defence. He explained what *The Awakened Conscience* was about: of all the paintings in the exhibition, he said, 'there will not be found one powerful as this to meet full in the front the moral evil of the age in which it is painted'. Debate continued. Hunt, seeing the success of his 'religious picture', determined that to meet 'full in the front' the Pre-Raphaelite ideals of authenticity and truth, he should take himself off to the Holy Land to paint more Bible pictures.

In 1855 and 56, while Hunt laboured abroad and Rossetti followed his own path, it was left to Millais to keep the Pre-Raphaelite flag aloft. His *The Rescue* was the hit of 1855, and at the 1856 Exhibition he showed a portrait and four major paintings: *The Random Shot* (concerning the French Revolution rather than the all too recent and painful Crimea); *Peace Concluded* (which although it *was* about the Crimea introduced the more sentimental approach he'd apply to future paintings); *The Blind Girl* (which, if even more tear-jerkingly sentimental, is so well painted as to remain one of his best works); and *Autumn Leaves* (a beautifully melancholy study of passing time, though with looser paint and unmistakeable signs of post-Pre-Raphaelitism). Now married to the spendthrift Effie, Millais was more concerned at the price his pictures would fetch than with their critical reception: 'I have already two thousand [guineas] certain in the pictures, and with every hope to make up another in the copyrights and other things,' he wrote to his wife – and that switch of attention from the critical to the financial shaped the rest of his career.

What, then, was the future for Pre-Raphaelitism? Of its three young founding fathers, Millais was drifting away, Rossetti talked the talk but never really belonged, and Hunt took longer and longer to produce his sporadic paintings. It was time for a second wave of enthusiastic practitioners to beat upon the shore.

1857 saw an exhibition billed as the First Ever Pre-Raphaelite Exhibition. It was organised by Madox Brown in a private house in Fitzroy Square and, as well as Brown himself and the Big Three (Rossetti, Millais and Hunt), the show mustered some twenty-two artists including John Brett, Charles Collins, Arthur Hughes, Robert Martineau, William Bell Scott, Thomas Seddon, Lizzie Siddal and W L Windus. And what pictures! Among others on the walls could be seen Ford's *The Last of England*; four from Rossetti: *Dante Drawing an Angel in Memory of Beatrice, Dante's Dream, Mary Magdalen at the Door of Simon* and a watercolour of *The Annunciation*; four pictures from Millais, three from Hunt, and six little pictures from Lizzie Siddal. Sales were modest, reviews were few – and most critics slated one of the four from Millais, his undoubtedly imperfect *Sir Isumbras at the Ford* in which, for once, he composed badly, making the horse ludicrously large and the picture generally out of true.

Critics sneered, delighted to find something they could pick upon.

Frederick Sandys, a relatively unknown artist at the time, parodied it in a famous cartoon, punningly entitled *A Nightmare*, depicting a weary carthorse carrying Millais, Hunt and Ruskin. It was ironic that Sandys made Ruskin share the nag with Millais: though Millais had stolen Ruskin's wife the critic had, till now, resisted the temptation to hit back. He'd been scrupulously fair to Millais in reviews, but now even he joined the attack upon the painting, highlighted the many 'errors and shortcomings in the work . . . too many to bear numbering'. To Ruskin, the painting was 'not merely Fall – it is Catastrophe'. It could be a turning point, warned Ruskin, in the artist's career. They were prophetic words for, in the opinion of most critics, then and since, 1857 saw the end of Millais as a practising Pre-Raphaelite, and his rebirth as a skilful but less careful commercial painter. It was this new Millais, unfettered by the principles of Pre-Raphaelitism, who would look to the market, see what it wanted, and meet the need.

He never lost his superb facility; while the subjects of his later paintings dulled or at times strayed into easy sentiment, the paintings themselves continued to be brilliantly executed. A married man wed to a spendthrift wife, Millais stepped away from the world of student idealism and high-flown principle into domains all too eager to embrace him: he became a hugely successful commercial artist and a paid-up member of the Academy.

But if the original Brotherhood had broken up, they were by now not the only Pre-Raphaelites. From the 1850s on an increasing number of progressive young artists joined the rebellion against the guidelines and strictures of the old Academy, to follow their own interpretation of Pre-Raphaelitism: truth to nature, meticulous detail, bright colours and *no chiaroscuro!* Who were these progressive new artists? One of the most important, Ford Madox Brown, was older than the lads who'd set up the brotherhood; he was looked up to by them and, for a few months, had Rossetti as his student. Brown was an independent-minded and, till late in life, commercially unsuccessful man, yet his brilliantly realised paintings were, and would remain, more Pre-Raphaelite than many of those produced by the original Brotherhood.

Early followers included Brett, Deverell, Hughes, Martineau, Sandys, Wallis and Windus, and a so-called 'Oxford Movement' emerged in the next decade based around Morris and Burne-Jones. Later still came followers – some more Pre-Raphaelite than the group's originators – including artists such as Crane, Dicksee, Holiday and, above all, J M Waterhouse. Let us look at these in more detail:

Henry Alexander BOWLER (1824–1903):

Bowler comes into the fringes of the Pre-Raphaelite artists – and indeed into any study of Victorian art – on the strength of one painting, *The Doubt: 'Can These Dry Bones Live?'* (now in the Tate). He spent most of his life in education, becoming headmaster of Stourbridge School in 1851 and moving through a number of positions until settling in the Science and Art Department of South Kensington Museum.

George Price BOYCE (1826–97):

Close associate and friend of the original Pre-Raphaelites (and, it is said, an even closer friend of their models!), Boyce trained as an architect, took landscape lessons from David Cox, and dallied with Pre-Raphaelitism when he became friends with Rossetti around 1849. (He commissioned *Bocca Baciata* in 1859 and took over Rossetti's Blackfriars studio in 1862.) Popular within the Brotherhood, he was later a close friend of Whistler and shared his interest in river effects. The son of a successful wine merchant, he was able to buy some works from his friends, and he appears in some of their pictures. He became an associate of the Old Water Colour Society in 1864 and a member in 1877, after which his paintings were largely watercolour landscapes. A handsome man, never short of funds, he had Philip Webb build him a house in Chelsea in 1869. He married in 1875.

John BRETT (1831–1902):

Born in Reigate, Brett was taught drawing by Richard Redgrave and became a student at the RA Schools but, after being introduced to Hunt at the home of Coventry Patmore, he took to the realism of the Pre-Raphaelites, and it was a painting in their style, *The Stonebreaker* (1858) that brought him to the attention of John Ruskin. 'It is a marvellous picture,' Ruskin wrote, 'and may be examined inch by inch with delight.' When Brett visited Italy and produced a finely detailed if, in Ruskin's words, 'wholly emotionless' *Val d'Aosta* (1859) Ruskin gave it several pages of coverage in his influential 'Academy Notes' and encouraged Brett to concentrate on the highly detailed, closely observed geological studies that Ruskin painted himself and admired in others. But Ruskin's stones would break John Brett. Ruskin favoured inland subjects, but Brett concentrated on coastal studies, sometimes off the west coast of Scotland but mainly in the English Channel and, in observance of the master, he dutifully produced scores of detailed but relatively dead studies. In the opinion of many, Ruskin had guided Brett into sterile waters in which his genius was drowned. Brett might respond by pointing out that he showed

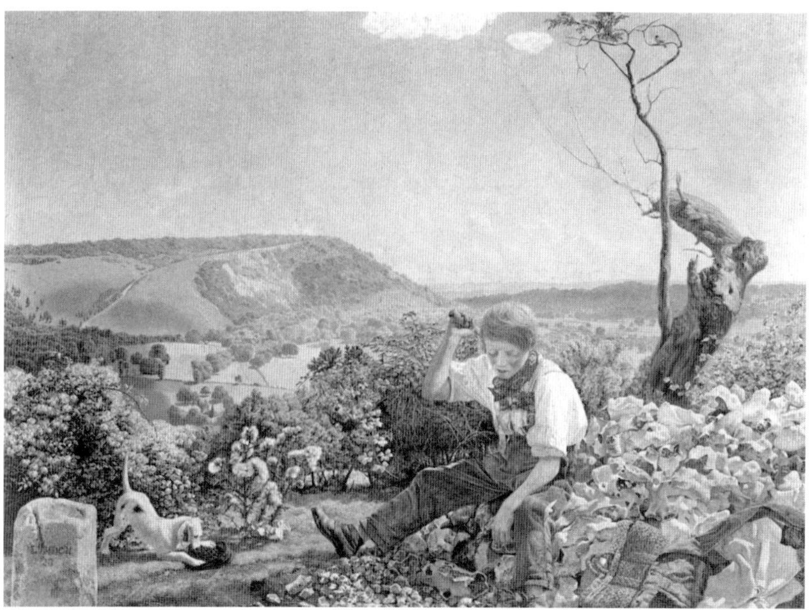

The Stonebreaker by John Brett (1857–8)

at every RA Exhibition from 1856 to 1901 (except 1863). Perhaps Brett stifled his imagination by relying on photographs taken on his trips. (Of *Val d'Aosta* Millais said the painting was 'a wretched work like a photograph of some place in Switzerland'. Some felt his own landscapes were not much better.) In middle age, the heavily-bearded Brett could have been mistaken at a glance for William Morris.

Ford Madox BROWN (1821–93):

A major artist whose reputation continues to increase, his career went through three phases. Born in Calais, brought up and trained in Belgium, his early works (generally landscape) showed continental romantic influences. He married his cousin in 1840, moved to London in 1844 and moved again to Rome in 1845 because of her failing health. She died there in 1846. His time in Europe exposed him to new trends in art, significant among which was the realistic fresco style of the German Nazarenes – the same movement which influenced the putative Pre-Raphaelites (more than it ever influenced *him*).

On his return to London his paintings, showing traces of new continental realism, led to his being one of the few contemporaries looked up to by the Brotherhood. Brown taught Rossetti privately for a few months and, although never officially of their number, was their match in the 1850s. A painting from that time, *The Last of England* (1852–5), now comes near the top in any poll of the nation's favourites. Inspired by the emigration to Australia of fellow artist Thomas Woolner (who had despaired of finding any success in his native country, but who would return a few years later) this iconic work shows Brown's second wife Emma as the young mother looking for the last time at her home shore, while his daughter Lucy is the doll-like poppet peeping out from behind a scarf. Emma had been Brown's model before he married her, while Lucy, child of his first marriage, would years later marry Rossetti's brother William. In another of Brown's paintings from that period, *Work* (1855), the heavily populated street scene is watched by the real-life literary lions, Thomas Carlyle and F D Maurice. (This six and a half foot wide picture took him twelve years to complete.)

The 1850s marked the pinnacle of Brown's career, if there ever was a pinnacle to his relatively unrewarded career. His quiet but revolutionary *An English Autumn Afternoon* was painted between 1852 and '54. It is

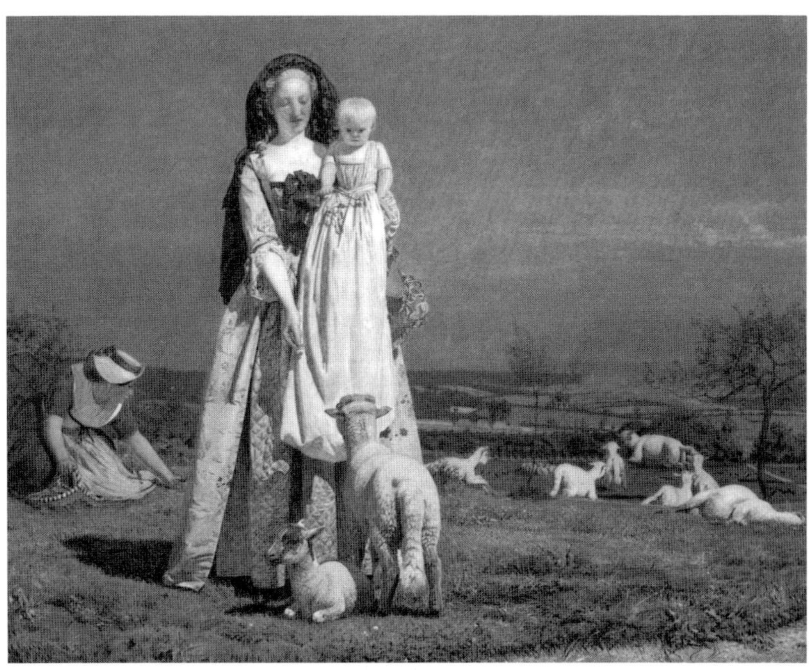

The Pretty Baa-Lambs by Ford Madox Brown

revolutionary not from its flattened oval framing and non-classical composition but from what was till then unlikely subject matter: an everyday view from the artist's rear window in Hampstead, a view that would be dismissed by Ruskin as being of insufficient interest to be recorded. (This is one of Ruskin's more spectacular misjudgements.) Like the Pre-Raphaelites themselves, Brown favoured working outdoors, *en pleine air* as the Impressionists would urge a little later, and in meticulous detail. He made several delightful studies around Hampstead, as well as the striking, if jarringly named *Pretty Baa-Lambs*.

Unlike other Pre-Raphaelites he struggled throughout his life to earn his living, and in later decades (roughly dating from the death of his 14-year-old son Oliver in 1874) he moved into his third phase, a more old-fashioned romantic style where he applied himself to historical and literary themes. These works are of little interest now and detract from his earlier work, though the murals he made in Manchester Town Hall, still on view there, retain their impact. But to see Brown at his best one has only to visit the City Art Gallery and Museum in Birmingham. Keener hunters may like to search for the more-than-competent works of his daughter Lucy (1843–94).

Edward Coley BURNE-JONES (1833–98):

It was not immediately obvious in the mid-1850s, when the pale, tall, lanky youth Ned Jones wandered onto the scene in the wake of the Pre-Raphaelites, that he would become one of the best-known artists of the century – and a largely self-taught one; he had no formal art training. He was, in 1856, an undergraduate at Oxford (along with William Morris) and in that year he met Rossetti. The Brotherhood itself had broken up, each artist going his own slightly different way, and Burne-Jones was happy to glide with Rossetti towards a dreamier, mythographic style of painting. On a more practical level, he became a director of and made numerous designs for William Morris's new design company, Morris, Marshall, Faulkner & Company (Rossetti and Madox Brown were fellow directors) where he was able to fuse Rossetti's romantic dreams and his own love of myth into the practical requirements of the Morris company. For these designs and for his stained glass work Jones leant towards religious allegory, Malory's *Le Morte d'Arthur* and other mainly Northern European myths. Examples of his stained glass can be found in churches throughout the country.

In the early 1860s Ned Jones (married to Georgiana after a four-year engagement) had become Edward Coley Burne-Jones: Coley was his mother's maiden name and Burne his aunt's married name. The hyphen was an affectation. He formed useful friendships with Frederic Leighton, Watts and Ruskin, with whom he and Georgiana visited Italy in 1862. In 1867, as an established if somewhat controversial artist, he and his wife took a house in West Kensington: The Grange – an old, dark red house, standing back from the road behind a wall and iron gate. The house, decrepit when they bought it (a ceiling collapsed within hours of their house-warming), was dark inside as well. In the tinted gloom were paintings and painted furniture created not only by Burne-Jones himself but by Rossetti and William Morris. In the garden was a mulberry tree, and at the end of the garden was his enormous studio, its walls hung with the gigantic pictures he worked on in later years. Some canvases he'd work on for years, working a while, putting it aside, coming back, leaving it – and some, of course, never were completed.

The influence of contemporary French art on his work is sometimes overlooked, but the aesthetic tendency – in literature, perhaps, more than the graphic arts – was established in France earlier than in Britain (their motto *Art pour L'Art* preceded Pater's 'Art for art's sake'; Baudelaire's *Les Fleurs du Mal* was published in 1857, decades before such works

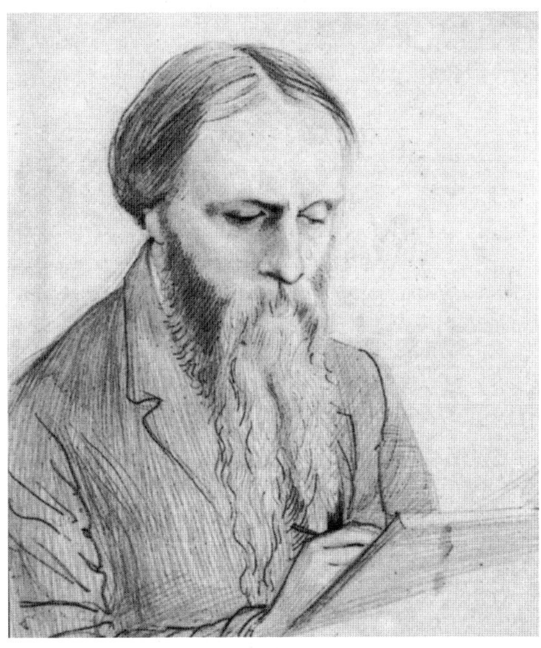

A sketch of Burne-Jones by his patron, George Howard

appeared in London). For the aesthetes, art and beauty counted more than science and morality, and Burne-Jones was an apostle in the 1870s: a picture should be 'a beautiful romantic dream of something that never was, never will be – in a light better than any light that ever shone – in a land no one can define or remember, only desire'. He peopled his paintings and his stained glass work with tall ethereal maidens against limpid backgrounds – the women beautiful, yet often lifeless, paper-thin and etiolated, without the luscious sexuality of Rossetti. His maidens, even when nude (as they often were) melted discretely into an overall design. A Burne-Jones heroine never lived, nor never will live, while Rossetti's shimmered from robust dreams.

Burne-Jones produced far more work than Rossetti (many painters did) and, although Rossetti saw himself, wrongly, as the leading light of the Pre-Raphaelites, it was Burne-Jones who had the greater influence, both as the century wore on and into the twentieth century. Burne-Jones led artists beyond naturalism and Victorian photo-realism into his own realm of symbolic aestheticism. He was, indeed, a leader of the Aesthetic Movement. For the Symbolists his allure was even greater in Europe than here; his work was lauded by late nineteenth-century French symbolists and twentieth-century giants of modernism such as Kandinsky and Picasso.

The Burne-Jones of those later years was a tall, thin, almost spectral figure – but why not let Graham Robertson, who knew him well, describe him to you?

> *His face with its great width across the eyes and brows, tapering oddly towards the chin, was strangely like his own pictorial type; its intense pallor gave it a luminous appearance added to by his large grey-blue eyes and silvered hair; his long coat and high waistcoat produced an impression indefinitely clerical; he wore a dark blue shirt and a blue tie drawn through a ring in which was set a pale blue jewel.*
>
> *He might have been a priest newly stepped down from the altar, the thunder of great litanies still in his ears, a mystic with spirit but half recalled from the threshold of another and a fairer world; but as one gazed in reverence the hieratic calm of the face would be broken by a smile so mischievous, so quaintly malign, as to unfrock the priest at once and transform the mage into the conjurer at a children's party. The change was almost startling; it was like meeting the impish eyes of Puck beneath the cowl of a monk . . .*
>
> *He saw colour with the eye of a jeweller; certain spaces in his design were to be filled up with various hues so as to make up a*

beautiful pattern; he coloured his drawing as a child will colour a black and white outline, and for his particular form of decorative art no method could have been better . . . In water colour he would take no advantage of its transparency, but load on body colour and paint thickly in gouache; when he turned to oil he would shun the richness of impasto, drawing thin glazes of colour over careful drawings in raw umber heightened with white; if he used pastel, it was to imitate oil; when he designed stained glass he did so in black and white cartoons without hint of colour and – most surprising of all – with no indication of the leading; when he drew for the woodcuts of William Morris, decorations in strong line, thick and black, he would do so in palest softest pencil, the drawing most delicate, the line shadowy and hesitating . . .

But as a master of line he was always unequalled; to draw was his natural mode of expression – line flowed from him almost without volition. If he were merely playing with a pencil, the result was never a scribble, but a thing of beauty however slight, a perfect design.

Within his lifetime Burne-Jones was extremely successful and, as his reputation grew, increasingly imperious, often dilatory, in completing his commissions. Constantine Ionides commissioned him to paint *The Mill*, a work that took the artist over ten years to finish. When he painted *The Three Graces* he portrayed Constantine's sister Aglaia (Mrs Coronio), Marie Spartali and – famously – Maria Zambaco.

For a man who looked a saint or, as Robertson put it, 'a priest newly stepped down from the altar', and whose works were noted for their beautiful but sexless maidens, Burne-Jones was less than saintly in his relations with women. He fell hopelessly in love with the beautiful, tumultuous Mrs Zambaco, and she with him. Impossible to hide, their affair became the talk of their friends. His wife tried at first to ignore it, then later to excuse it – an approach which astounded her friend Rosalind Howard, who noted in her diary in 1869, 'She still won't admit that Mm Z was deceitful. As for E.B.J. she says he takes all the blame on himself & says Mm Z is innocence & truthfulness itself.' The affair lasted for several years and when Jones ended it Maria Zambaco fought back with all the passion of a Greek beauty scorned. It was around this time, ironically, that William Morris fell in love with Mrs Burne-Jones.

The Mill was by no means the only work that took Burne-Jones years to finish. His series of twelve paintings based on the story of Cupid and Psyche (inspired by William Morris's long ballad *Earthly Paradise* and intended as a tapestry frieze) was begun in 1869, but by 1878 only four

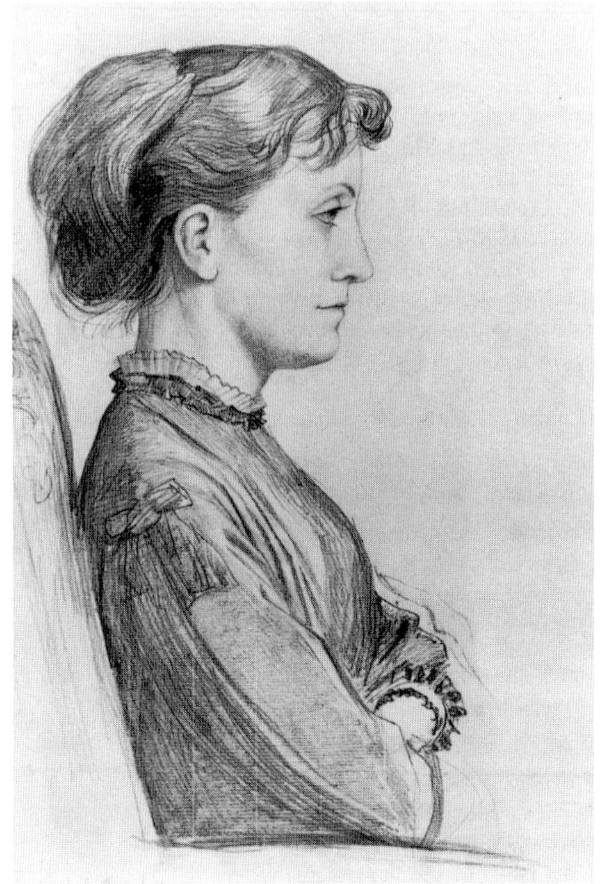

Georgiana Burne-Jones, drawn by George Howard

of the twelve canvases had been completed. (He'd been canny enough to have his patrons Rosalind and George Howard buy the bare canvases for him first.) When the Howards finally protested, Burne-Jones called on the younger artist Walter Crane to help. But the partnership did not go well, both artists criticising the other's contributions. Burne-Jones told Howard that Crane didn't understand the paints he was using, and pointed out that some of his work could be rubbed off with a duster.

Secure in his reputation, comfortably housed in The Grange, cosseted by his long-suffering wife Georgiana, Burne-Jones floated serenely above the earthly world. A famous portrait of him at that time, when he was in the midst of painting his vast *Golden Stairs*, shows him tall and lean as one of his own creations, wispy of beard and Arcadian of gaze, descending an enormous stepladder as if from clouds above. W Graham Robertson has a splendid anecdote about him then, telling of the time his new man-servant came in to announce the arrival of a new model:

> 'Please, sir, your Aunt Nelly.'
> 'My Aunt Nelly?'
> 'Yes, sir.'
> 'But – I haven't got an Aunt Nelly.'
> 'No, sir? Gave that name, sir.'
> 'But – what have you done with her? Where is she?'
> 'Ran straight up to the studio, sir.'

The artist bounded upstairs, opened the door and disclosed not Aunt Nelly but a male model, who introduced himself with a heavily accented 'Antonelli'. Burne-Jones hesitated. 'Buon giorno,' cried the model – to which the artist replied, 'Quite right. Burne-Jones – that's the name.'

William Shakespeare BURTON (1824–1916):

A splendidly-named follower of the Pre-Raphaelites, best known for his *Wounded Cavalier* (1856) which *The Athenaeum* (never the best judge of modern art) called 'the most remarkable picture in this year's Exhibition'. He'd won their gold medal in 1851 for *Delilah Begging the Forgiveness of Samson in Captivity*. Though his career continued throughout the century he was plagued with breakdowns in health and never lived up to that early promise.

Charles Allston COLLINS (1828–73):

A lesser member of the Pre-Raphaelite Brotherhood, but an 'official' one as, although not one of the original seven, he exhibited with them at the notorious Academy exhibition of 1851. He submitted for the final time in 1855 and turned to literature – an unsurprising choice, given that his older brother was Wilkie Collins and that he, Charles, married Dickens's daughter Kate in 1860. (Earlier that decade he had proposed to but been rejected by Christina Rossetti.) His *Convent Thoughts* now seems less of a piece with the others than it did then. And he only wrote two novels.

James COLLINSON (1825–81):

Unlike the similarly-named Charles Collins, Collinson was a legitimate member of the original Pre-Raphaelite Brotherhood. Like Collins, he proposed to Christina Rossetti. She rejected them both. Brought into the Brotherhood by Rossetti (though, as a devout Catholic, he resigned from it on religious grounds in 1850) Collinson managed to plough his own furrow, tending towards carefully executed indoor scenes which he kept free of the symbolic overlays beloved of fellow members. Manchester Art Gallery has his best known *Answering the Emigrant's Letter* and the less known but fine *A Son of the Soil*. He was renowned also for falling asleep at the drop of a paintbrush.

Walter CRANE (1845–1915):

As a follower of Burne-Jones he could, at a pinch, be classed among the Pre-Raphaelites, but I have placed him among the Illustrators.

Walter Howell DEVERELL (1827–54):

A friend of Rossetti's and reputed to have 'discovered' Lizzie Siddal working in a hat shop (though this is disputed), Deverell hung around with the Pre-Raphaelites, obliged as a model occasionally but, probably due to the ill-health (Bright's Disease) which killed him in his twenties, produced relatively little work. Well-regarded by his friends, he was nominated to replace Collinson in the original Brotherhood, though the group never got round to formally electing him. Apart from his first significant picture, *Twelfth Night* (1849–50), only *The Pet* (Tate Gallery) is really known now. At the 1848 RA Exhibition he showed *Margaret in Prison*, a painting now lost.

Sir Frank DICKSEE (1852–1928):

Though he spanned the centuries, Dicksee remained a Victorian artist in mood, drawn as he was to literary, mythographic and, at times, Pre-Raphaelite themes. Thus his election to the Presidency of the Royal Academy in 1924 supported the age-old complaint that the RA was as backward-looking as ever.

William DYCE (1806–64):

A deeply religious man (High Church), Dyce was a polymath, a scientist, musician, historian and, above all, fine artist – one of the few to be looked up to by the young Pre-Raphaelites, and one of the few established artists of the mid-century prepared to learn from *them*. His later paintings are clearly influenced by their dictates, as are many of his paintings by his High Church beliefs – though it should be noted that he had been influenced by *their* influencers, the German Nazarenes in the 1820s, before any Pre-Raphaelite had heard of them. Of his many works the most famous is *Pegwell Bay* (1858, now in the Tate) in which the foreground figures – added afterwards by Dyce – are (from the right) his wife, her two sisters and his son. It is only after one has studied the meticulous and beautifully lit landscape detail for some time that one notices the faint trail of Donati's comet in the sky. Notable religious works include *Joash Shooting the Arrow of Deliverance* (1844) and *Jacob and Rachel* (1853). A fine early portrait was *George Herbert at Bemerton*.

John Rogers HERBERT (1810–90):

Many mid-century artists can be said to have been influenced by the Pre-Raphaelites, but Herbert influenced *them*. His sun-bleached *Our Saviour Subject to His Parents at Nazareth* (1847, now at the Guildhall Art Gallery) immediately reminds us of Millais's later *Christ in the House of His Parents* (1850). Like the PRB, Herbert was criticised for 'Roman tendencies' (he converted to Catholicism) and, more than any of them, he looked and sounded the part: dark and bearded, with piercing eyes, and much given to preaching about the nobility of art. Influenced in his turn (as were the PRB) by the German school of Nazarenes, he painted a good number of stirring Bible scenes, some of which were copiously reproduced for home display.

Arthur HUGHES (1832–1915):

A softer, more sensitive, at times over-sentimental, part-way Pre-Raphaelite who submitted his *Ophelia* for the RA Exhibition in the same year Millais submitted his. (Hughes's *April Love*, 1856, and *The Long Engagement*, 1859, might seem again to stray into Millais territory.) But Hughes was always his own man; his paintings have their own charm, his colours remind one of early Italian masters (before Raphael), and his book illustrations are unsurpassable (see under Illustration). He did his best work when young. *Home from Sea* (1856–62) is particularly effective. In his most famous painting, *April Love*, his wife Tryphena is believed to have supplied the face; it was painted originally in costume but later changed to modern dress. *The Long Engagement* was even more reworked. Painted originally as a Shakespearian *Orlando in the Forest of Arden*, it was rejected by the RA, so Hughes entirely revised it, painting out Orlando (and perhaps the original Rosalind, though there is some uncertainty about this) and inserting a clergyman and his all too patient love.

Millais used Hughes's head for *The Proscribed Royalist*.

WILLIAM HOLMAN HUNT (1827–1910):

In his memoirs Hunt claimed to have founded the Pre-Raphaelites – and although that is disputed, he certainly flew its flag the longest. The first of his paintings to be exhibited at the Royal Academy, *The Flight of Madeline and Porphyro* (1848) – a conventional Academy title – bore all the hallmarks of Pre-Raphaelitism, though the movement had not been founded. (That came a few months after.) In 1850 and '51, through all the storms that beset the movement, then later still as the artists became accepted, Hunt's pictures never strayed from the Pre-Raphaelite creed, remaining sharp-edged, brilliantly lit, immaculately executed and, in different ways, packed with arresting images, if sometimes overweighted with symbolism.

His apparently naturalistic painting, *Strayed Sheep* (1852), represented the church's pastoral flock straying too close to the doctrinal edge – just as in *The Hireling Shepherd* (1851) the sheep, unwatched by their pastoral master, were seen to stray into forbidden fields. His matted and frankly hideous creature in *The Scapegoat* (1855), up to its shins in Dead Sea shallows, stands suffused in guilt and purple, cast out by man. The symbolism of his most famous and most reproduced picture, generally known as *The Light of the World* (1851–3), seems obvious: Christ refused entry at the door. Yet, suggested Diana Holman Hunt from tales told within the family, that door – encrusted with ivy to show it had not been opened for many years (a far from original metaphor) – was painted first without Christ beside it and without Hunt having a clear idea of who or what he should place there. How easily, one feels, he could have added a different person to make yet another version of *The Long Engagement*. But Christ stepped in, and the rest is history. (In his 1895 *The Importunate Neighbour* Hunt returned to that moonlit door with dust and encrustations swept away: the man at the door knocks in vain for food, while two dogs slurp contentedly at food left out for them.)

The dogmatic, vehement, vigorous Hunt never lost his fervour. As the Brotherhood descended into squabbles and sexual tangles (from which Hunt was not entirely unencumbered) he painted on – both in England and the Middle East where he famously placed his easel and rifle side by side in the desert while he worked, and where more than once he defended himself in stout Victorian manner. In the last decade of his life he was working on two typically Pre-Raphaelite pictures, *The Lady of Shalott* and *The Miracle of the Holy Fire*, but his sight was fading – this for a man who had been gifted with astonishingly sharp long sight. He died practically blind.

Hunt was a large and powerful man, a workaholic, obsessive, dogmatic and flummoxed by love. His first known affair (which may have been no more than an affair of the heart; certainly it was brief) was with Emma Watkins, the model for the temptress in *The Hireling Shepherd*, but his long-lasting, hopelessly fraught and misguided romance was with the urchin model Annie Miller, shared in every sense with the other Pre-Raphaelite artists, who Hunt courted, became engaged to, tried to educate, struggled with even after he knew she'd been unfaithful, and eventually lost to a more worldly-wise and richer man-about-town. After their affair had ended, when it became known that Hunt had sold his *Finding the Saviour in the Temple* for a record sum, Annie tried to blackmail him over their previous relationship.

Frequently short of money (in part because he was so long in finishing his 'more important' works) Hunt painted a number of commercial portraits, and among his portrait pieces are studies of his family including: a famous self-portrait done when he was just 14; a grander, yet sadder, self-study (1875); his married sister and her daughter (*Mrs Wilson and her Child*, 1850); his nephew Teddy Wilson (*The King of Hearts*, 1862); his uncle and benefactor, Thomas Combe, as well as his aunt Martha Combe; his mother-in-law *Mrs George Waugh* (painted 1868); his first wife Fanny Waugh (a portrait in 1866, plus his better-known use of her in the commemorative *Isabella and the Pot of Basil* painted while he mourned her); Edith, his second wife, Fanny's sister (*The Triumph of the Innocents* and other more personal studies); his son Cyril (1876); his daughter Gladys (*Miss Flamborough*, 1882); his son Hilary (*The Tracer*, 1886); et cetera. (The marriage to Edith was strongly opposed by her family and, as such marriages were illegal in Britain, had to take place abroad.) His useful if self-aggrandising memoirs, published in 1905, annoyed the descendants of his Pre-Raphaelite companions, but helped cement his own position as 'The True Pre-Raphaelite': the title of his biography by Anne Clark Amor, published in 1989. His ashes lie in St Paul's Cathedral.

John J LEE (fl 1850–60):

Little known outside his native Liverpool, he worked mainly in illustration, in the Pre-Raphaelite manner. He is believed to have included a self-portrait in his *Sweethearts and Wives* (1860) in which the women bid farewell to their men at Liverpool Docks.

Sir John Everett MILLAIS (1829–96):

A child prodigy, one of the founder members of the Pre-Raphaelite Brotherhood, he was enormously successful throughout his life (and pretty much ever after). He was the youngest ever prize-winner at the RA

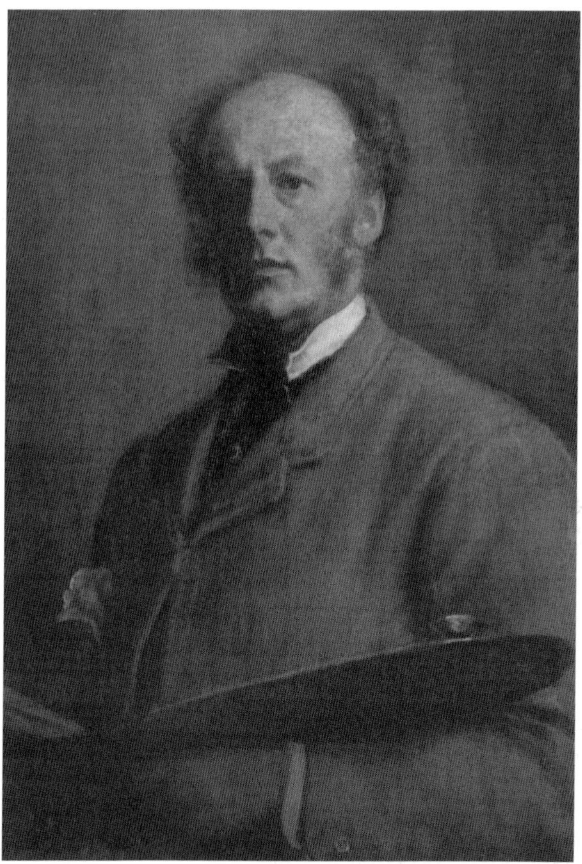

A Millais self-portrait of 1880

Schools but some of his early paintings, familiar and revered as they are now, aroused controversy. The biggest storm blew up over his 1850 masterpiece *Christ in the House of His Parents*, seen by many as sacrilegious; according to Charles Dickens the picture depicted Christ as 'a hideous, wry-necked, blubbering, red-haired boy in a nightgown'. His mother (the Virgin Mary!) 'would stand out from the rest of the company as a monster in the vilest cabaret in France or in the lowest gin-shop in England,' Dickens continued, in what must be one of the most spectacular misjudgements of his life. Mary was modelled by Mary Hodgkinson and Christ by Noel Humphreys (son of the illustrator).

Millais continued in Pre-Raphaelite vein for the first half of the 1850s with wonderful works such as *The Bridesmaid* (for which the model is believed to be an unknown 'Miss McDowall'), *The Return of the Dove to the Ark*, *The Woodman's Daughter*, *Mariana*, *Ophelia*, *The Blind Girl* and *Autumn Leaves*. Of these, *Ophelia* has become the most famous, partly from the quality of the work and partly through his use (or misuse) of Lizzie Siddal to model the drowning Ophelia. Practically everyone knows the story of Lizzie lying in a bath in which the water, initially warmed by candles underneath, cooled to room temperature, while she lay still and never complained. Some say she caught a chill that day which brought about her early death, but that is romantic fantasy. She was never well, and she died of consumption and over-use of laudanum.

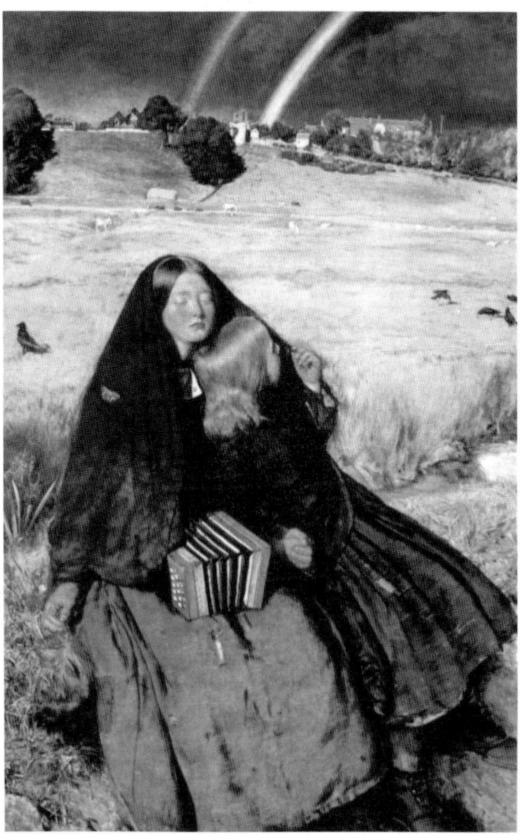

Millais's haunting *Blind Girl* (1854–6)

Yet the sentiment, or sentimentality, of *The Blind Girl* and other early works and their appeal to a general public led Millais to stray from Pre-Raphaelite tramlines towards genre and narrative paintings. He had, in any case, wrecked his relationship with their champion: in 1853 he had fallen for, and in 1855 had taken away and married, Ruskin's ex-wife Effie. (Ruskin, it should be said, continued to praise Millais's paintings.) But the length of time required to make PRB pictures – every leaf and every petal meticulously delineated – irritated Millais and he began to skimp on detail.

He was a superbly accomplished painter and, even when he skimped, his works were technically far above most rivals. He could hit the public nerve: few well-brought-up Victorians could fail to like *The Boyhood of Raleigh* (1870), *My First Sermon* (1863) and, worse (though still brilliantly executed), *Bubbles* (1886) and *Cherry Ripe* (1879). His portraits and landscapes, if without deeper meaning, were finely done. Portraits ranged from family members to major public figures: his wife featured in several major works; daughter Effie was *Red Riding Hood* (1864) as well as appearing in both *Sermon* pictures; daughter Alice was *The Picture of Health* (1874) and *The Crown of Love* (1875). His portraits pleased and flattered their subjects – and earned good money: a half-length, he told F G Stephens, brought £1,000 while a head and shoulders fetched £500. He painted Dickens on his deathbed, and the last portrait of Disraeli, seventeen days before he died; he painted Tennyson, Gladstone, Cardinal Newman, Sir Arthur Sullivan, and a number of society's *belle dames*. Freed from the taint of Pre-Raphaelitism he became eminently respectable – so much so that when, in 1870, he exhibited *The Knight Errant*, showing the rescue of a naked young lady tied to a tree, he failed to find a buyer. Other painters might, and did, paint female nudes, but it wasn't what the public expected from Mr Millais, and the aberrant painting languished unsold for four long years.

That, though, was an untypical aberration in his career. Accepted by both the public and the Academy, he was made a baronet in 1885 (the first artist to be thus honoured) and was elected President of the RA in 1896, by which time, sadly, he was a sick man. At his inaugural address his voice was so faint that many could not hear him, and a few months later his life faded away. He was buried at St Paul's.

William MORRIS (1834–96):

Famous as he is, Morris barely earns a place in a book of Victorian artists. He *could* paint, though *Queen Guenevere* (1858) is his only known oil painting; it's a too carefully worked portrait of Jane Burden (his future wife) in his idea of medieval dress – and even this painting is said to have been completed by Rossetti and, perhaps, by Madox Brown. Morris was founder of Morris, Marshall, Faulkner & Co (established 1861) and it is for his prolific, beautiful and innovative designs (a near-impossible combination of achievements) that he is remembered. Those designs, of course, grace many a house today.

Dante Gabriel ROSSETTI (1828–82):

If Holman Hunt was the founding father of Pre-Raphaelitism, Rossetti was its driving spirit. These two men, with Millais, were the real artists among the original seven of the Brotherhood. Rossetti, who was never comfortable in the Academy Schools and who had been an errant pupil under Madox Brown and (a strange choice) John Sell Cotman, was the archetypal rebel student – moody, restless, alternately idle and frenetic. A less competent artist than his two fellows, he could, at his best, produce the more beautiful pieces. His pencil work and his handling of colours could be sublime (when he could be bothered to finish).

He was Cockney-Italian, son of an Italian political refugee and an English mother, and was brought up in a warm, lively, artistic household – 'an Italian of the fourteenth century who happened to reside in London,' claimed his friend Val Prinsep. His sister was the poet Christina Rossetti and his brother William (a fellow founder of the PRB) became a noted art critic and chronicler of the Brotherhood. Rossetti, who could have stepped straight from *La Bohème*, is generally assumed to have had affairs with each of his main models. He climaxed his turbulent on-off affair with Lizzie Siddal by marrying her shortly before her death, and by having all his poems buried with her in her coffin – then by changing his mind later and having her and the coffin exhumed so he could rescue the precious pages. His affair with the more voluptuous and more relaxed Fanny Cornforth mellowed into a friendship which, to the irritation of his friends and family, continued until his death. Real criticism should perhaps be reserved for his stealing away Janie Morris, née Jane Burden, wife of his friend William Morris, and for forcing Morris himself into a form of impotent *ménage à trois*.

Rossetti was both poet and artist, and his literary works were useful in giving the PRB greater literary and intellectual credibility. Being Rossetti, he managed to become embroiled in a famous public spat with the (then better-known) poet Robert Buchanan, following an article Buchanan wrote for the *Contemporary Review* entitled 'The Fleshly School of Poetry'. Rossetti responded with 'The Stealthy School of Criticism'.

Rossetti will always be judged among the finest Pre-Raphaelite artists – even if, in the opinion of more observant critics, he ignored most of the

Pre-Raphaelite credo. He began with *The Girlhood of Mary Virgin* (1849) and *Ecce Ancilla Domini* (1850) – both pictures of the Virgin and both using his sister as model – before giving vent to his real obsessions, beautiful women, the Italian poet Dante, and the Arthurian legend as spun by Malory and Tennyson (though Rossetti made comparatively few Arthurian paintings, leaving the field to fellow artists like Burne-Jones). What he could have achieved is hinted at in his famous woodcut, *The Maids of Elfin Mere* and *The Blue Closet* (watercolour, 1856–7, in which, although Lizzie has the starring part, May Morris peeps in, top left). A notable religion-inspired pen-and-ink drawing of the time was his *Mary Magdalene at the Door of Simon the Pharisee* (1858) in which Burne-Jones models Christ, and Swinburne the Pharisee. (Ruth Herbert was Mary.) In that year Madox Brown said of Rossetti: 'His forte, and he seems to have found it out, is to be a lyrical painter and poet, and certainly a glorious one.'

So in thrall was Rossetti to the poet Dante that, as a young man, he switched the order of his names to put Dante first. Among his Dante-inspired paintings one thinks of *Dante's Dream at the Time of the Death of Beatrice* (dawdled over from 1870–81 and based on an earlier watercolour from 1856; Jane Morris was Beatrice and Marie Spartelli the mourner on the viewer's right), *Dantis Amor* (1859, only part painted by Rossetti), *Dante's Vision of Rachel and Leah* (1855), *Dante's Dream* (1856), and the incomparable memorial to Lizzie, *Beata Beatrix* (1864–70). His enthusiasm for things medieval (and beautiful women) inspired paintings such as *St Catherine* (1857, Lizzie Siddal as the model), *Regina Cordium* (1860, Lizzie again), another version of *Regina Cordium* (1866, Alexa Wilding as the beauty[1]), *Girl at a Lattice* (1862, Madox Brown's servant as the model), *Fazio's Mistress* (1863, Fanny Cornforth), *The Blue Bower* (1865, Fanny again), the somewhat outrageous *Venus Verticordia* (1864–8, showing a nude unknown beauty, apparently a cook: 'a very large young woman, almost a giantess', noted William Allingham), *Monna Vanna* (1866, Alexa Wilding) and *The Beloved* (1865–6, a painting originally intended as a Dante/Beatrice study but changed by Rossetti as he thought the central model, Marie Ford, though beautiful, not right for his conception of Beatrice). His *The Bower Meadow* (1871–2) was begun in homage to Dante (note the apparently Italianate background) but changed to a more general Italianate study; the models were Alexa Wilding and Maria Stillman. *La Ghirlandata* (1873) is a study of nothing other than beauty; the central woman is Alexa Wilding again, and both the angels are William Morris's sister May. There is a tendency for the features of all these models to blend into a single archetypal

'Rossetti woman' – something his sister observed as early as 1856 when, in her sonnet 'In an Artist's Studio', she wrote 'One face looks out from all his canvases / One selfsame figure sits or walks or leans.'

The troubled affair between Rossetti and Morris's wife Jane began in the late Sixties, and from then on she came to dominate his pictures. She sits uncomfortably fingering her wedding ring in *La Pia de' Tolomei* (1868–80: begun early in their affair but left uncompleted for years) and stands holding her fateful box of troubles as *Pandora* (1869). One of the most attractive Jane portraits is *La Donna della Fiamma* (1870). She appears again in the moody and much-reproduced *Prosperine* (1873–7),

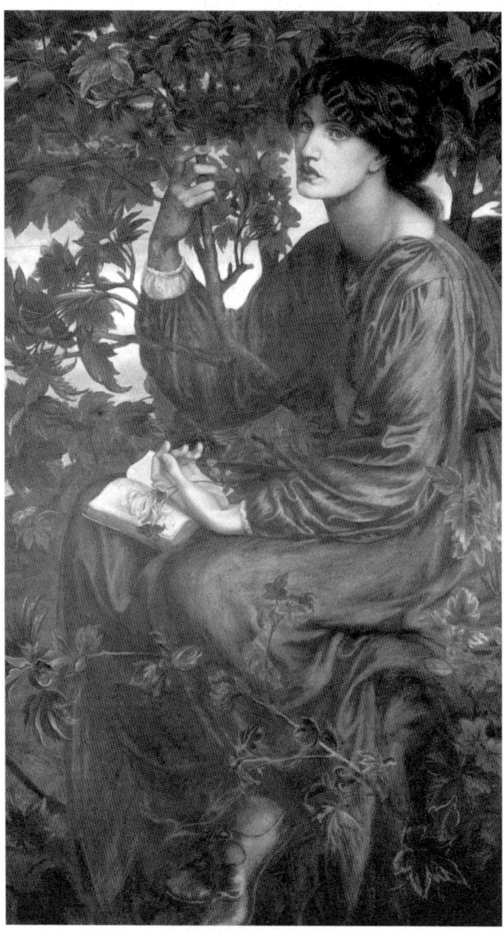

Rossetti's *Day Dream*, 1880

and is wistful in *Astarte Syriaca* (1875–7). By then the ailing Rossetti was taking his time over another version of *Pandora*, this time in chalk, with the never slight Janie looking massive and challengingly bare-shouldered.

In 1879, when Constantine Ionides saw a drawing Rossetti had made of Jane reading a book while seated in a tree, he commissioned a painting from it. Rossetti asked a steep 700 guineas and took over two years to complete the commission. That painting was the lovely *The Day Dream*. (Constantine was lucky to get it at all; Rossetti was notoriously slow and unreliable, and on his death in 1882 left many works unfinished.) Rossetti had been unwell from the early 1870s, increasingly dependent on chloral, alcohol and laudanum. He became both paranoid and, when not with Jane Morris, morose and housebound, severing friendships. In his final year a new edition of his *Poems* was published, along with *Ballads and Sonnets*. He died on Easter Sunday, 'half blind and suffering a great deal of pain', said his brother William. Christina and his mother sat beside him at the bedside.

John RUSKIN (1819–1900):

One of the most important figures in nineteenth-century art: a fine artist himself (his drawing better than his painting) and the leading critic of his day. Born to rich though stiflingly devoted parents and encouraged by them from infancy into adult aesthetic pleasures, he studied and analysed art in all its forms with formidable rigour. Travels through England in his teens (especially the Lake District) were followed by travels through Europe in mountains and cities of culture. His monumental *Modern Painters* came out in five volumes from 1843 to 1860 with an authority far beyond what might be expected from a man in his twenties. Throughout his life he continued to lecture and write – the lectures appearing as pamphlets, in magazines and in volume form and, surprising as it may seem today, being lapped up by the public. His preferences – though he was wide in his tastes – were for the medieval and the Gothic but, most of all, were for honesty, clarity and 'the good'. To observe closely and record accurately was his maxim, as practised in his own geological and botanical studies. 'Go to nature,' he wrote, 'in all singleness of heart, rejecting nothing, selecting nothing, scorning nothing.'

His status was such that when, in 1851, he came to the defence of the much-criticised young Pre-Raphaelites, their reputation transformed almost overnight. Similarly, his defence and constant advocacy of Turner kept the great man's flame alight. Yet in the Fifties his reputation survived a marital assault which would have destroyed a lesser man and which, today, would have been examined, re-examined and pursued by the media till it destroyed him. His wife divorced him on the grounds of non-consummation (a charge he refused to fight), after which she married John Everett Millais, one of the artists Ruskin had defended and supported (and to whom Ruskin would continue to be fair and generous in his writings for years to come).

Ruskin's writings ranged beyond art into society and how it should be organised – he was, to some extent, the nineteenth-century plain man's Plato – and he continued to draw and paint meticulously. Late in his life his razor-sharp mind failed him; he became obsessional, irrational and even odder than he had been in personal relationships, particularly with women and young girls. Even his artistic judgement wavered, leading him late in life to become embroiled in a ridiculous libel case with Whistler, one of whose paintings, Ruskin said, was like 'flinging a pot of paint in the public's face'. He was, at the time, in the throes of a mental breakdown – perhaps from overwork, perhaps from the libel case, no one can be sure. In the last two decades of his life Ruskin became increasingly hermit-like, immured in his home beside Coniston in the Lake District, where he died.

FREDERICK SANDYS (1829–1904):

Born in Norwich, the son of a professional painter called Sands (he altered his name around 1855), he began with topographical and natural history illustrations before being exhibited at the RA in 1851. Amused initially by the new Pre-Raphaelite craze – he lampooned them in his famous cartoon of Sir Isumbras – he later became friends with one of the subjects of that skit, Rossetti, though Millais never forgave him. Sandys, said Jeremy Maas, was perhaps the 'one outstanding portrait painter' of the Pre-Raphaelite movement, and he remains equally well-regarded as a book illustrator. Little surprise, then, that the RA, with typical bull-headedness, failed to hang his best picture, *Medea* (1868), due to 'lack of space'. The ensuing outcry forced them to hang it the following year, when it was greatly praised.

Sandys married Georgiana Creed in 1853 but the marriage was not a success. In 1864 he tried to divorce her but, under the rigorous divorce laws of the time, he failed. He was, by that time, living with Mary Jones, the model with whom he would spend the rest of his life. He was a handsome, frequently broke, and extravagant man – which helped endear him to fellow artists like Rossetti. (They shared a house in Cheyne Walk for a year.) Though he lived to 1904 his best work stems from the 1860s and 70s.

Elizabeth SIDDAL (1829–62):

More famous as the model and muse of the Pre-Raphaelites and especially Rossetti, whom she married a year or so before her death, Lizzie Siddal became, under Rossetti's tutelage, a moderately accomplished painter in her own right. Her drawings had a naive if childlike charm but her colours smacked suspiciously of her lover's palette. She was the daughter of a generally impecunious cutler in the Old Kent Road (and was born in July 1829, not 1834 as she maintained, and her name then was Siddall: Rossetti changed it). Introduced to the Pre-Raphaelite circle as a model, she became Rossetti's lover and eventually his wife (in 1860). Rossetti's fierce promotion of her as an artist persuaded the normally wiser Ruskin who, perhaps as a means of keeping a grasp on the elusive Rossetti, agreed to buy everything Lizzie painted. She, to her credit, resisted, and tried to establish herself without him. She produced over 100 works, with or without Rossetti's aid, and showed several at the 1857 First Pre-Raphaelite Exhibition at Russell Place. (See more on her under *Models*.)

Simeon SOLOMON (1840–1905):

A talented and original Pre-Raphaelite whose career was shattered in 1873 when he was arrested and charged for soliciting in a gents' lavatory. He was abandoned by most of his friends and potential customers and,

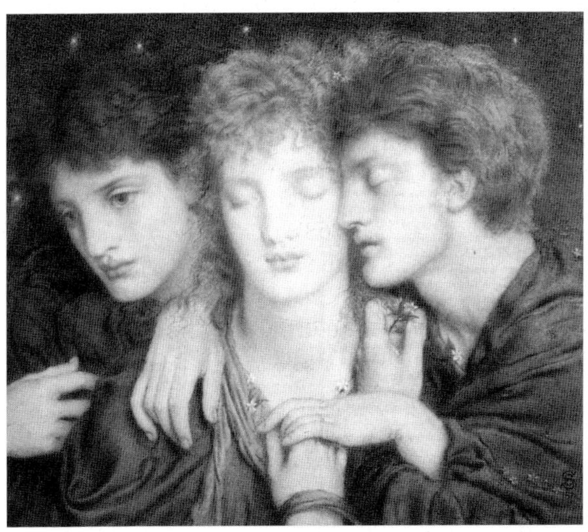

The Sleepers and the One that Watcheth (1870) – Simeon Solomon's recurring theme of a couple and the outsider

presumably in despair, became hopelessly addicted to alcohol. How he dragged his ravaged frame into its sixties is a mystery. Solomon's tragedy deprived us of a fine artist, both in watercolour and in black and white: he first exhibited at the RA months before his eighteenth birthday. A number of his paintings and engravings depict in detail the customs and observances of the Jews (he was Jewish, and his family prominent in the Bishopsgate Jewish community). The engravings appeared in Victorian magazines and some of them, unexpectedly, in the famous picture book, *Dalziel's Bible Gallery*. In acute contrast is the work he produced in collaboration with one of his friends, the poet Swinburne, whose pornographic novel *Lesbia Brandon* and long poem *The Flogging Block* he illustrated. Solomon's last years were spent in dire poverty; he lived in dosshouses and worked sporadically as a pavement artist and shoelace-seller.

JOHN RODDAM SPENCER STANHOPE (1829–1908):

Seen as a late follower of the Pre-Raphaelites, though his style really owed more to Burne-Jones, Stanhope was the son of John and Lady Elizabeth Spencer Stanhope of Yorkshire. He had the means to mix with London's finest artists, from Watts to the Pre-Raphaelites. (He travelled with Watts to Budrum in Asia Minor and rented a studio below Rossetti's in Chatham Place.) Ill-health persuaded him to move to Florence in 1880, where the climate must have suited him, as he lived for twenty-eight more years.

HENRY WALLIS (1830–1916):

Unfairly characterised as 'a one-painting painter' although he exhibited some thirty-five pictures at the RA between 1854 and '77, Wallis was initially lauded by Ruskin as a Pre-Raphaelite. The work for which he earned instant fame, *Chatterton* (1856), is a wonderfully tragic study of the young suicide lying beneath an open window through which the sun burns into sunset. The model for the young poet was George Meredith and the scandalous twist was that two years later Wallis ran off with Meredith's wife, seen here in a pencil sketch made by Wallis and kept by him until his death. Wallis's one other painting of note is *The Stonebreaker* (1857).

JOHN WILLIAM WATERHOUSE (1849–1917):

Often thought of as a late Pre-Raphaelite, he'd be very late indeed as he wasn't born until the year that they were founded. Of the relatively few paintings he produced in Pre-Raphaelite style, *Ophelia* (1889) is a gorgeous example, as is his sensual six and a half foot 1888 oil, *The Lady*

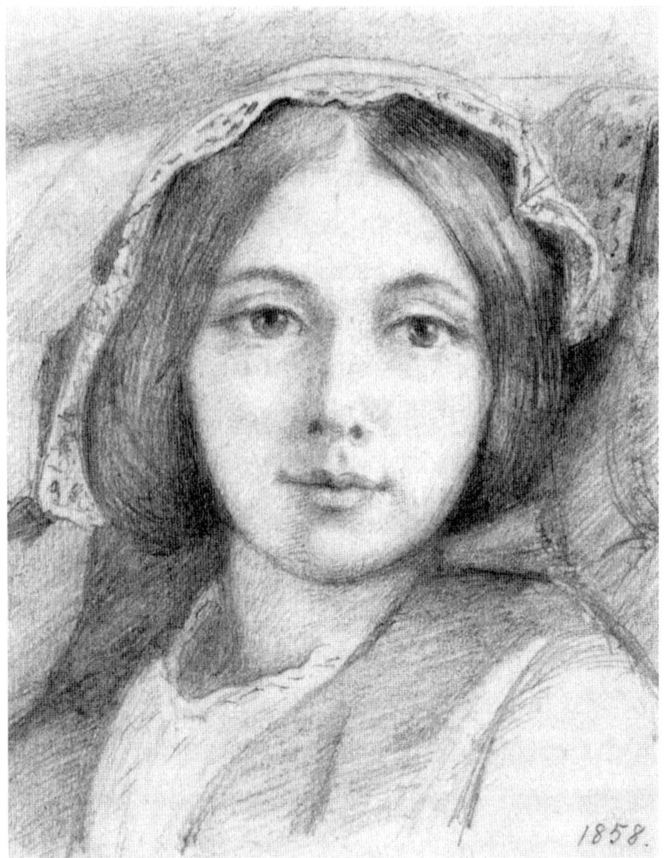

Mary Ellen Meredith painted by Wallis a year after she left her husband

of Shalott. Such works have eclipsed those that formed the bulk of his output and, indeed, Pre-Raphaelitism has been 'read into' paintings he no doubt thought of as Classical. (His earlier works were more in the style of Alma-Tadema.) Born in Rome but schooled in Leeds, his first RA exhibit was a Roman allegory, *Sleep and his Half Brother Death* (1874), and he continued in a broadly classical style until the quite different *Shalott*.

William Lindsay WINDUS (1822–1907):

An early convert to the Pre-Raphaelite cause, he is sometimes called 'the first provincial Pre-Raphaelite'. (He was born in Liverpool.) Ruskin, for some reason, took against him and delivered a scathing dismissal of what was to become Windus's best-known work, *Too Late* (1859), and the criticism was enough to shake the young man's confidence and lead him towards safer work. The narrative painting *Burd Helen* (1856, which Ruskin liked) was his next best-known piece. Windus lost a son early in his marriage (before his wife died in 1862), from which time comes his haunting *Study of a Dead Child, the Artist's Son* (1860). Never strong in confidence, he gave up painting altogether in 1862. In 1880 he famously made a bonfire of all his unsold works.

THOMAS WOOLNER (1825–92):

One of the original seven members of the PRB, invited in by Rossetti, yet never really a true adherent. Slightly older, he had been exhibited at the RA first in 1843. A poet also, he knew Coventry Patmore, whose plea to Ruskin caused him to speak up for the Brotherhood in 1851. Shaken by the barrage of criticism, Woolner emigrated to Australia the following year to dig for gold – with predictable results. He returned to London in 1854 to re-establish himself as the only sculptor among the seven. (How much he was really a part of them is debatable.) His pieces, especially his portrait medallions, were finely made and became increasingly sought-after. He married Alice Waugh in 1864 and was to become Holman Hunt's brother-in-law – twice: Hunt married Alice's two sisters. The first time was acceptable but the second, when Hunt married his dead wife's sister, proved too much, and the two men fell out.

REACTIONS TO PRE-RAPHAELITISM:

During the first decade of Pre-Raphaelitism, critical responses were polarised between the staunchly for and the determinedly against. As that decade continued and as more artists incorporated Pre-Raphaelite techniques into their works, critics and customers learnt to live with the new wave. Some critics, though past their initial shock, still quibbled at the over-indulgence, the fussiness, the subordination of imagery to cold realism. To Hunt's *Finding the Saviour in the Temple* one of the less polarised responses at the time – one which would find an echo in some quarters today – came in a private letter from Edward Fitzgerald to his friend George Crabbe in 1860. Fitzgerald explained why he

> *didn't care a straw for Holman Hunt's Picture. No doubt, there is Thought and Care in it: but what an outcome of several Years and sold for several Thousands![2] What Man with the Elements of a Great Painter could come out with such a costive Thing after so long*

> *waiting! Think of the Acres of Canvas Titian or Reynolds would have covered with grand Outlines and deep Colours in the Time it has taken to niggle this Miniature! The Christ seemed to me only a wayward Boy: the Jews, Jews no doubt: the Temple, I dare say very correct in its Detail: but think of even Rembrandt's Woman in Adultery at the National Gallery; a much smaller Picture, but how much vaster in Space and Feeling! Hunt's Picture stifled me with its Littleness. I think Ruskin must see what his System has led us to.*

To Fitzgerald, as to many others, Ruskin was seen as an integral part of this new-fangled Pre-Raphaelitism – whatever it was. Many Victorians asked exactly that: what it was, what it meant, and what it was trying to say. Even now, with hindsight, it is easier for us in the twenty-first century – though less easy than some might think – to define *who* was a Pre-Raphaelite than to say what Pre-Raphaelitism was. Raphael, after all, was not mentioned in their 1848 Manifesto. They aspired, as students usually do, to freshness and excellence and to the study of Nature, and they opposed, as students usually do, conventionality and the teachings of the old. Hunt and Millais, at first, took inspiration from Nature; Rossetti took his from religion, Dante and the Middle Ages. All three – again, at first – tackled social problems of the day: prostitution, drunkenness, emigration and vice. Frannie Moyle (author of *Desperate Romantics*) has said they were arguably the first movement to show – indeed, to glorify – women other than saints in moments of ecstasy and agony.

But increasingly they shifted their gaze from their own time to earlier: Hunt chose the Bible, Millais literature and history, and Rossetti, before abandoning himself almost entirely to portraits of idealised women, lost himself in the medieval fictions of Malory, Scott and Tennyson. The original Brotherhood had been the brainchild of three fellow students, but there were four other founding members: Thomas Woolner, James Collinson, F G Stephens and William Rossetti. What of them?

Woolner became one of the century's leading sculptors, though – apart from the realism of his sculpted portrait medallions – his work showed little anyone could call Pre-Raphaelitism. Collinson never lived up to his early promise; Stephens switched to art criticism (becoming a leading critic, and therefore a useful ally); and William Rossetti, although no artist, was to prove invaluable to the group as archivist, promoter and administrator.

That leaves us with the main three. Hunt was undoubtedly a Pre-Raphaelite; from the start he had the clearest idea of Pre-Raphaelite principles, and he never wavered from them – even if his dogmatic adherence to their demands caused him to labour meticulously over each of his major works, most of which took him years of careful tedium to complete. Of the three principal originators, only he stuck painstakingly and obsessively to his last. Millais, the most naturally gifted, began as a keen Pre-Raphaelite but found the demands too restricting: why, he asked, slave for years over a single painting when he could turn one out just as effectively in days or weeks? Ruskin, in his 1854 lecture on Pre-Raphaelitism, had declared that 'one of the chief reasons for the violent opposition with which the school has been attacked by other artists, is the enormous cost of care and labour which such a system demands from those who adopt it.' Even to an artist as naturally gifted as Millais, the Pre-Raphaelite manner demanded an 'enormous cost of care and labour' and, though he didn't mind the hard work, he did mind taking so long over each picture. The longer he took, the less he could produce. The less he produced, the less he could sell. By the mid-1850s he had abandoned Pre-Raphaelite strictures in favour of comfort and commercial success.

Rossetti, the man who had talked most about the movement's principles, never really followed the creed at all. His paintings, gorgeous and original as they were, were not accurate representations of or inspired by nature; they did not show 'truth'; they did not conform to Ruskin's criteria of 'absolute, uncompromising truth in all that it does, obtained by working everything down to the most minute detail, from nature, and from nature only'. Nor were his pictures 'painted to the last touch, in the open air, from the thing itself'. Rossetti could more accurately be described as a Romantic.

Two names often associated with the movement are Burne-Jones and William Morris. They were friends, especially with Rossetti, though that friendship was to become painfully tangled as each man fell for another's woman. Rossetti seduced Jane Morris, forcing Morris into a relationship, almost certainly platonic, with Georgiana Burne-Jones while her marriage rotted around her. Burne-Jones had lost his heart and will to various models, but it was his dramatic affair with Maria Zambaco that unsettled his wife. Georgie stood by her husband, and Morris never lost his fondness for her. Somehow Morris and Burne-Jones overcame these challenges to continue their friendship: indeed, Burne-Jones rather ignored, and perhaps was grateful for, Morris's attachment to Georgie. Art comes above all.

But could Burne-Jones and Morris be called Pre-Raphaelite? Certainly the two men were inspired by themes of medievalism, myth, religion and classical literature. But no one, surely, could call a painting by Burne-Jones (in accordance with Ruskin's dictum) 'painted to the last touch, in the open air, from the thing itself'. Burne-Jones almost never painted in

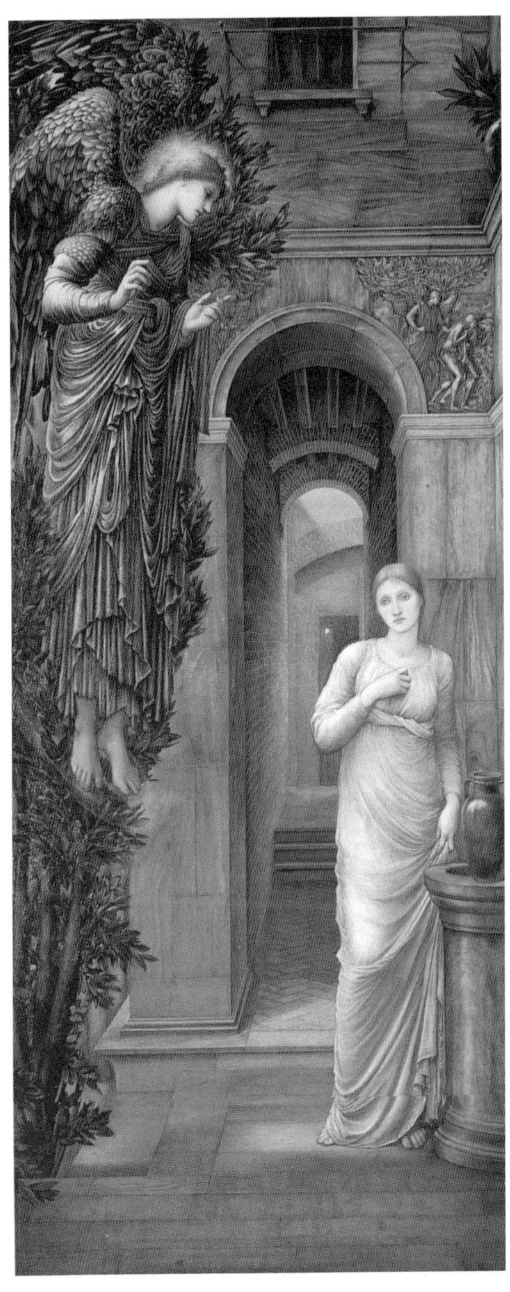

Burne-Jones's *The Annunciation* with Julia Stephen as the Virgin (painted 1876–9)

the open air. If one can categorise him at all, Burne-Jones was a 'mythographic' painter – as, in many of his works, was Rossetti. William Morris, though a brilliant designer, was hardly a painter at all: his one serious attempt in the Pre-Raphaelite genre, *Queen Guenevere* (1858), was a good try but not a great painting, and it was in any case completed for him by (either or both) Rossetti and Ford Madox Brown.

Late in the century came John William Waterhouse, perhaps the last great artist in the Pre-Raphaelite style, along with Thomas Cooper Gotch, 1854–1931, strong in the 1890s, and Eleanor Fortescue-Brickdale, stronger in the early twentieth century – each sometimes derided as derivative. But their paintings tick all the boxes in Ruskin's list: minute detail, painted from nature, and – as Ruskin also stipulated – 'in contradistinction to the present slovenly and imperfect style'. True followers, but too late. The whole Pre-Raphaelite movement fell out of fashion in the twentieth century. By the 1960s, when anything more than two years old was square, Pre-Raphaelite paintings were lumped together with the most meretricious Victorian canvases. But the Sixties were their nadir: in 1965 Burne-Jones's four-painting series *The Seasons* was sold for a laughable £65; eight years later, in America, it fetched $37,800. The climb-back had begun to the million-pound prices of today.

NOTES

1 There is another *Regina Cordium* modelled by Mrs J Adam Heaton, a friend's wife.

2 Hunt forced the dealer Gambart up to a record-breaking £5,500 – and although Gambart made him reduce the price later, the dealer always maintained that it was the highest price paid for a modern picture in England.

Chapter Two

PORTRAITURE
A Good Likeness

In the nineteenth century, portrait artists found themselves less reliant on patronage and less restricted to producing images of paymasters and their families. They could look about and choose their subjects. Landscapes no longer had to be backgrounds to stately homes or well-fed owners. Portraits needed no longer to be of the rich – though they did still have to sell, and hence, when artists broadened their vision they tended to look not to the labouring classes but to the famous. From their portraits we can now put a face to almost every well-known nineteenth-century name

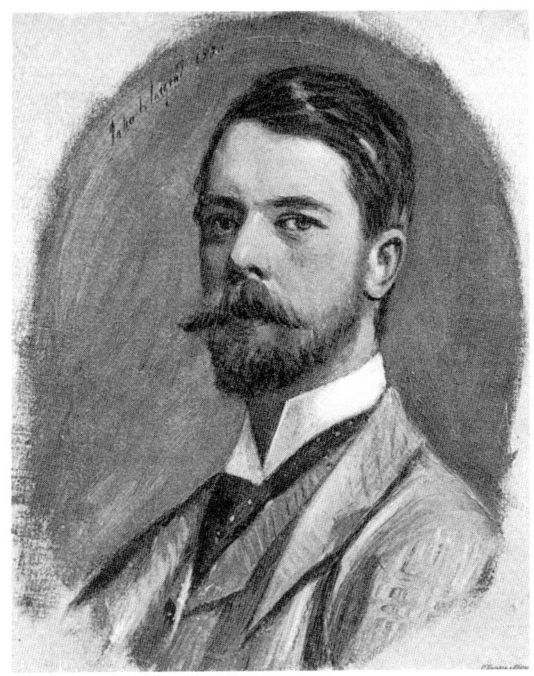

A self-portrait of John Singer Sargent

– politicians, actors, writers, soldiers, the beautiful and the damned. And halfway through that bustling century, photography broadened the vision further, capturing images first from the photographer's studio, then outside in the streets, in the countryside, on the beaches and in people's homes.

Not only could anybody be the subject, but everybody could see the pictures. Until the nineteenth century, books, magazines and newspapers had been restricted both by technology and price to the few who could afford them. No longer. Demand grew for illustrated reading matter – woodcuts and engravings, followed by mechanical reproduction, then photographs. Illustrations decorative or informative showed how things worked and where they were, what they looked like and what *people* looked like. Fun as it was to see drawings of Fagin and Oliver Twist in a monthly part-work, it was just as interesting to see who the author was, and what *he* looked like. Nineteenth-century readers, like today's, loved to see pictures of celebrities, be they drawings or paintings engraved for print or, as the century progressed, in photographs. For most of the century, given the technology of the time, pictures reproduced more clearly from engravings (hand-cut in the early decades, photographically reproduced from the mid-century on). Photographs might be 'real' but were murky, blurred and grey, lacking the sharp clear black and white of engravings. All of which favoured the artist over the photographer. But for us today, when we look back at the legacy of those portrait artists and photographers we see that, while artists left us images of famous people, photographers – who increasingly could 'snap' – were happy to record images of everyday or anonymous folk.

In the National Portrait Gallery, some 18 per cent of the 500 Victorians portrayed are artists, another 16 per cent are literary figures, and 11 per cent are statesmen. Add the next group – travellers and explorers, 10 per cent – and we've gone past half the total. Naval and military commanders make the next 8 per cent, as does a combined group of scientists, engineers and inventors. Actors and dramatists have 5 per cent, churchmen about 3.5 per cent, philanthropists 2 per cent, followed by small sets of architects, musicians, judges et cetera. By today's standards, commerce and industry seem surprisingly poorly represented, while the everyday, non-famous teeming multitudes are hardly there at all.

Working people seldom commission portraits, high-earners saw little need, but for artists, portraiture was their wage. Almost every artist earned at least part of their income from portraiture, so they painted people who could pay them. In this chapter we look at some of those portraitists.

James ARCHER (1823–1904):

Scottish artist whose early paintings had seemed faintly Pre-Raphaelite cum Arthurian before he turned to portraiture.

John BALLANTYNE (1815–97):

Competent portrait artist whose most interesting works for us today are the large studies he made of famous artists at work in their studios. Among others, he captured Holman Hunt, Sir Edwin Landseer (working on his Trafalgar Square lions) and Sir Francis Grant.

Thomas Jones BARKER (1813–82):

War artist and portraitist, eldest son of Thomas Barker (1767–1847). He studied in Paris from 1834 where he achieved a considerable reputation, selling some paintings to King Louis Philippe. On his return here in 1845 he began exhibiting at the RA, carving out a career as a respectable painter of portraits and scenes of historical, literary, religious, genre, hunting and war interest. Though successful commercially he was less so with critics.

Charles BAUGNIET (1814–86):

An above-average engraver and portrait artist.

Charles BAXTER (1809–79):

Famous for his 'Keepsake'-style portraits of imaginary beauties, often purporting to be peasants, maids or docile maidens, Baxter's all-but-airbrushed lovelies were tasteful enough to grace the most respectable domestic wall. His finely executed works are popular with collectors of Victoriana and can still be found in the V&A museum.

William BEWICK (1795–1866):

A portrait and historical painter who studied under Haydon and achieved as little success as did most of that man's students. In 1848 Bewick retired to all intents to Haughton-le-Skerne, near Darlington, where he was able to live comfortably. He was no relation to Samuel Bewick, the wood-engraver.

Sir William BOXALL (1800–79):

Sir William's success is puzzling. He attempted landscape and historical painting with little success, turned to portraiture but was said to rarely produce a good likeness (though among others he was commissioned to do Wordsworth and the Prince Consort), yet in 1866 he became director of the National Gallery. (He was the compromise choice against at least three others: Landseer, J C Robinson proposed by the Queen, and a civil servant proposed by the Prime Minister.) Having got his post he virtually stopped painting.

Julia Margaret CAMERON (1815–79):

Her innovatory style of portrait photography, using the camera to create art studies rather than mere portraits, together with her access to celebrity models, earns her a place here. She was one of the famous Pattle sisters.

Margaret Sarah CARPENTER, née Geddes (1793–1872):

A largely self-taught portrait painter, critically and commercially successful, so much so that she exhibited more often at the RA (156 works) than did any other woman artist although, being a woman, she was never elected to it. Married to William Carpenter, keeper of prints and drawings at the British Museum, and mother of eight children (three died in infancy), she earned more than her husband and, despite her current lack of fame, was the most successful woman artist of her day.

Alfred Edward CHALON (1780–1860):

Dismissed now as one of the 'Keepsake' artists, he was (like his brother Henry, 1770–1849) a court painter to royalty. Chalon, though based here, was French and spoke French to his admiring clients. Alfred specialised in flattering portraits, Henry in equally flattering animal studies.

George CHINNERY (1774–1852):

One of those Victorians who took the conventional image and trampled it to dust. He began conventionally at the RA Schools, and became a young and successful portrait artist and miniaturist. He married, had two children, but threw it over for a new life in India, initially alone, then with his family. By the time his wife arrived, Chinnery was earning £500 a month from portraiture but had fathered two more children and was mightily fond of opium. Eventually (1825) he fled a mountain of debt by setting sail for China. Again his wife was slow in coming after him – but the rest of the tale can be found in the Foreign Climes chapter.

Charles West COPE (1811–90):

One of the winners in the House of Lords competition that shattered Haydon, Cope's later paintings included an interesting (and much reproduced) *Selecting Pictures for the Royal Academy* (1876, now in the RA, unsurprisingly). This seven foot wide painting includes portraits of Millais,

Leighton, Grant and Cope himself, among others. Other works include far more domestic studies; he was particularly good at children. In Cope's own childhood he broke his arm and was forced to carry around a small oyster barrel to straighten the elbow. But his left arm remained crooked and useless for the rest of his life.

Lowes Cato DICKINSON (1819–1908):

A portrait painter who, although he took up painting relatively late, was well-thought-of in his day, though he was little more than competent, in truth. He was one of the founders of the London Working Men's College where, together with Ruskin, he taught art.

Count Alfred Guillaume Gabriel D'ORSAY (1801–52):

Though famed more as a fine-looking libertine and bankrupt (and society's darling) and, despite his apparent homosexuality, as companion to the liberated Countess of Blessington, the French dandy D'Orsay also found time to paint and sculpt. He painted Wellington in 1845, after which the famously prickly general declared himself so satisfied that he would never sit to anyone else. D'Orsay's social contacts gave him access to subjects from the Queen down, and even today some sixty-one of his sketched portraits are in the National Portrait Gallery.

John DOYLE (1797–1868):

Successful portrait artist, remembered more for having taught and encouraged his gifted son Richard.

Eden Upton EDDIS (1812–1901):

Successful portrait painter with many famous clients, exhibiting often at the Royal Academy. His most successful genre painting, of a child on the beach, was affectionately titled *Going to Work* (1869).

Richard EVANS (1784–1871):

There are few artists prepared to describe themselves as copyists, but Evans, a capable portrait artist, was an exception. As a fledging artist he had been so poor that his friend David Cox lent him some of his own Indian ink sketches to copy and sell. Later, while still intending to be a portrait painter, he found employment making copies of Sir Thomas Lawrence's portraits of the royal family. He continued combining the two skills, and on one famous occasion informed the director of the South Kensington Museum that their Roman antique fresco of *Ganymede*

Feeding the Eagle was in fact one of his copies. Some of his own works are held by the National Portrait Gallery, but Evans painted little in the last twenty-five years of his life.

William Powell FRITH (1819–1909):

Though primarily a genre painter (see that chapter) his first paintings were either portraits or set in previous ages. A superbly capable painter, his portrait of the young wife of the dealer Gambart is an exquisite thing. His 1853 *The Artist and his Model* (or *The Sleepy Model*) contains a useful self-portrait and two of the model herself, an Irish orange-seller who not only fell asleep but, just before doing so, made the wonderful observation that 'gentlemen is much greater blackguards than blackguards is'.

Sir Francis GRANT (1803–78):

The rich were happy to be painted by him, partly because he was considered, rightly, one of the finest portraitists of his day and partly because he was rich. (He didn't begin painting till his thirties.) Son of the Laird of Kilgraston, educated at Harrow, lavish spender of his inheritance, Sir Francis fitted comfortably into any stately home – though, interestingly, the Queen didn't think much of his work. His models were the aristocracy, and he was duly rewarded with the Presidency of the Royal Academy.

Mary GRANT (1831–1908):

Portrait artist, not to be confused with Mary Jane Seacole (née Grant), the famous nurse at the Crimea.

Sir George HAYTER (1792–1871):

Queen Victoria's reputation for primness gets a shake from her championing and eventually knighting George Hayter who, early in life, had disgraced himself matrimonially: it was she who appointed him her portrait and historical painter, and he repaid her with a number of suitably august portraits. His other works were eminently respectable.

Sir Hubert von HERKOMER (1849–1914):

Best known today for his genre work (see that chapter), Herkomer worked in various fields, mastering different media, including illustration, oil studies, enamels, metalwork and etching, but supplemented his income from commercial portraiture. In the Eighties and Nineties he was better known for portraiture than for his other work.

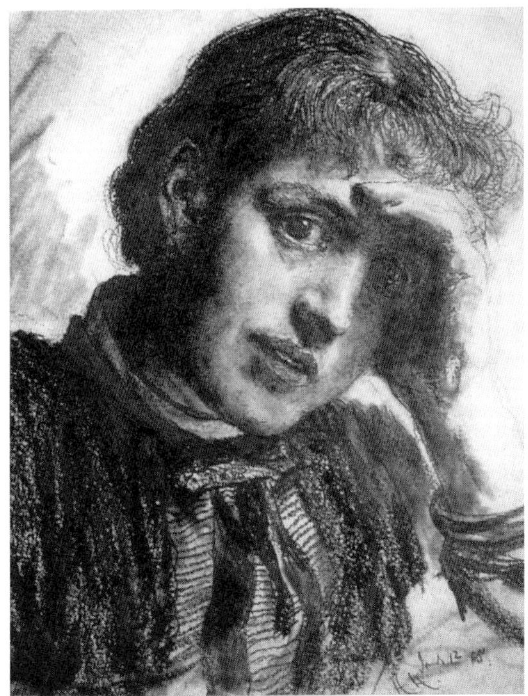

Herkomer's pencil sketch of his wife

Francis HOLL (1815–84):

The most successful of the Holl family of engravers, he engraved commercial copies of works by artists like Frith, and made portraits also. His father had been an engraver, as were his brothers William Holl the younger (1807–1871) and Charles (1810–82). Francis's son was Frank Holl, 'the English Velasquez'.

Francis Montague (Frank) HOLL (1845–88):

A portraitist and illustrator, notably for *The Graphic*, who produced nearly 200 portraits in his relatively short life in a style which led to his being dubbed 'the English Velasquez'.

Louise JOPLING (1843–1933):

Born Louise Goode, the fifth child of a Manchester railway contractor, she married Frank Romer, private secretary to Baron Rothschild, a marriage which took her into circles that helped obtain her the finest instruction (in Paris, naturally). On Romer's death she married J M (Joe) Jopling, a watercolourist and friend of Millais (who painted a striking portrait of Louise in 1879). Louise herself went on to become a celebrated portrait artist and to found her own art school for women artists. The portrait of her by Millais was bought by the National Portrait Gallery in 2002 for £430,000.

John Prescott KNIGHT (1803–81):

The son of a comedian known as Little Knight, John Prescott was a hard-working portrait artist (he needed the money) who produced well over 200 portraits in oils, as well as other works, some military, some religious. (He became a deacon of the Catholic Apostolic church in 1847.) In 1831 he married Clarissa Isabella Hague, who was herself an accomplished painter of still-life and domestic scenes.

Richard James LANE (1800–72):

A portrait artist, sculptor and, principally, lithographer. He produced many lithographic portraits and, in 1837, was appointed lithographer to the Queen, and three years later to Prince Albert.

Samuel LAURENCE (1812–84):

In his day a much-admired portrait painter, noted for his portraits of famous literary figures, among whom he socialised. If his works are less thought-of now, it is only because his portraits are too much of their time – but that, of course, is why so many are in the National Portrait Gallery.

Sir John LAVERY (1856–1941):

A better painter, perhaps, than human being. When he and his sister were in their twenties she became pregnant and, to get her out of the way, he sent her to America. When she returned, pregnant again, he rejected her a second time, and two days later she drowned herself in the Clyde. Before long he bought and insured a studio, which quickly succumbed to a mysterious but financially profitable fire. He used the proceeds to quit Glasgow for London and Paris. By the mid-80s he had returned to Glasgow to become one of 'The Glasgow Boys' (a group which had spurned him a few years earlier). Much of his work in the next decade was with the help of photographs (he was a keen photographer) and, being respectably saleable, they helped establish him as a dull but reliable portraitist.

Charles Hutton LEAR (1818–1903):

Not to be confused with Edward Lear, Charles was a fine portrait artist.

Alphonse LEGROS (1837–1911):

French-born, a poor student, he began by painting scenery at L'Opéra in Lyons before being accepted into the École Impériale de Dessin in Paris, where fellow students included Fantin-Latour and Rodin. Fantin-Latour introduced him to Whistler and the three ganged together as the Société des Trois. Whistler brought Legros to London in 1861, where he soon nestled in with progressives like Watts and Rossetti, before exhibiting at the RA for the first time in 1864. Always in debt, never sure whether to make his career in Paris or London, the decision was finally settled when in 1876 he was appointed professor at the Slade School of Fine Art. He became a British citizen in 1880 and in that year helped found the Society of Painter-Etchers; he was an accomplished printmaker. Working at the Slade made him disciplined and conventional – certainly in his portraiture, for which he found himself much in demand by 'society' sitters. Meanwhile he continued in a Symbolist vein, producing interesting works such as his six plates, *Death and the Woodcutter* (*c*.1875–1906) and a longer series, *The Triumph of Death* (*c*.1892–1900). He married the conventional with the new.

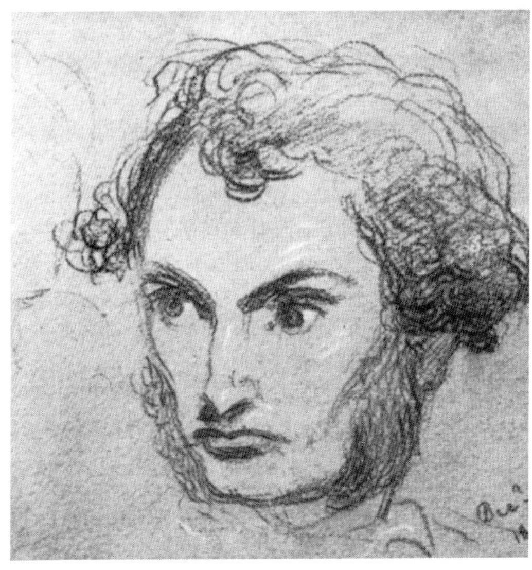

C H Lear's dynamic sketch of Maclise

Charles George LEWIS (1808–80):

Brother to J F ('Spanish') Lewis and son of Frederick Christian, he was a less skilled artist and made his career with engravings and portraits.

Frederick Christian LEWIS (1779–1856):

A superb engraver (signing his works F.C.Lewis) and portrait artist, he was father of J F and C G Lewis, both of whom he taught.

Violet LINDSAY (1856–1937):

A noted beauty (Mrs Patrick Campbell described her as 'the most beautiful thing I ever saw') she married the Marquis of Granby and became therefore Marchioness (Mrs Henry Manners), but despite her high position and income she was a fine artist, working in pencil and silver-point, and also as a sculptor (a sad but fine example is the tomb she sculpted in memory of her beloved son, Lord Haddon). Among her portraits are those she made of the aristocratic bright young things known as the 'Souls', in which she was an actively bohemian member. Having borne her husband a daughter and two sons, she allowed herself to look wider: her second daughter is said to have been fathered by Disraeli's former Private Secretary, and the third (who went on to become Lady Diana Cooper) by Harry Cust, the highly intelligent if errant Conservative MP for Stamford, Lincs. A selection of her portraits was published in 1900 as *Portraits of Men and Women*.

Henry Duff LINTON (1816–99):

Engraver and portraitist, the son of the polemical wood-engraver William James Linton (1812–97). Linton's was one of the larger wood-engraving companies.

HRH Princess LOUISE (1848–1939):

The Duchess of Argyle was a justly celebrated portrait artist, though she is remembered today more for her long affair with the sculptor Edgar Boehm, who is said to have died of a heart attack while making love to her.

John Seymour LUCAS (1849–1923):

Very unfashionable artist and likely to remain so, specialising in studies of merry characters in 'period' costume. Once popular with a section of the lower middle classes. He should not be confused with the earlier John Lucas (1807–74), who *was* a portrait artist.

Sir Daniel MACNEE (1806–82):

A leading Scottish portrait painter who, unlike many, remained in Scotland. Appreciated both for his art and his conversation, he became President of the Royal Scottish Academy in 1876.

Thomas Herbert MAGUIRE (1821–95):

Engraver and portrait artist.

Sir William John NEWTON (1785–1869):

Portraitist and miniature painter who was a founder member of the first Photographic Club (formed by amateur 'calotypists' in 1847).

John PARTRIDGE (1789–1872):

A Scottish portrait artist who, while working in London, was for some years patronised by the new Queen, though he never quite fitted the top rank. He was uncle to the twentieth-century *Punch* cartoonist Bernard Partridge.

Stephen PEARCE (1819–1904):

Painter of portraits and horses, including the Queen's horses.

Henry Wyndham PHILLIPS (1820–68):

Portrait artist, the son of the greater but pre-Victorian portrait artist, Thomas Phillips (1770–1845) who was a Professor of Painting at the Royal Academy and known for his portraits of the famous, mainly writers.

Henry William PICKERSGILL (1782–1875):

A worthy if dull painter of celebrity portraits, especially of military men, yet he was seldom out of work. His son, Henry Hall Pickersgill (1812–61) followed him as an artist (mainly of historical subjects) while his wife, Jeanette Caroline Pickersgill (1814–85), exhibited often at the RA, and had the distinction of being the first person to be legally cremated in Britain. Henry was uncle to F R Pickersgill.

James PRYDE (1866–1941):

A portrait artist and designer of posters and stage sets, his main success in the nineteenth century came when he collaborated with Nicholson as the Beggarstaff Brothers to produce striking posters and prints, some of which were then issued in expensive book form. Pryde himself had no real success till the twentieth century, and he supplemented his income in the Nineties with occasional portraits and stage work.

HENRIETTA RAE (1859–1928):

A fine portraitist, often overlooked, best known for her paintings of wistful young lovelies. In 1905 her biographer, Arthur Fish, acknowledged her ability with the wonderfully patronising words, 'in spite of her sex she is an artist, and a successful artist, too'. She lived, of course, in a world where most artists were men and where any woman associated with art was regarded with suspicion. So, though capable of better, she tended to paint what she could sell.

While a student at the Royal Academy Schools (1884) she met and married a fellow artist, Ernest Normand. In those days women at the Schools were excluded from life classes, yet when she began her professional life she concentrated on tasteful nudes, two of which were in the Academy exhibition of 1885. Nevertheless, as Fish wrote in his biography, the idea of a woman painting nudes 'attracted a certain amount of adverse criticism from the irresponsible section of the public which sees in this class of subject nothing but impropriety or indecency'. Fish writes of one critical letter to which Rae's less censorious doctor suggested she 'should reply to the letter and state that she had recently given birth to a son "who came into the world entirely naked", which fact seemed to suggest to her that there was no impropriety in representing the human form as it was created'. Her husband's paintings, interestingly, attracted no such criticism.

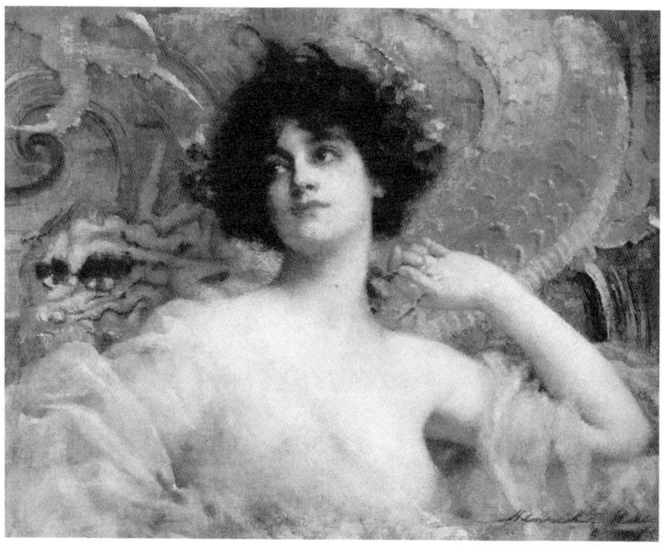

Henrietta Rae's *Portrait of a Young Beauty*

In 1890 she and her husband studied for a while in France, where they became converted to Impressionism – a conversion which found little favour when they came home. Henrietta hit back with a great success at the 1894 Academy exhibition: a characteristic *Psyche before the Throne of Venus*. By the end of the Nineties their 'lapse' had been forgiven, and she was invited to join the Hanging Committee at the Liverpool Autumn Exhibition (she was the first British woman to judge at any major public exhibition). That same year (1899) she painted one of the murals for the Royal Exchange. Frederic Leighton painted another.

George RICHMOND (1809–96):

The son of the miniaturist Thomas Richmond and close friend of Samuel Palmer, Edward Calvert and William Blake, he and his friends ('The Ancients') worked in Kent and London. George began, like his father, as a miniaturist, went through a visionary patch with the Ancients, but switched to portraits in the 1830s. An early commission to paint William Wilberforce made his name, after which he became one of the century's leading portrait artists, creating some 2,500 portrait works.

Walford Graham ROBERTSON (1867–1948):

Though fairly well-regarded in his day, it is not as an artist that Robertson is remembered but for his chatty memoirs of the turn of the century art and theatre scene, *Time Was* (first published 1931 and running into three editions that year). He was rich enough to be a keen patron of the arts also.

Sir William Charles ROSS (1794–1860):

Portrait artist and fine miniaturist who, reaching his sixties, gave up as, in his regretful view, photography had supplanted paint.

William ROTHENSTEIN (1872–1945):

It was the turn of the century before he came to prominence, mainly for his society portraits, but two of his early volumes of lithographic portraits were *Oxford Characters* (1896) and *English Portraits* (1898).

Richard ROTHWELL (1800–68):

Born in Athlone and trained in Dublin, an early member of the Royal Hibernian Academy, he alternated between portraits and genre painting.

Henry Thomas RYALL (1811–67):

An engraver and portrait artist. He began in the 'stipple' format but moved into what for him was to be the more lucrative area of large-scale reproductive engravings (often in mezzotint). His skill in this medium led to his being made historical engraver to Queen Victoria, and he was always in demand by publishers for high-quality reproductions of other artists' work.

JAMES SANT (1820–1916):

A genre and society portrait artist, who, from the number of his paintings still found in corners, seems to have been in permanent employment.

JOHN SINGER SARGENT (1856–1925):

Though Sargent was American his ability to make superb portraits made him a favourite with the British aristocracy and wealthy classes. Much in demand though he was, his deftness did not always endear him to rival artists, who sometimes remarked on his 'facility' rather than his undoubted talent. Yet there was no guarantee that his paintings would flatter their subject: something of their essential nature – be it their selfishness, even stupidity – often peeped through. Sargent didn't help matters by occasionally letting slip his attitude to his sitters, as with his portrait of three sisters, daughters to the chairman of the Vickers armaments manufacturers, of whom Sargent complained that he had to go to the 'dingy hole'

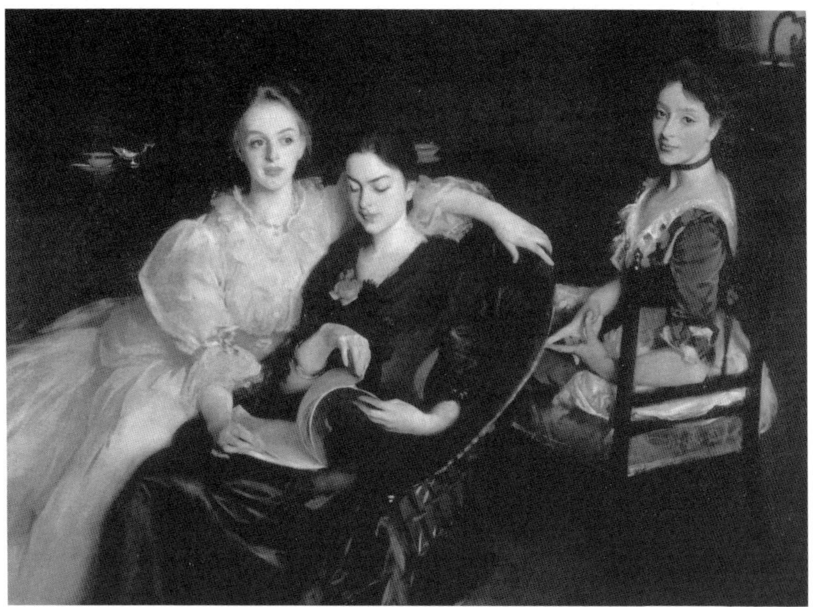

Sargent's *The Misses Vickers* (1884)

of Sheffield to paint 'three ugly young women'. Either his words or his picture serves us false, for he shows Florence, Mabel and Clara to be, if not raving beauties, far from ugly. His 1889 portrait of *Ellen Terry as Lady Macbeth* became the sensation of the year.

Sir James Jebusa SHANNON (1862–1923):

James Jebusa Shannon was an American portraitist who produced most of his finest work in London, a city to which he came in 1878 when he was just 16 to attend the National Art Training School in South Kensington

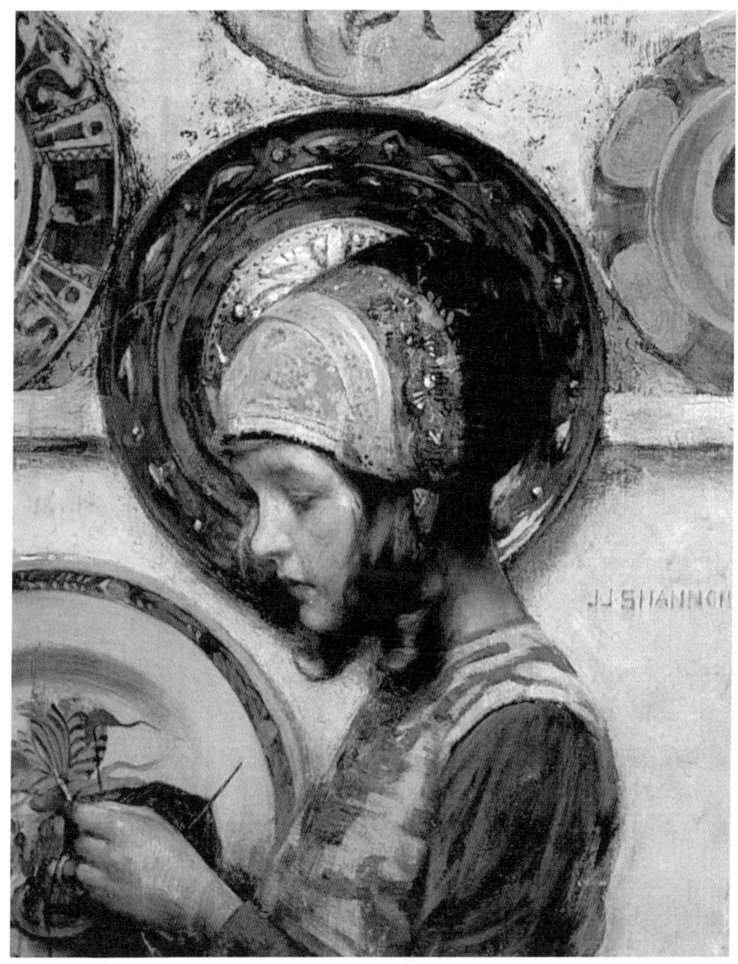

J J Shannon painted his daughter Kitty for this gorgeous piece, *The Purple Stocking*

under Edward Poynter. It was Poynter who gave Shannon his first significant commission, recommending the student to Queen Victoria as the artist to paint a portrait of her Woman of the Bedchamber. Victoria liked the result, had it shown at the Royal Academy, and commissioned another. The success was enough to persuade Shannon to set up in Chelsea. (He later moved to Kensington.) It was his marriage in 1886 and, more importantly, the birth of a first daughter in 1887 that convinced him that, to earn an income, he should concentrate on portraiture. (A brief break from that determination came in 1888 when his *Myrrah* was bought by the biscuit-maker Peak Frean for use on their tins.)

A portrait he made that year was, fortuitously, of Violet Manners, Marchioness of Granby, and cousin to Coutts Lindsay, joint founder of the Grosvenor Gallery. (Her own works were exhibited there.) He painted her several times and, through her, was introduced to the influential circle of young aristocrats calling themselves The Souls, several of whom he painted. Shannon knew the value of contacts; he had already helped found two arts institutions, the Chelsea Arts Club and the New English Art Club, and in 1891 he helped found the Society of Portrait Painters. The following year he was able to buy a plot of land in Holland Park Road next door to Frederic Leighton. The house he had built contained a 40-foot long studio with a window 25 feet high. By this time, and indeed well into the twentieth century, J J Shannon was regarded as one of the finest, perhaps *the* finest, portraitist in the land. His nearest rival was the fellow American, John Singer Sargent. The Royal Academy made Shannon a full Academician in 1909, and in 1910 he became President of the Royal Society of British Portrait Painters. He was knighted in 1922, having by then been for four years confined to a wheelchair, and he died in 1923.

Sir Martin Archer SHEE (1769–1850):

A Grand Manner portraitist who, as President of the Royal Academy from 1830 till his death, was seen by most of the young progressive school as the epitome of the old, the out of date and the obstructive. He dismissed young Millais's talent: 'Better make him a chimney-sweep than an artist,' and he told Watts's father, 'I can see no reason why your son should take up the profession of art.'

Frank STONE (1800–59):

The father of Marcus was perhaps a better – and more emphatic – artist than his more famous son, even if he wasted much of his time on pretty 'Keepsake' portraits of often imaginary young ladies.

James Rannie **SWINTON** (1816–88):

In his day, a fashionable Scottish portrait artist, given to life-size works in crayon or oil (often drafted in crayon and finished in oil). Eighty-five of his works were exhibited at the RA.

Robert Scott **TAIT** (1815/16–97):

A photographer more than a painter but remembered for his unquestionably accurate depiction of Thomas and Jane Carlyle in their sitting room – accurate (despite their carping) because the painting was derived meticulously by Tait from his photographs. His unpainterly perspective comes from the camera – but so does the accuracy. Jane Carlyle hated the tablecloth ('frightful') and the size of the dog ('as big as a sheep'). Carlyle hated having the photographer/artist under his feet for a year (who wouldn't?): 'Tait has been steaming about all day with his photographing (very malodorous) apparatus.'

Dorothy **TENNANT** (1851–1925):

Illustrator and portrayer of street urchins – despite being the wealthy daughter of society hostess Gertrude Tennant and, from 1890 to 1904, the wife of explorer Henry Stanley, who moved in with Dorothy and her mother and, when mother and daughter were not away travelling, lived for nine years in their London house. When Stanley died, Dorothy married his doctor. Henry James, who was never likely to marry her, called Dorothy: 'the delicious Dolly, one of the finest creatures I have met.' Earlier, in 1876, she met G F Watts on the Isle of Wight and they remained friends for years (he painted her in 1876, and painted her younger sister Eveleen as well). She had her own studio by then (in Richmond) and had posed for Millais (in his 1875 *"No!"*). She was a fine animal and child painter.

James **THOMSON** (1787–1850):

When the 15-year-old Thomson was sent from Northumberland to London his boat took nine weeks to arrive and by the time his family heard from him they'd given him up for dead (teenager, away from home at last, first time in London . . .). After a seven-year apprenticeship as an engraver, he became adept at both plain and stipple engraving and at etching, but became best known for his portraits, largely of pre-Victorian notables.

Henry **TONKS** (1862–1937):

His career spans the centuries and he appears in the biographies of a number of twentieth-century artists, but in style Tonks is more a late

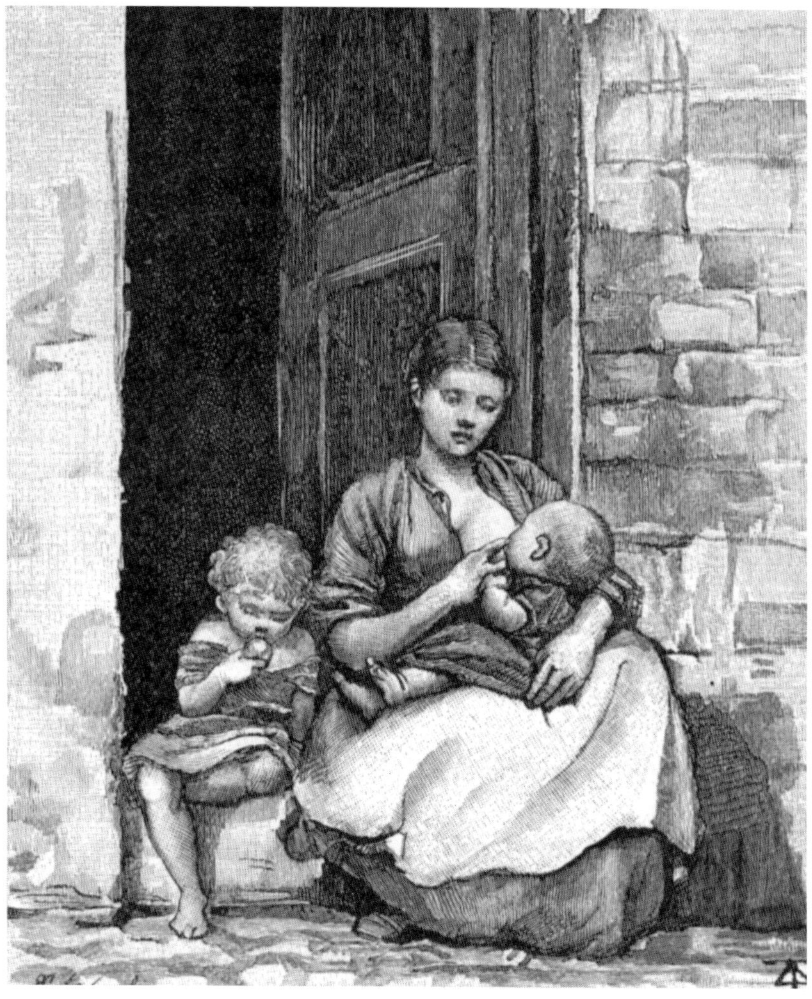

Dorothy Tennant's harsher vision of *Mother and Child*

Victorian than an Edwardian artist, his slightly old-fashioned, correct manner inevitable, perhaps, for one who taught art (which is why he appears in the biographies) and who had to impose rules and rigour on young twentieth-century students. His range was wide (he eventually became an official War Artist) but perhaps the best of his Victorian works were his portraits.

Charles TURNER (1774–1857):

An engraver and portrait artist, the finest mezzotint engraver of his day, producing around 1,000 in his lifetime. Among artists he engraved was J M W Turner (no relation) with whom he eventually had a falling-out (as did many people) but the two Turners made it up and JMW made him an executor of his will.

Elizabeth WALKER (1800–76):

Her father was the engraver Samuel William Reynolds (1773–1835), and she became both a skilled engraver (learnt from her father) and a miniaturist talented enough to become Miniature Painter to King William IV. Among her many works, Elizabeth Walker (aka Elizabeth Reynolds) painted miniatures of five Prime Ministers. Her husband William (1791–1867) made his living as an engraver too, making over 100 portrait engravings in stipple and mezzotint, though late in life he switched to commercial portrait photography.

Dame Ethel WALKER (1861–1951):

Though she was to become a long-lived and well-thought-of portrait and still-life artist, particularly accomplished in painting nudes, she produced little of note in the nineteenth century (or little has survived) and has to be regarded as a twentieth-century name.

Sir John WATSON GORDON (1788–1864):

Scottish painter of portraits and, earlier in his career, historical subjects. He portrayed Sir Walter Scott several times, and James Hogg as *The Ettric Shepherd* (Hogg's pseudonym). He became President of the Royal Scottish Academy in 1850.

Francis John WILLIAMSON (1833–1920):

Portrait artist and student of J H Foley.

Franz Xavier WINTERHALTER (1805–73):

A society portrait artist who will never fade from memory as he produced some of the most emblematic portraits of the new Queen Victoria. German, born in the Black Forest, he had established an earlier reputation on the continent for his portraits, including some of European royalty. He did not come to Britain until 1842, when he was commissioned by the Queen and her Consort, and he produced his first portrait of her in 1843. He was capable of almost photographic realism before the camera had been invented – which makes his portraits of Victoria and her coronation

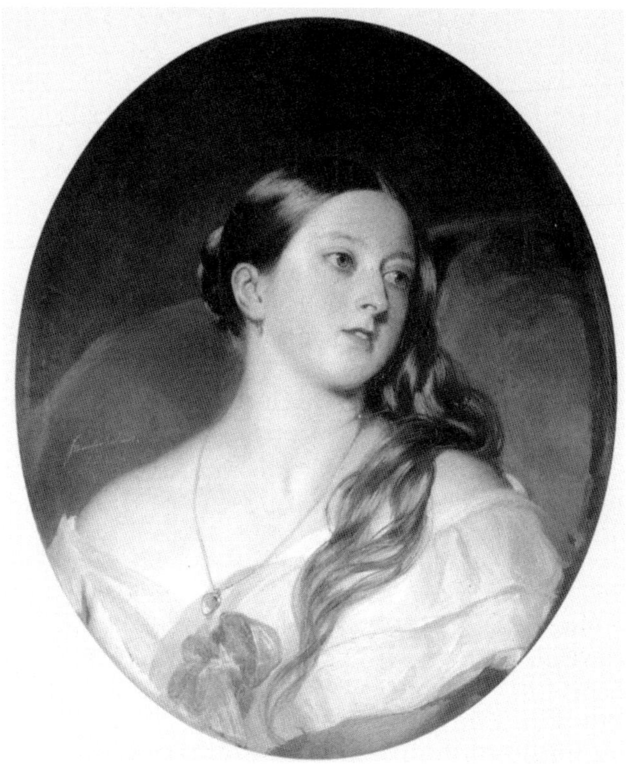

The Young Queen painted by Winterhalter in 1843

especially valuable as historical documents, if nothing more. He was an archetypal court painter; his own wife, in his portrait of her dated 1863, poses wonderfully dressed, looking every inch a queen. But, though he became a personal friend of the Queen, he was never much liked by fellow artists; Eugène Delacroix considered him 'not a bad fellow, but a terrible bore', and Ruskin gave one of his shorter judgements: 'a dim blockhead'.

Among other portraitists you might look out for: Rudolph LEHMANN (1819–1905) and Louisa STARR-CANZIANI (1845–1909).

Chapter Three

LANDSCAPE
The World About Us

Victorian paintings glow with light, so it's easy to forget the conditions in which many were produced, for Britain is not noted for its long bright daylight. American author Henry James, in a letter complaining that one day he had to light a candle at eleven in the morning to read, wrote: 'The weather is hideous, the heaven being perpetually instained with a sort of dirty fog-paste, like Thames-mud in solution.' Winter fogs could last a week, and a break of a few days might be followed by another week of fog. (In the 1890s it was calculated that London saw fifty-five days of fog a year.) Luke Fildes once calculated, gloomily, that in the worst four months of winter he'd had barely fifteen hours of light per week to paint by. He was one of several artists to commission a glass house as a studio. Frederic Leighton was another; he had top architect Aitchison build him an iron and glass studio in 1890. Fildes joked that the base of it was large enough to support the Eiffel Tower.

Art exhibitions in spring forced artists to complete their pieces in winter months when light was feeblest, and it wasn't until 1897 that the galleries of the Royal Academy were lit by electricity. So it's little surprise that some

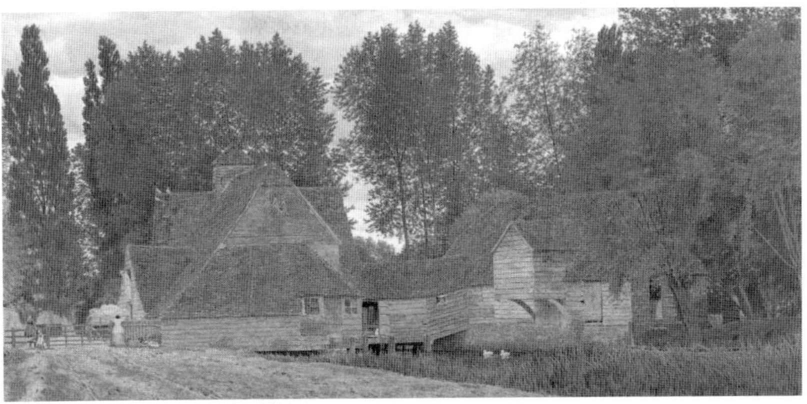

The Mill on the Thames at Mapledurham (1860) by G P Boyce

artists forsook daylight altogether: Walter Sickert recommended working entirely by artificial light as it was constant and unchanging; Linley Sambourne drew his black and white illustrations by gaslight through the night, using an engraver's globe to throw a beam of light onto his board – a common if not essential practice among engravers earlier in the century. Other artists, if they could afford it, went abroad.

Here are some of the artists who worked in and caught the atmosphere of the open countryside.

Helen ALLINGHAM, née Paterson (1848–1926):

Of the Birket Foster school of charming rustic (they were near neighbours in Surrey) she was a feistier woman than her charming watercolours suggest, promoting herself to publishers in a way thought unbecoming in a woman. She married the poet William Allingham and, partly through him, met Tennyson, Carlyle and Ruskin.

Richard ANSDELL (1815–85):

Noted painter of Scottish landscapes, many of which were reproduced as engravings for the domestic interior, and those engravings provided much of his income. Ansdell suffered from being contemporary with and painting the same subjects as Edwin Landseer. Some felt Ansdell was the greater artist, but he never produced a *Stag at Bay*, and thus was doomed to second place. But what a magnificent second he was. In the mid-1850s, after twenty years of Scottish landscape, Ansdell switched much of his attention (though by no means all) to Spain, where his landscape and genre studies had less obvious competition. Some of these works were painted in collaboration with John Phillip. Other paintings saw Ansdell collaborate with Frith and, early in his career, with Thomas Creswick. He also painted some very good large-scale portrait groups, such as *The Waterloo Cup Coursing Meeting* (1840); for several years in the 1970s, curiously, this painting held the auction price record for Victorian paintings.

Henry John BODDINGTON (1811–65):

Son of the important pre-Victorian artist Edward Williams senior, Henry adopted his wife Clara's surname to distinguish himself from other members of his artistic family. He is known mainly for his Home Counties, and occasionally Welsh, rural landscapes.

Thomas Shotter BOYS (1803–74):

A fine watercolourist whose pure (some would say too pure, too uninvolving) landscapes are keenly collected today. Many of his studies came from leisurely tours of Europe. He was the first artist to exploit chromolithography, learnt in Paris.

Frederick Lee BRIDELL (1831–63):

A promising landscape artist who died too young to develop fully. The dramatically-lit *Coliseum by Moonlight* is his finest work.

Henry BRIGHT (1810–73):

Landscape artist of the Norwich School, whose best works have a fine outdoor feeling.

Richard BURCHETT (1815–75):

A landscape artist of whom the only well-known work in a public collection is *A Scene in the Isle of Wight*, now in the V&A. He was a rebellious man of vigorous attitudes, contesting authority both in education (he was a troublesome headmaster at the Government School of Design) and in the Church (he converted to Catholicism). Late in life he devoted his energies to farming, without success.

Sir George CLAUSEN (1852–1944):

Though he lived for nearly a half century under Victoria, Clausen is considered a twentieth-century artist. If his work now seems conventional, it did not then: his style was continental rather than English – so much so that in 1876 *The Times* critic mistook him for a 'very clever Dutch painter' – and his continental realism continued to mark him out. From the 1890s his style progressed from realism and he became increasingly regarded as a *pleine air* artist. His standing remained high and in 1895 he became a teacher at the Royal Academy Schools. (In 1904 he was made professor of painting. He would be a war artist in WWI.) His knighthood came in 1927.

George Vicat COLE (1833–93):

In his day he was a hugely successful landscape and genre artist, capable of fine work both in modest and large-scale canvases – e.g. the painterly *Pool of London* (1888) – though his breakthrough came with *Harvest Time, Painted at Hombury Hill, Surrey* (1860) painted while he was in an earlier Pre-Raphaelite phase. His father was the landscape artist George Cole (1810–73) while his son, Reginald George Vicat Cole (1870–1940), also painted landscapes. There is an unrelated George Townsend Cole (1810–83), Portsmouth-born, self-taught and very competent.

William COLLINS (1788–1847):

A solid landscape and coastal scene artist, though his reputation was overshadowed by the similarity of his work to that of his mentor David Wilkie and, in the view of some, to the works of John Constable. In later years his reputation took a second knock when it was outshone by that of his son, Wilkie Collins, author of *The Moonstone*.

David COX (1783–1859):

The son of a Birmingham blacksmith, Cox began dabbling with paint while confined to bed after breaking his leg – dabbling, in that the first products of one of England's finest watercolourists were painted kites. Fortunately he also made copies of prints around the house, copies of sufficient quality to encourage his parents to pay for painting lessons. For a while he was a stage set painter but by his early twenties he had exhibited at the Royal Academy. For all the delicacy and invention in his art, Cox was a professional, and his finest works mingled with workaday pieces, pleasant and saleable. Many of his later paintings were made on the same batch of (literally) wrapping paper – fortunately a large batch – which gave a characteristically rough and flecked texture to his work. When asked about those flecks (embedded in the paper) he famously replied, 'Oh, I just put wings on them and they fly away as birds.'

Cox's oil paintings belong to the last two decades of his life. They carry much of the freshness and movement of his watercolours, and seem advanced for their day. The best, perhaps, is *Rhyl Sands*. David Cox senior's son, David Cox junior (1809–85) imitated his father's style and, although their works can occasionally be confused, he was not his father.

Thomas CRESWICK (1811–69):

A landscape watercolourist of the kind the establishment approved – accurate, correctly composed and unexciting. Practically all his landscapes included water – a stream or river of some kind – and at the Memorial Exhibition of his paintings it was felt worth pointing out that one of them did *not* contain water.

James Jackson CURNOCK (1839–91):

A Bristol landscape artist, son of James, a genre and portrait artist, praised by Ruskin for his clear and tranquil *The Llugwy at Capel Curig* (1873/4).

Francis DANBY (1793–1861):

A stand-out artist from the early decades, his style combined the sublime palette of Turner with the vision of John Martin. His sunsets and light effects, though less wild than Turner's, were as stunning in their way – and more 'correctly' executed – while his visionary pieces which again, were more 'correctly' executed than John Martin's, could be mistaken for the work of twenty-first-century fantasy artists. But if Danby the artist stuck more closely to the rules than did either Martin or Turner, Danby the man did not. His wife went off to live with another artist, Paul Falconer Poole, and Danby took a mistress. When she and Danby moved to Geneva he took his seven children, along with his mistress's three, with him – but he did not divorce his wife. The scandal, at the peak of his career, wrecked his reputation (he was about to be elected an RA). On Danby's death, Poole married his ex-wife. (The work of neither of Danby's artist sons – James, 1816–75, and Thomas, 1817–86 – should be mistaken for their father's.)

William DELAMOTTE (1775–1863):

A landscape artist, born in Weymouth, who lived most of his life in and around Oxford. Most of his best work was before Victoria's reign. A son, Alfred William, was a lesser landscape artist; another son, splendidly named Freeman Gage, was a wood-engraver; and his youngest son, Philip Henry (1821–89), was a pioneer photographer who became Professor of Fine Art at King's College in 1879.

Peter DE WINT (1784–1849):

Though he lived little more than a decade into Victoria's reign, De Wint was prolific and produced plenty of fine watercolours up to his death. Of Dutch/American origins (hence his name) he was born in Staffordshire, moved to London, began in oils but soon found watercolour to be his métier. His lovely atmospheric landscapes are much collected, although often the original luscious colours have faded, leaving the paintings only ghosts of what they were. He also painted in oils, but they were never as popular as his watercolours.

Charles EARLE (1832–93):

A prolific watercolourist who, though born in London, spent a great deal of time exploring the British countryside for his paintings. He also took working holidays on the continent.

Myles Birket FOSTER (1825–99):

Born in North Shields but moving to Tottenham when he was 5, Foster began as an apprentice engraver for Landells (where he met his lifelong friend Edmund Evans) but was almost immediately engaged as an artist

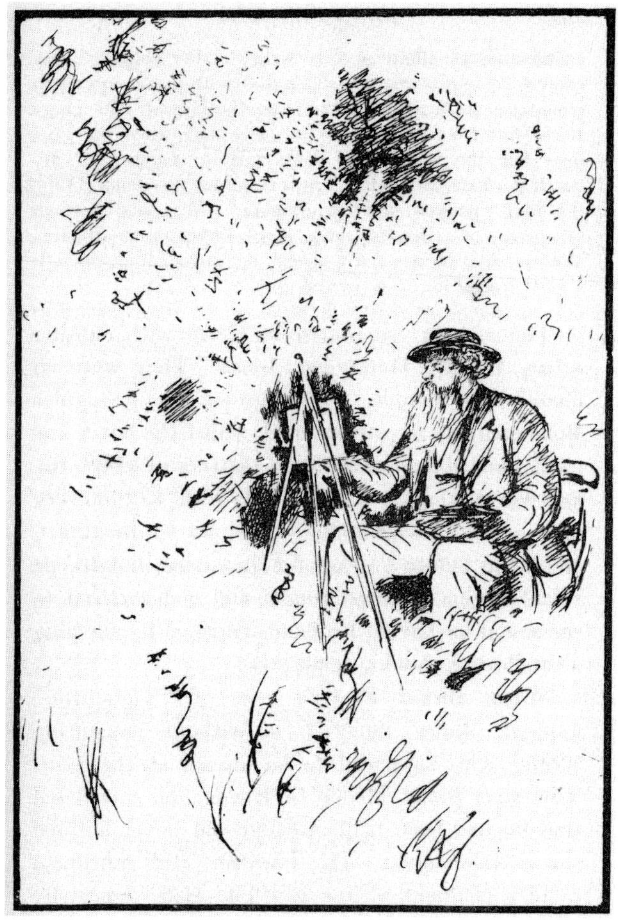

Birket Foster sketched by Charles Keene

rather than a mere 'cutter'. By the time he was 21 he was confident enough to leave Landells and set up as a professional artist/illustrator, mainly for *Punch* and the *Illustrated London News*, and before long was producing pretty pictures for poetry and drawing-room table books (and for the annual *London Almanack*). From 1858 he worked almost exclusively in watercolour (he was self-taught) and, to those who know his works from reproduction, it can come as a surprise to realise how small many of his finely detailed pieces are. Plenty are less than 4 inches by 6.

He was the archetypal artist and illustrator, equally at home in watercolour and black and white, and as such he fell out of fashion for the first half of the twentieth century, though he is collected again today – so much so that fake Fosters abound. They did in his lifetime; even he once went into a shop to ask why a watercolour of his in the window was so cheap. They told him it was a chromolithograph. Collectors today who can't afford his watercolours (or the many convincing prints masquerading as such) can always fall back on the books he illustrated.

His works are rose-tinted, charming and sentimental but, conventional and commercial as they may seem, Foster the man was popular with fellow artists. He lived for thirty years (till 1893) near Godalming in Witley, at 'The Hill', a house decorated by William Morris and Burne-Jones – a house he often threw open to locals and visiting artists for amateur theatricals, entertainments and parties. Evans married Foster's niece, Miss Brown, in 1864, and that same year Foster wed for the second time, marrying J D Watson's sister. 'Mine has been a very uneventful life,' he wrote in 1895, 'but one that my art has made very pleasant to me.'

George Arthur FRIPP (1813–96):

A Bristol-born watercolourist, well enough regarded to become Secretary to the Society of Painters in Water-Colours in 1849. He produced mainly landscapes (sometimes a touch lurid) and in the 1860s was commissioned by the Queen to sketch at Balmoral.

Alfred Augustus GLENDENING (1861–1907):

Landscape artist, usually of Kent scenes.

John GLOVER (1767–1849):

A larger-than-life (he weighed 20 stone) and largely pre-Victorian landscape artist, he was of the late classical style, and is thought to have invented the split-brush technique he used when painting foliage. He travelled extensively through Britain, and at the age of 63 emigrated to Australia. He was a farmer's son, self-taught as an artist, but became a drawing master and ran his own drawing school. He continued exhibiting in London till his death.

Frederick GOODALL (1822–1904):

Half-forgotten now, yet one of the most richly rewarded artists of his day, he was known mainly for his landscapes, with scenes from Britain, Ireland and northern France, then later, after visiting in 1858, for Egyptian and Biblical paintings – which can seem dreary to us today (while his rare fairy pictures are quite charming). He won his first award, a Society of

Arts silver medal, when he was just 14, and at the peak of his career he regularly earned more than £10,000 a year. His older brother Edward Angelo Goodall (1819–1908) was one of Britain's first war artists, and painted at the Crimea. His younger brother Walter (1830–99) was a fine watercolourist, largely of crisp rural scenes, but he became paralysed in 1875, a condition which sadly worsened until his death.

Albert GOODWIN (1845–99):

A Kentish landscape and genre painter who trained with Arthur Hughes and Madox Brown (who forecast a great future for him as a landscape painter). Goodwin produced bright and airy pictures and was a notable exponent of the stipple effect.

William Henry GORE (fl 1880–1920):

A watercolour painter of mainly rural scenes, simple if romantic, often exhibiting at the Royal Academy.

William W GOSLING (1824–83):

Popular in his day, if variable in quality, London-born Gosling was known mainly for his carefully-composed rural settings, often including sheep. He was given to titling his works with supposedly apposite poetic quotes.

David (1802–70) and Mrs David Octavius HILL, née Amelia Paton (fl 1863–74):

He was a Scottish landscape painter who, as the century progressed, made use of photography to help create some quite enormous pictures, exemplified by a vast group portrait of 470 Scottish ministers resigning in 1843. (During the 1840s Hill had a part share in a photographic business, and some of his own photographs are very good.) Miss Paton was an artist before she married him.

John Evan HODGSON (1831–95):

Painter of genre, landscape and historical pictures, and an exhibitor at the RA from 1856 to '93 – i.e. almost all his adult life. From 1882 to '95 he was Librarian and Professor of Painting at the Academy. Practically all his paintings from the last two decades of his life were inspired by his travels to north Africa in 1868.

John William INCHBOLD (1830–88):

Leeds-born landscape painter, the son of a newspaper proprietor, his early landscapes showed Pre-Raphaelite tendencies which led to his being at first praised and later criticised by Ruskin. He was especially good at mountains, lakes and mists.

Cecil Gordon LAWSON (1851–82):

A fine landscape artist in the Dutch manner, who died tragically young. He achieved limited fame with *The Minister's Garden* (1878) and was promoted, to little effect, by the critic Edmund Gosse. He was the son of the Scottish portrait painter William Lawson (fl 1819–1864).

Benjamin Williams LEADER (1831–1923):

It helps if an artist gives himself a more memorable name than Ben Williams, and this Ben had the additional excuse that he wanted to distinguish himself from the unrelated Williams family of artists. Hence did B W Leader create himself. He was one of the best and more individual landscape artists of his day. Coming to maturity around 1850, it was inevitable that his early work should be influenced by the Pre-Raphaelites, but he soon moved on to his own, softer palette, one more suited to the British climate. His landscapes were of several different areas – from Wales (largely around Betws-y-Coed), to Scotland, the English Midlands and West Country – and his most famous, one of the nation's favourites (though by no means one of the critics' favourites) is the quintessentially English *February Fill Dyke* (1881). The mud in that picture still looks wet; the sky and the damp grassy furrows are damp and chill. The artist, bizarrely, claimed he had painted 'A November evening after rain.'

Edward LEAR (1812–88):

Best known for having invented the limerick and for his books of amusingly illustrated comic verse, Lear was a superb landscape artist whose reputation has only improved since his death. Despite his own wry words, 'How pleasant to know Mr Lear', he was a depressive whose epilepsy made him solitary and shy. At the age of 19 he published his *Illustrations of the Family of Psittacidae, or Parrots*, and many of his paintings can be found in John Gould's magnificent *Birds of Europe* (1832–37). His work earned him the sponsorship of Lord Stanley and it was for Stanley's grandchildren in 1846 that Lear produced *The Book of Nonsense* with its limericks and quirky illustrations.

Though still epileptic and frequently unwell, he was a restless and inveterate traveller, moving through Europe, Arabia, India and Ceylon. From these travels came his many delicate landscapes, in pen and ink, in watercolour and in oil. In a telling letter to a friend he wrote, 'I think it will be long before I settle again in London. The constant interruptions there – the organ grinding, the penny post, the frequent callers, and the uncertain state of light is fatal to my chance of doing my best.'

Frederick Richard LEE (1798–1879):

A landscape artist in the traditional style, who nevertheless made a comfortable living from his work.

John LINNELL (1792–1882):

The long-lived, fiercely religious and demanding father-in-law to Samuel Palmer was a prolific landscape artist of the old school (much use of brown and dark green), who could nevertheless imbue his countryside studies with 'Englishness' and fill his skies with almost apocalyptic movement. The paintings sold: he left over £200,000 in his will (an enormous sum then).

John MARTIN (1789–1854):

One of the most easily recognised artists, especially when working in black and white. His dramatic landscapes, frequently with biblical overtones, are overwhelming (if sometimes flawed in technique) and the more garishly coloured could grace the covers of fantasy novels today. Enormously popular in his time (before Victoria), he was facing ruin when she was crowned, but his untypical, portrait-packed *Coronation of Queen Victoria* brought him back to fame. He soon faded to near-obscurity before being re-recognised in the second half of the twentieth century. His mezzotints to *Paradise Lost* are stunning and often reproduced.

Horatio McCULLOCH (1805–67):

A fine Scottish landscape painter, especially in watercolour, who defined the Scottish landscape for non-travelling patrons. Nevertheless, his most successful painting was the historical *Glencoe* (1864), which as a print sold by the thousand.

Robert Gustav MEYERHEIM (1847–1920):

As his name suggests, he was not British, though he captured the mood of the English countryside with great skill. Born in Danzig, the German Meyerheim came to London in 1875 and never left – even through the difficult period (for a German) of the First World War.

George William MOTE (1832–1909):

An interesting if little-known landscape painter, self-taught, a gardener by occupation (for Sir Thomas Phillips, of Broadway) who painted in an individual, almost primitive style, and who was eventually able to make art his profession – though, perversely, his best works are from the early years when painting was still his hobby.

William James MÜLLER (1812–45):

Bristol-born landscape, and occasionally genre, painter of quite an advanced style who spent much of his short life travelling and painting what he saw – throughout England and Wales, much of Europe, Egypt (in 1838) and Lycia (1843–4).

John O'CONNOR (1830–89):

Irish landscape artist who came to London in 1848 having spent his teens painting stage scenery. No surprise, then, that he found work doing the same for the Haymarket and Drury Lane. But from 1855 he began exhibiting the landscapes – British, European and some from India – for which he is known.

Samuel PALMER (1805–81):

It is generally held that his best works were his earliest – be they the delicate landscapes or the visionary pieces influenced by William Blake – but Palmer's early period ended around the time Victoria came to the throne. He married that year, and his new and domineering father-in-law, John Linnell – despite having been an admirer of Blake himself – is blamed for having led Palmer away from what he did best. (The need to earn money may have played a part; Palmer's early pieces were lovely but did not sell.) In Victoria's reign Palmer concentrated on landscape and historical subjects – etched or in watercolour – and, though they may lack the dreamlike qualities of his early works, they can be just as beautiful.

Henry PETHER (fl 1828–65):

He and his brother Sebastian (1790–1844) painted romantic landscapes in the 'picturesque' style – as did their father, William 'Moonlight' Pether (1738–1821), seen by some as a forerunner to Atkinson Grimshaw. Before Sebastian settled down to moonlight studies he is said to have invented the stomach pump. He died of consumption.

William Bell SCOTT (1811–1890):

Son of the Edinburgh engraver Robert Scott and brother of the artist David, William trained first as an engraver while at the same time writing poetry. When he moved to London in 1837 he mixed with established but conventional artists like Frith and Egg (though he also knew Dadd). In 1843 he

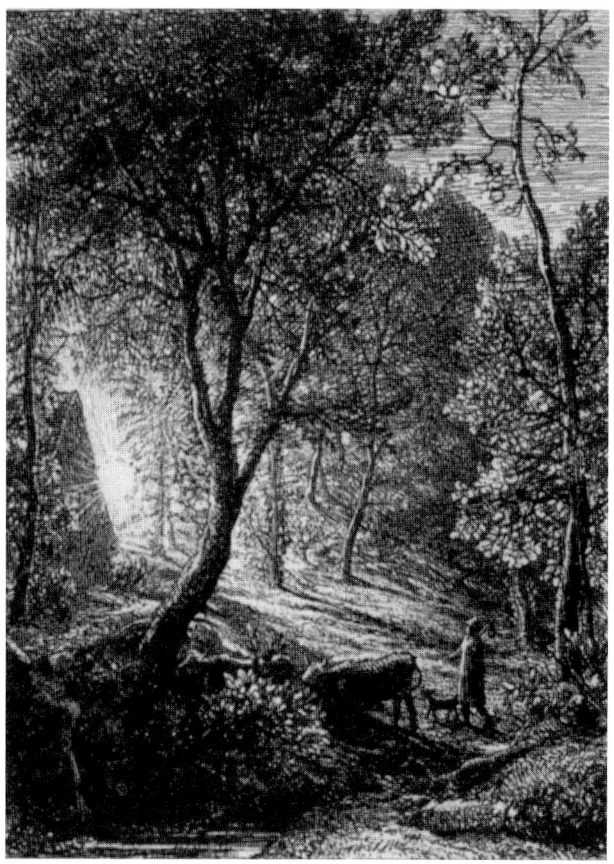

A typical woodland scene: engraving by Samuel Palmer

began a twenty-year spell at the Government School of Design, Newcastle. Rossetti admired his poems, and Scott contributed to *The Germ*. After his move back to London in 1866 he and Rossetti grew closer, and from 1870 they were neighbours in Cheyne Walk. He was a minor landscape painter, though he painted a striking portrait of Swinburne (who was then, but not later, a friend).

Alfred SISLEY (1839–98):

So associated was Sisley with the Impressionists that he is sometimes left out of surveys of English painters. He was born in Paris to a well-off English father, received his training in France, exhibited at French salons and worked in France all his life, apart from brief spells in England in 1881 and '97. He never sold as well as friends like Renoir (who painted his portrait twice) and, in truth, Sisley's life was a sad one. When he died, after contracting cancer of the throat, he had not got round to completing naturalisation papers and died, therefore, an Englishman. The obituary in *The Magazine of Art* noted sadly that his pictures were 'not altogether acceptable either to artists or to the art-loving public'.

James SMETHAM (1821–89):

A painter, etcher and portrait artist whose influences were William Blake, Wesley and the Pre-Raphaelites. He gave up portraiture because of what he considered the unbeatable competition of photography, and changed his focus to land and seascapes. Though devoutly religious, his beliefs did not wreck his friendship with the hedonistic Rossetti and he was happy to sometimes include pagan figures in his landscapes. He maintained a friendship with Ruskin also. Sadly, he died insane.

Alfred STANNARD (1806–89):

One of the better specialists in landscape and marine work of the Norwich School. His talented daughter, Eloise Harriet Stannard (1829–1915), on the other hand, specialised in sumptuous indoor still-lifes and flower studies. The Stannard clan also contained a Mrs Joseph Stannard (1803–85) and an artist daughter Emily. Whether Henry (?–1920) and his son Henry John Sylvester (1870–1951) Stannard were directly linked is less certain.

Philip Wilson STEER (1860–1942):

Very much in the French Impressionist mould, his delicate landscape and coastal studies mark him out from most of his contemporaries. Progressive as he seemed in the late nineteenth century, he made little progress in the twentieth, other than to concentrate more on portraiture, his weaker suit.

John Frederick TENNANT (1796–1872):

A London boy who moved out, first to Bexleyheath, then to Hendon. He began in genre but turned to landscape, unconsciously documenting the unspoilt land that would soon become suburbanised.

Joseph Mallord William TURNER (1775–1851):

England's greatest colourist. A revolutionary, in that he can be said to have anticipated Impressionism and Abstract Expressionism. An often cantankerous, never obsequious misfit from the lower classes who was

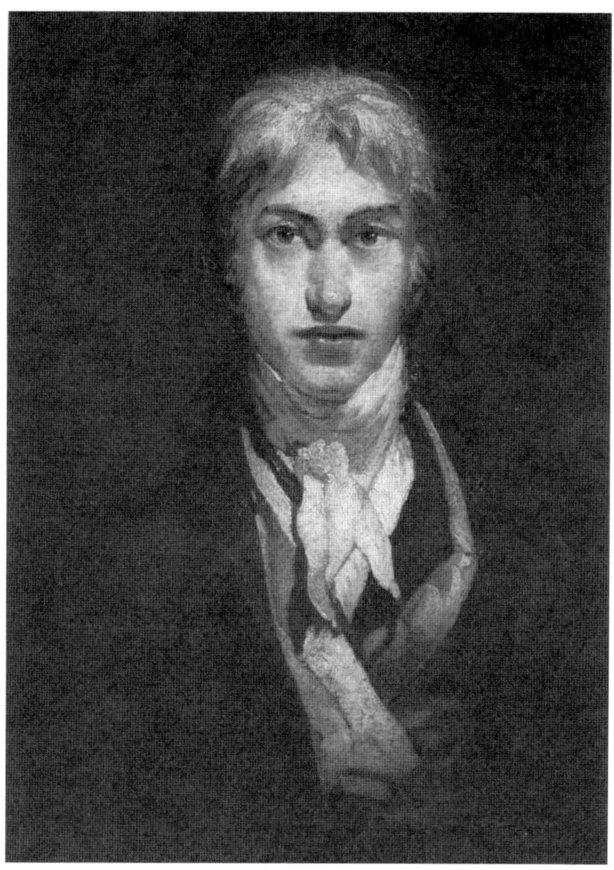

Self-portrait of the young Turner (about 23)

lauded by the aristocracy. A lecturer who was barely articulate. A private man who bequeathed all his paintings to the public. It is not a matter of deciding which of his paintings were revolutionary; it is more a question of finding those which were not: some of the early classical pieces, perhaps, some of his vignettes. Of the many astounding, utterly innovative masterpieces one might select from the best-known: *The Fighting Téméraire*; *Rain, Steam and Speed*; *Ulysses deriding Polyphemus*; and *Peace – Burial at Sea* – but the list is almost endless. Of his aristocratic patrons the most consistent would have been Lord Egremont, whose house, Petworth, was made available to Turner for years; this patronage was repaid hugely, and while *Interior at Petworth* is the most famous painting, Turner's *Music Party* made there is the author's favourite.

Turner was a Londoner, the son of a barber and, though he joined and was active in the Royal Academy and had grand patrons, he made no attempt to elevate his status or to pretend to be anything other than he was. He dressed shabbily, carelessly, and lived at addresses he wouldn't give out. In the last years of his life he kept a shambolic, badly maintained, leaking studio in Queen Anne Street but lived secretly in a small house off Chelsea's Cremorne Road with his presumed mistress Mrs Booth (he was known to the neighbours as Mr or sometimes Admiral Booth, never as Mr Turner). Poorly educated, he struggled to express himself in words; his lectures were gap-filled mumbles, the texts he wrote to accompany his pictures were well-nigh incomprehensible – some, at times, came the closest he ever did come to pretentiousness. He was a secretive man: how he achieved his effects was not something he imparted willingly, though it is known that his range of methods included, occasionally, throwing paint at his paper and soaking it in a bucket of water, then watching the paints run when he hauled it out. In this, as in so many things, he was a modernist.

An artist this individual, self-willed and innovative was bound to be inconsistent. Not every picture worked. Though, like most artists, he destroyed many of his failures, he kept many too – leaving them lying around his dreadful studio among the clutter. Some have come onto the market or have been exhibited, but they don't detract from his status and, if Turner had known they'd still exist a century and a half after his death, he would have laughed. In his studio when he died, among works he had refused to sell, was *The Fighting Téméraire*. The legacy he *gave* to the nation comprised some 350 of his paintings and an astounding 20,000 drawings and watercolours.

William TURNER (1789–1862):

His dates are not dissimilar to those of his near namesake and, although both Turners were landscape artists and watercolourists, this one was the more conventional. He exhibited at the RA from 1807 and became a very young Associate of the Society of Painters in Water-Colours in 1808. He is often designated 'of Oxford' (where he lived) to help distinguish him from JMW.

Robert Thorne WAITE (1842–1935):

This long-lived Cheltenham-born watercolourist achieved his best results in rural scenes, either Cotswold or South Downs (he lived the last part of his life in Bournemouth), though he passed some years in London also.

Edmund George WARREN (1834–1909):

The son of the painter Henry Warren was a particularly realistic landscape and genre painter, so much so that he was criticised for his photographic likenesses. Ruskin thought his works 'mechanical'. But many, including buyers today, admire his technical virtuosity, seen at its best in the many studies of sunlight filtering through the trees.

Frederick Waters WATTS aka Frederick William Watts (1800–70):

A landscape artist in the style of Constable, to an extent some have thought plagiaristic, but a very able painter nevertheless. Few can be blamed for assuming his *A Suffolk Landscape* with its cart stuck in the millpond beneath fine trees to *be* by Constable. His middle name was Waters, not William, though he is often wrongly called so.

James Thomas WATTS (c.1850–1930):

Born in Birmingham and trained at the Birmingham School of Art, he was well-placed to fall under the spell of the Pre-Raphaelites, and his often charming landscapes show careful fidelity to their precepts and Ruskin's rules. He moved to Liverpool in 1874 and became as much, if not more, associated with that city as with Birmingham.

Josiah WHYMPER (1813–1903):

With his brother Ebenezzar [sic] he founded a famous firm of wood-engravers, providing illustrations for many Victorian books and magazines. An engraver himself, Whymper was also a landscape artist in the style of Samuel Cox.

Daniel Alexander WILLIAMSON (1823–1903):

A good middle-rank landscape artist and close friend of W L Windus, with whom he shared painting holidays in the Lake District.

Edmund WIMPERIS (1835–1900):

Watercolour landscape artist in the style of Cox, and a wood-engraver, concentrating on landscape to make up for the fact that his human figure-work was weak. Wimperis first exhibited in the year of Cox's death and eventually became Vice-President of the New Society of Painters in Water-Colours. His three sisters were also artists, as were his two sons.

Chapter Four

MARINE PAINTING
Our English Coasts

An island nation would be expected to produce fine marine artists. We have a long coastline, spectacular coastal scenery and a maritime history through peace and war. Throughout the centuries men have given their lives on the seas about us, to defend the nation or simply to bring us food. They have died, and their loved ones have mourned them. There is no lack of subject matter: in the nineteenth century it was no idle boast to say that Britain was the foremost maritime nation in the world; London was the world's mightiest port. Bristol, Newcastle, Liverpool and Glasgow contrasted with the many small fishing ports scattered along our shores and, even before railways made the seaside more accessible, our inland people had rediscovered the beaches and coastal scenery.

Frith's *Ramsgate Sands* showed the British holidaymaker in full Victorian panoply, while Tuke showed lonesome paddlers in absorbed contemplation, foam at their ankles, sun on their shins. Stanfield, Cooke

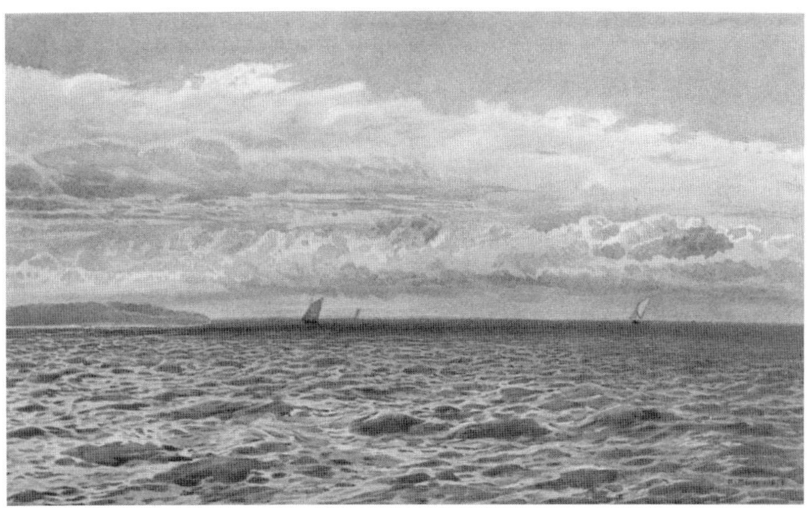

(The other) Henry Moore's *A Sunny Day in the Solent* (1873)

and Roberts dramatised the Navy and battles with watery weather. Artists of the Newlyn school revealed the knotty detail of wooden fishing boats buffeted by the waves. Turner fêted our fighting ships or the greater glory of a setting sun. The coasts themselves attracted disparate artists: John Brett, William Dyce and Holman Hunt from the Pre-Raphaelites; Bramley, Forbes, Langley and Frederick Hall from Newlyn; Tissot for Society; Steer and one might say James Smetham for British Impressionism. Artists sketched and painted in oil while perhaps excelling in that essentially British – nay, English – medium of watercolour: Edward Duncan, Copley Fielding, the Brothers Joy. Many artists turned to the sea as a break, a vacation from their usual genre, though some specialised in the marine.

Frank BRANGWYN (1867–1956):

Much of his finest work was produced in the twentieth century but by the end of the nineteenth he had already carved out a reputation as a fine marine artist. He began the last decade of the century with an extended tour of the East, a tour that brightened his palette which had, before then, been inclined to monochrome.

Sir Oswald Waters BRIERLY (1817–94):

Marine Painter to Queen Victoria, and fine depicter of historical naval scenes. His work, not surprisingly, can be found today at the National Maritime Museum in Greenwich.

George CHAMBERS (1803–40):

Chambers had a short and active life, despite the chronic ill-health which would take him to an early grave. From humble beginnings he went to sea at the age of 10 and by his mid-twenties his marine studies were being exhibited at the Royal Academy.

Edward William COOKE (1811–80):

Cooke had no formal training as an artist but was taught by his workaday artist father, yet he rose to become a Fellow of the Royal Society and a favourite artist of Queen Victoria. He was both a fine marine artist and an accomplished botanist and scientist. Some of his work is in the National Maritime Museum.

Edward DUNCAN (1804–82):

A marine and landscape painter highly regarded in his time though somewhat ignored today, seen at his best in watercolour.

Vandyke Copley FIELDING (1787–1855):

He painted mainly marine subjects, in watercolour (many of which have subsequently faded), and was greatly praised by Ruskin: 'No man has ever given, with the same flashing freedom, the race of a running tide.' His reputation has since faded like his watercolours.

Stanhope Alexander FORBES (1857–1947):

A leading member of the Newlyn School and a founder of the New English Art Club, Forbes was a major figure in late Victorian (and early twentieth-century) painting and, for those today who have little taste for realistic genre painting, his pictures can be seen as revealing glimpses into Victorian life. His marine studies are equally well made, and examples of his work are in the Tate and other galleries. Cook, Hardie and Payne, the biographers of his artist wife, Elizabeth Adela Forbes (1859–1912), describe her husband as 'a somewhat prosaic male artist with a brilliant wife' within the '"Newlyn brotherhood of the palette"'. The Canadian Miss Forbes is generally thought to have damaged her career by marrying Stanhope, who married one of his students three years after Elizabeth died.

Charles Napier HEMY (1841–1917):

Mainly remembered for his fine marine subjects, finely rendered and, at times, so realistic that the use of photographic assistance is suspected.

James Clarke HOOK (1819–1907):

A largely forgotten but able painter of marine and coastal scenes, sometimes 'prettified' with human interest. His early works were of historical bent.

The Brothers JOY, William (1803–60?) and John (1806–59):

Both were born in Great Yarmouth, and both were fine watercolourists of marine and occasional genre scenes, spending much of their later years together at Chichester. They often collaborated on their paintings.

Henry MOORE (1831–95):

It is unfortunate for an artist to have the same name as a more famous one, but the Victorian Moore (the brother of Albert) was, of course, unaware of the twentieth-century sculptor. He was essentially a marine painter, and a fine one, better perhaps than his contemporaries saw. He showed the sea in all its moods.

William Clarkson STANFIELD (1793–1867):

A leading marine painter, brought up by the sea and, after a spell in the Merchant Service, press-ganged into the Royal Navy, from which he retired injured (tripping over an anchor). Yet he retained his love for the sea. He and his close friend David Roberts painted scenic effects for the Theatre Royal, Edinburgh and London's Drury Lane, and collaborated on huge dioramic seascapes while working separately on their own paintings. When Roberts died in 1864 Stanfield was inconsolable and died three years later. Stanfield's dioramic work (series of tableaux on cycloramic or unrolling backcloths) encouraged him to over-dramatise his works, which can be like action stills from spectacular melodrama.

Henry Scott TUKE (1858–1929):

Born in York, he moved to Falmouth as a child, studied at the Slade, then moved to Newlyn, where he became allied with, if not a full member of, that school before returning to Falmouth in 1885. His coastal and beach scenes often include softly-painted young men and boys frolicking gently in the spume.

John WARD (1798–1849):

Born in Hull, it is perhaps no surprise that he specialised in painting ships.

Charles William WYLLIE (1853–1923):

A marine artist of fair talent, though he has always lain in the shadow of his brother. Their father was a less well-known artist, William Morison Wyllie (*c.*1819–1895).

William Lionel WYLLIE (1851–1931):

More talented than his brother Charles, he painted mainly marine subjects, usually though not always contemporary, and between 1870 and '90 provided illustrations to *The Graphic*. From around 1880 an increasing number of his paintings were of maritime and industrial life on the Thames and Medway, and in the twentieth century he painted naval and military subjects. In Wyllie's paintings one can almost feel the wind and rain, and hear the creaking of the timbers.

Chapter Five

GENRE
Work & Everyday Life

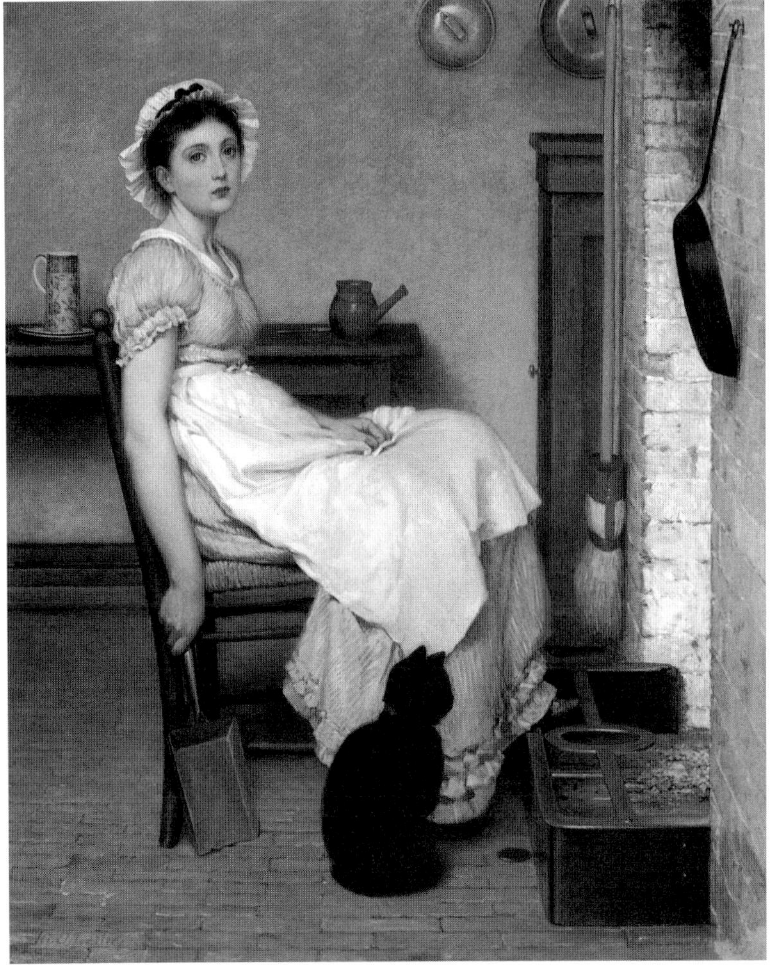

Her First Place by G D Leslie

Genre is an odd word to have attached itself to what is, in effect, one genre among many. In art it has come to mean pictures of everyday life, usually contemporary life, with the picture small in scale and suitable for display in a domestic interior. It often has a narrative or moral element. Though the genre had existed earlier, it first flourished in seventeenth-century Holland: think of those easy-to-live-with pictures of peasant life, domestic interiors, drinking scenes and rustic pleasures. The nineteenth century added scenes from urban life: street and railway scenes, back yards, parlours, kitchens, basements, dining rooms – anywhere people

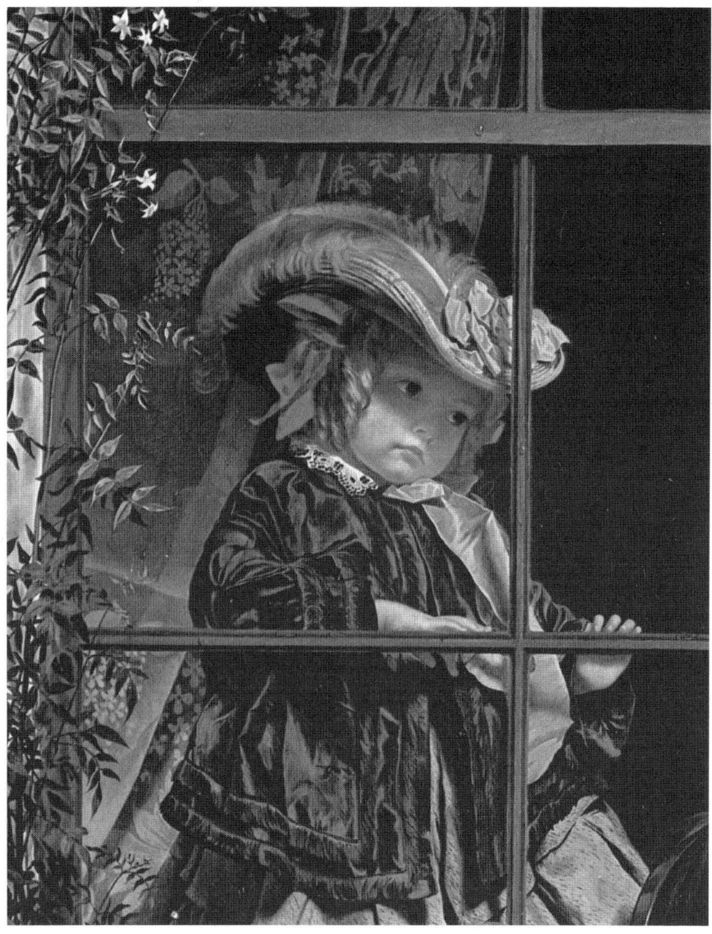

No Walk Today by Sophie Anderson

recognised, not necessarily as part of their own lives but as part of the bustling world in which they lived. Whatever the setting, it was populated with recognisable types although, again, not necessarily 'folk like us'. Peasants, urchins, vagabonds, drunks – fallen women even – and servants were as likely a subject as was paterfamilias and his brood.

Much of our interest today lies in how people dressed and what they did. Everyday behaviour was lovingly recorded: Mulready's *Choosing the Wedding Gown* and Faed's *The Mitherless Bairn* contrast with the massive crowd scenes of W P Frith. Genre paintings showed the seaside (Frith's *Ramsgate Sands*), how people got there (*To Brighton and Back for 3/6d*, Charles Rossiter), how they travelled in town (Egley's *Omnibus Life in London*), how they ate (Frith's *Many Happy Returns of the Day* versus Charles Hunt's *A Coffee Stall, Westminster*), how they shopped (Hicks's hectic *Billingsgate* against Clausen's sedate *Spring Morning, Haverstock Hill*). All human life, indeed, was there – from George Smith's *Fondly Gazing* (at her baby) to Martineau's *Last Day in the Old Home*.

Who were the artists, then, whose works reveal the Victorian world to us today?

Sophie ANDERSON (1823–1903):

Best remembered – perhaps *only* remembered – for her much-reproduced *No Walk Today*. Although in 2008 that painting sold for £890,000 at Sotheby's (before buyer's commission took it above the million), Anderson's smaller portrait, *Little Bo Peep*, of the same little girl (assumed to be her daughter) sold for a mere £12,000 the following year.

Thomas ARMSTRONG (1832–1911):

A lesser member of Du Maurier's 'Paris Gang', he trained on the continent before returning to London around 1860. He worked then mainly on decorative panels, and his paintings had the decorative appeal appreciated by the Aesthetic movement. In 1881 he became Director of Art at South Kensington.

John Henry F BACON (1868–1914):

London-born painter of mainly genre scenes, though he also produced historical works. He exhibited at the RA from 1889.

Frank BRAMLEY (1857–1915):

A leading member of the Newlyn School and a founder member of the New English Art Club. Though considered by some to be brutally realistic then, his well-made paintings seem typically Victorian today – *A*

Hopeless Dawn (now in the Tate), much-reproduced in its day, exemplifies his sentimentality.

Philip Hermogenes CALDERON (1833–98):

Founder of the St John's Wood Clique, a group of artists including W F Yeames, H S Marks and G A Story, which aspired to ape the rebellious spirit of 'The Clique' (a more effective 1837 anti-Academy movement) but with no noticeable effect. Calderon was the son of a Spanish priest who eventually became a professor at King's College. Although with *Broken Vows* (1856) he began in a Pre-Raphaelite vein, he moved into the safer waters of genre painting.

R W CHAPMAN (fl 1855–61):

Little is known of this realistic genre painter, though his *Posting the Letter* of 1857 suggests a pleasing ability.

James CHARLES (1851–1906):

A founder member of the New English Arts Club, whose palette was lighter and fresher than most of his genre contemporaries. *Christening Sunday* (1887) shows his wife as the young mother.

Eyre CROWE (1824–1910):

Crowe is an artist who nowadays turns up more often in biographies than in galleries, perhaps because, as a cousin of Thackeray and the Prinseps, he had easy access to literary and artistic circles. His well-painted genre studies give interesting if uncritical views of Victorian life.

Augustus Leopold EGG (1816–63):

A leading exponent of Victorian realism whose works, conventionally beautiful as they seem now, were mildly revolutionary in their day; Egg was a founder member of 'The Clique' which, in 1837, set out to challenge the orthodoxy of the RA. He had a penchant for historical and literary subjects (he was a friend of Dickens and acted with him in amateur theatricals) and, though he was tempted by the accuracy of the Pre-Raphaelites, clung to his own, almost super-realist, social documentary style, varying from the (for its time) harrowing *Past and Present* trilogy (1858), warning women against infidelity, to the lovely *Travelling Companions* (1862), depicting two demure young ladies in a railway carriage, carrying no moral message at all.

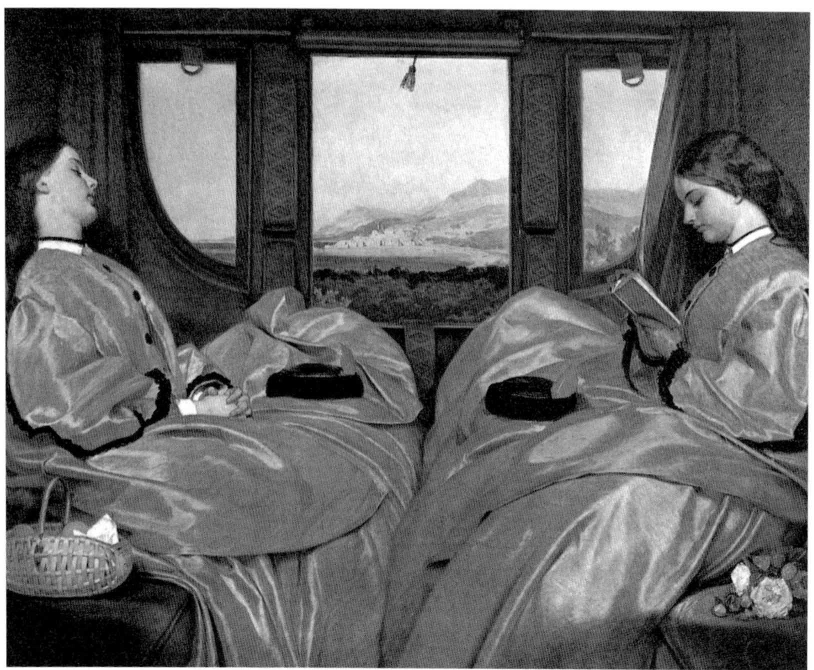

The Travelling Companions by Augustus Leopold Egg

William Maw EGLEY (1826–1916):

The son of a portrait miniaturist, he became a leading genre painter whose paintings carried the high gloss and meticulous finish associated with the Pre-Raphaelites, though he was not of their number. After an early period (mid-Forties to mid-Fifties) painting historical and literary subjects, he moved on to paint scenes from contemporary life, somewhat romanticised. In his *Omnibus Life in London* he used friends and relatives to model the fourteen passengers, and could be said to have employed a Pre-Raphaelite attention to detail in the bus itself, on which even the pasted advertisements were meticulously recorded. But in the mid-Sixties he moved on again, this time to the less interesting theme of eighteenth-century costume pieces. Despite being a painfully slow worker, he is reputed to have produced and offered for sale over 1,000 works.

Alfred ELMORE (1815–81):

Always in the second rank, yet always there, Elmore's range ran from historical to genre paintings. *On the Brink* (1865), showing a woman agonising over a young man's suggestion, is one of the few Elmore paintings you are likely to see today.

THOMAS FAED (1826–1900):

A Scottish genre painter, best at scenes from Sir Walter Scott and of rural poverty, such as his *The Mitherless Bairn* (1855). Much of his income came from prints made of his paintings.

SIR LUKE FILDES (1843–1927):

A graduate of the School of Art in Chester and the School of Design in Kensington (to which he'd won a scholarship), he began his artistic career as an illustrator in popular magazines such as *Once a Week*, *Good Words* and *The Graphic*. His first sketch for *The Graphic* encouraged Dickens to commission him to illustrate *Edwin Drood* – which Dickens, of course, died before completing. It was at Dickens's funeral that Fildes conceived the picture that would make him famous: *The Empty Chair, Gad's Hill Ninth of June 1870*. The sketch appeared first in *The Graphic* but was such a success that it was issued as a print of which thousands of copies were quickly sold. Fildes's watercolour version was hung at the Academy the following year. He promptly ceased to be a 'wood-drawer' (designing engravings to be printed from wooden blocks) and became a painter. At this early stage in his career he dithered between sentimental genre scenes, such as he'd often done for *Once a Week* and *Good Words*, and the social comment pieces he'd sometimes made for *The Graphic*.

It was in 1874 that he exhibited his second most famous picture, the dramatically realistic *Applicants for Admission to a Casual Ward*. Crowds in the Academy were so large and so determined to view his canvas that it had to be guarded by a policeman and an iron railing. Models for this piece, he claimed in the *Strand*, were drawn from life in the London streets where he would select his disreputable and filthy subjects, place them on brown paper, and ring them round with disinfectant. When the cotton-spinner and manufacturer Thomas Taylor bought *Casual Ward* (for £1,250) he hung it in the art gallery of his country house in Oxfordshire and displayed it to the public every Wednesday.

Fildes's later work blended social realism with sentiment, tugging at the heartstrings with subjects such as *The Widower* and his famous study of a forlorn attendance at the deathbed of a child: *The Doctor*. Fildes was knighted in 1906.

STANHOPE ALEXANDER FORBES (1857–1947):

Forbes is mainly a marine or coastal painter, but this leading member of the Newlyn School made a number of interesting genre studies too. Indeed, some of his coastal and fishing paintings can be best described as coastal genre. See under Marine.

MYLES BIRKET FOSTER (1825–90):

Described in more detail as a Landscape artist, many of Foster's studies are rural genre. See under Landscape.

WILLIAM POWELL FRITH (1819–1909):

He was possibly the only nineteenth-century artist to take up painting not because he wanted to, but because his ambitious parents forced him. Publicans in Harrogate, they sent him to Sass's Academy in Bloomsbury, after which he joined the RA Schools in 1837 and exhibited the following year. As his early inspirations were literary (scenes from Dickens, Goldsmith, Shakespeare and Scott) his first paintings were either portraits or set in previous ages. Typical was *English Merry-Making a Hundred Years Ago* made in 1847. A cheerful painting he made of *Dolly Varden* began a lifetime friendship with Charles Dickens.

It was a visit to Ramsgate in 1851 that inspired his first great panorama of contemporary life, *Ramsgate Sands* (also known as *Life at the Seaside*) which he exhibited at the RA in 1854, a year after he was elected to it. He had found his métier. The painting was a sensational success and was bought by Queen Victoria. (As can happen with royal patronage, her agents had to claim royal prerogative and apply royal pressure to persuade a reluctant dealer to part with it. He was canny enough to keep the engraving rights, which earned him a fortune anyway.) Frith followed with more in the same vein: *Derby Day* (1858), *The Railway Station* (1862), *The Salon d'Or, Homburg* (1871), *Private View Day at the Royal Academy* (1881). Each of these, like *Ramsgate Sands*, attracted crowds so large and thrusting that crush barriers had to be erected before them when they were displayed. By then Frith had learned about fortunes from engraving rights, and he never again let them go cheaply.

When we think of Frith today we think first of his social life panoramas – but he preferred to paint historical and literary subjects, portraits and, in one series, *The Road to Ruin* (1878) and *The Race For Wealth* (1880), he became quite Hogarthian. Among his smaller pictures his *The Artist and his Model* is both amusing and charming, and portraits like the one he made of the dealer Gambart's young wife show all too clearly why their owners prized them. Famed as he is for realism, he should not be

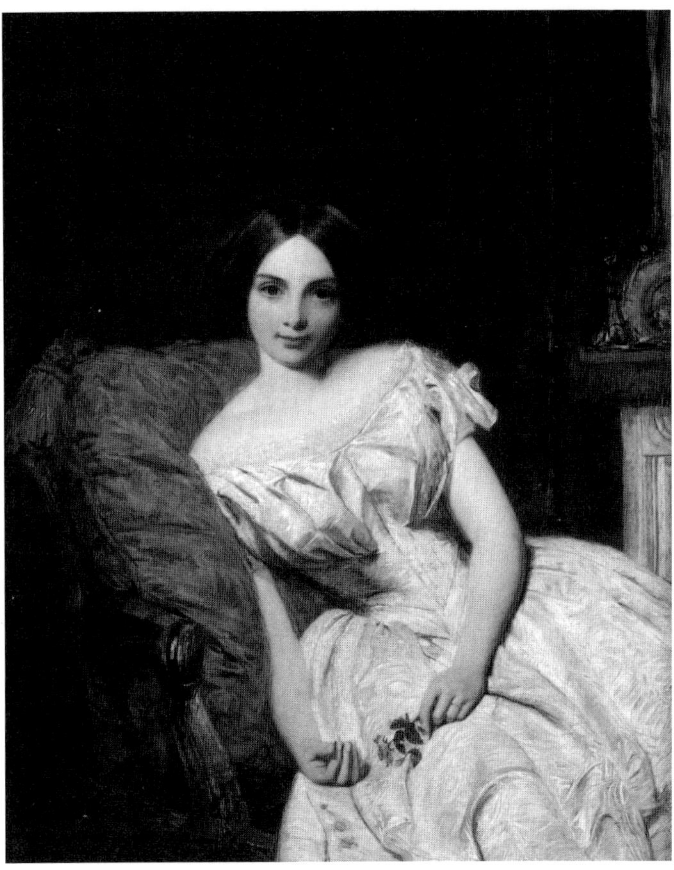

Frith's *Portrait of Annie Gambart*, the art dealer's 16-year-old wife

confused with the great photographer of Victorian life, Francis Frith. In the Mercer Art Gallery his home-town of Harrogate houses a collection of his works.

Norman GARSTIN (1847–1926):

Born in County Limerick, he trained at the Royal Academy in Antwerp (in Paris also) before going to Newlyn in 1886 to join the Newlyn School of painters. His most famous painting is *The Rain it Raineth Every Day* (1889) satirising, perhaps, the British holiday, with its depiction of a rain-soaked Cornish promenade. Garstin became a regular contributor to the *Studio Magazine.*

Tom GRAHAM (1840–1906):

Produced some attractively Impressionistic paintings, especially of Scottish west coast fishing village scenes. He modelled as the husband in Orchardson's narrative picture *The First Cloud*.

John Atkinson GRIMSHAW (1836–93):

He is known today as the Moonlight Painter. His night-time studies, sometimes rural but often and, even more effectively, lonely urban settings, are endlessly reproduced – as indeed, some have claimed, they were from his studio, which operated like a factory, where students and trained employees combined to turn out canvases under the direction of the great man. Certainly there is a sameness – but it is a sameness that succeeds in being both appealing and impressive. He was criticised for being 'too realistic' – by critics, not by his customers – and his realism was much aided by his practice of projecting a photograph onto a canvas and painting through it. Grimshaw preferred autumnal and wintry weather, with mist and streaky sunset and gaslight on dampened pavements. He lived and worked most of his life in the north of England.

Earlier in his career, in the 1850s and 60s, when like most young artists he was affected by the Pre-Raphaelites, his works were suffused with daylight and sun. At this time, unsure of his métier, he also produced some glowing interiors suggesting Tissot, along with some neo-classical works and a few rather symbolist studies of female nudes. His son, Louis Grimshaw (1870–1943) was a skilful painter himself, and collaborated with his father in his late years.

Frederick HALL (1860–1948):

A leading figure in the Newlyn School, settling there in 1884 and staying till 1896, he is, in part, a Victorian artist – even though most of his Victorian output has disappeared. After 1896 his work became more conventional and less interesting.

Frederick Daniel HARDY (1827–1911):

A popular genre painter in his day, specialising in children and domestic interiors. His brother George also painted, and both were members of Kent's Cranbrook colony of artists. His realistic interiors provide useful references to everyday life at the time.

Sir Hubert von HERKOMER (1849–1914):

An immigrant to Britain in 1858 from Bavaria, he followed the sensible route for an artist who meant to live by his trade, beginning with illustrations for *The Graphic*, the best of which he reworked in oils, before finding success with *The Last Muster: Sunday in the Royal Hospital, Chelsea* (1875). Between 1885 and '94 he was Slade Professor at Oxford, having in 1883 opened the Herkomer Art School in Bushey, near Watford. By then he was working in various media including enamels, metalwork and etching. He dabbled in writing for the theatre and earned good money from commercial portraiture, though he continued to work in social realism: *On Strike* (1891) was biting enough to create a minor sensation. Portraiture was important to Herkomer, bringing him over £250,000, a huge sum then. He also earned a significant part of his later income from designing stage sets, and he lived long enough to act, direct and produce set designs for the cinema. Married three times, his first failed after four years; his second to a Welsh nurse, Lulu Griffiths, was shattered by her death after a year; his third was to her sister Margaret. At the time it was illegal to marry a deceased wife's sister, and he had to renounce British citizenship (he regained it in 1897). In memory of his second wife he built and lived in an extravagant mansion named 'Lululand'.

George Elgar HICKS (1824–1914):

After abandoning a career in medicine he produced a number of interesting, if not particularly imaginative, studies of Victorian urban life in the Fifties and Sixties, useful for their accuracy (in the style of a lesser Frith) if rather obvious in their morals. *Changing Homes* and *The Wedding Breakfast* are two of his best-known works, though perhaps the posed crowd in his *The General Post Office: One Minute to Six* (1860) delighted his contemporaries more. He was still exhibiting in 1892.

John Callcott HORSLEY (1817–1903):

One of the winners in the Palace of Westminster fresco competition who moved from high-minded historical pictures to more saleable (and to us more interesting) genre studies later – they being less mawkish than those of his rivals. He was a member of the Cranbrook colony.

Charles HUNT (1803–77):

A genre painter of contemporary life, often with children.

Haynes KING (1831–1904):

Born in Barbados, he came to London in 1854 and exhibited at the RA from 1860 to 1904. He was a landscape and genre painter whose paintings often carried memorable titles such as *The Anxious Look-out* (1860), *Homeless* (1872), *Flirtation and Jealousy* (1874), *Approaching Footsteps*

(1883) and *The New Gown* (1892). In 1904 King committed suicide by jumping in front of a train at Swiss Cottage station.

WALTER LANGLEY (1852–1922):

Born in Birmingham from humble stock, he trained as a lithographer before moving to Newlyn in 1881, where he helped form the 'Newlyn Art Colony'. Though initially a watercolourist, the work of his fellow Newlyn artists encouraged him to try his hand at oils, *In Memorium* (1883) being his first major oil. His paintings of fisherfolk are particularly memorable, with *Among the Missing* (1884, watercolour) the best-known. Other works include *The Sunny South* (1885) and *Never Morning Wore to Evening but some Heart did Break* (1894).

HENRY LE JEUNE (1819–1904):

His name betrays his Flemish origin and there is something of the old Flemish – certainly of the previous century – in many of his studies of well-behaved children, but he was born in London. A fairly conventional painter – his *Liberation of the Slaves* (1847) was purchased by Prince Albert – he was at his best with children: *Early Sorrow* (1869) and *Children with Toy Boat* (1865) are good examples. He was curator of painting at the RA Schools from 1848 to '63.

THOMAS JAMES LLOYD (1849–1910):

Tom Lloyd was born in London and lived in some rural south-east locations, which he recorded in his watercolours. First exhibited in 1870, he was regarded as one of Britain's finest watercolourists. Today's market might think of chocolate boxes.

THOMAS MACKAY (fl 1893–1913):

A collectable Liverpool artist about whom little is known. He painted genre scenes in Britain and abroad, and was an extensive traveller.

THOMAS FALCON MARSHALL (1818–78):

Born in Liverpool, and best-known in his day there and in Manchester, he painted portraits, historical subjects, and modern life studies with the dirt taken out.

ROBERT BRAITHWAITE MARTINEAU (1826–69):

He never decided whether his work was in the social realist or Pre-Raphaelite mould, though posterity has placed him in the former. He was a student for a while with Holman Hunt and perhaps learnt his attention to detail from him, although his most famous painting remains the classic story-picture *The Last Day in the Old Home* in which the demon drink (here, untypically, champagne) has forced a family from their house.

William McTAGGART (1835–1910):

McTaggart came from a poor background (his father was a crofter) and when he found a place at the Trustees' Academy in Edinburgh he had to support himself through portraiture. In the 1860s he broadened into genre landscape studies, often with children, and in 1870 he became an Academician at the Royal Scottish Academy. Many of his later Scottish landscapes had a social comment or at least a genre element.

Arthur MELVILLE (1855–1904):

One of the Glasgow Boys and an innovative artist, noted for his colourist genre pictures in the 'Kailyard' mould and for his sundrenched watercolours (after travels in the Middle East) using a technique dubbed 'blottesque'.

John MORGAN (1822–85):

Successful in his day if overlooked now, he specialised in genre and children studies.

Augustus Edwin MULREADY (1855–1938):

Known mainly for his London street scenes, often including street children. He was a member of the Cranbrook School and the grandson of William Mulready. (His father Paul was an artist too.)

William MULREADY (1786–1863):

A very competent narrative painter who seems typically Victorian and too sentimental for modern taste. In his later years he painted nudes, but few could get excited by them. He also worked as an illustrator, and his skill here led to his being invited to design the first pre-paid postage envelope (1840) but the design was publicly mocked and parodied, causing it to be swiftly withdrawn.

Mulready had four unruly sons, all of whom became artists, and Michael (1807–89) collaborated with his father on some works. This can cause confusion in accurate accreditation. Mulready's respectable paintings contrast with his tempestuous lifestyle: he was pugilistic, probably violent (certainly unfaithful) to his wife and, unsurprisingly, was often out of funds. All this was hidden from his public at the time.

HENRY NELSON O'NEIL (1817–80):

A founder member of 'The Clique'. At the start of Victoria's reign, in common with other members, he abandoned young ambitions to work on saleable genre and historical themes. *Eastward Ho! August 1857* (painted that year and showing troops leaving for India) is his most famous painting, alongside its companion, *Home Again* (1858–9). His *The Parting Cheer* (1861) is thought by some to be Britain's most important mid nineteenth-century painting on the emotional subject of emigration; it sold in 2004 for £450,000.

GEORGE BERNARD O'NEILL (1828–1917):

Dublin-born genre painter who stuck to his chosen path even as it was petering out.

SIR WILLIAM QUILLER ORCHARDSON (1832–1910):

Best-known for his dramatic studies of well-off domestic life (literally dramatic; they can look like scenes from plays), though he began by painting historical and literary subjects. A Scot who trained at Edinburgh's Trustees' Academy, he worked his way forward via a period of 'Regency' pictures (a popular Victorian sub-genre, now disliked) but, once he found his métier, sat supreme. Disdained by (then modern) critics like Whistler and George Moore, and out of fashion for much of the twentieth century, he can now be seen as one of the finest narrative painters of the century; the first of these paintings being *The Social Eddy* (1878). His pair of 4-foot wide plasma screen-like productions, *The Marriage of Convenience* (1883) and *The First Cloud* (1887) have been much reproduced, if only as emblematic book jackets.

WILLIAM ORPEN (1878–1931):

Prolific turn-of-the-century artist, most of whose work falls outside our period. He was proficient in watercolour, oil and pencil, and is frequently underrated due to the ease with which he 'turned them out' and to the fact that he wasn't afraid to say so.

EMILY MARY OSBORN (born 1834):

Genre artist about whom little is known, despite her being one of the more successful women artists of the Victorian era. She exhibited often at the RA and received commissions from the Queen and, therefore, from other wealthy patrons. Her *Nameless and Friendless* (1857), showing a restrained but desperate woman attempting to sell a painting to a picture dealer, is justifiably familiar. Some romantic souls have suggested it is the

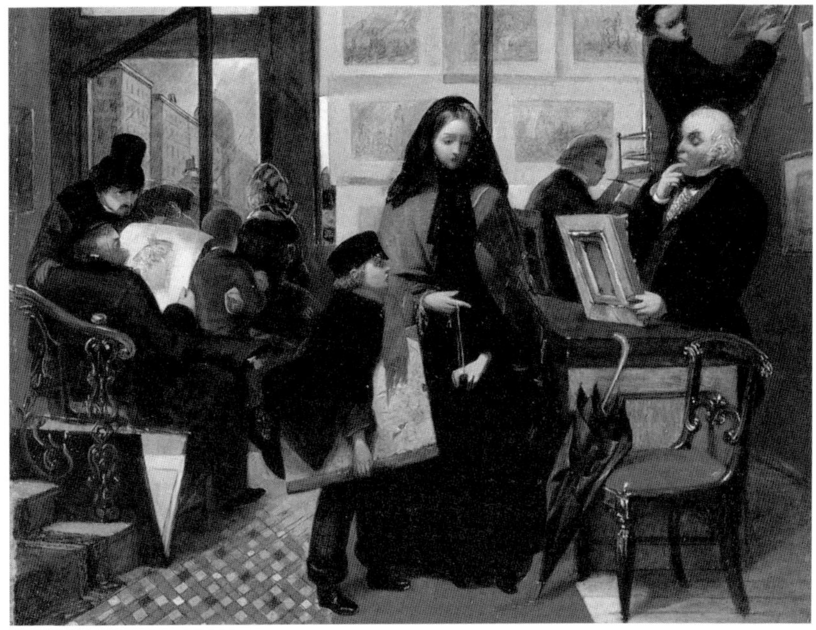

Nameless and Friendless by Emily Mary Osborn

artist herself, though she was never that desperate. She lived well into the twentieth century.

GEORGE O OWEN (fl 1887–1926):

Birmingham-based watercolour painter of genre and landscape scenes, formally composed.

JOHN PETTIE (1839–93):

Scottish genre artist, sentimentally inclined but skilful, inclined towards the historical and Sir Walter Scott. When he first moved to London he lodged with fellow Scots W Q Orchardson and Tom Graham. A hard-working, competent painter, he was more appreciated in his day than he is now.

JOHN PHILLIP (1817–67):

Scottish genre painter from humble beginnings (his father was a soldier) and a founder member of The Clique (when he was 20) whose works were little more than pleasant Scottish genre until he visited Spain in 1851.

The bright sun seems to have released something hitherto hidden within him, and his Spanish paintings overflow with life and sunshine. Before the Fifties were out he had become known as 'Spanish Phillip' – though one shouldn't overlook his 1858 portrait of Prince Albert in highland dress.

Frederick Richard PICKERSGILL (1820–1900):

A contemporary of Millais at the RA Schools, he was a painter of literary and historical subjects, together with portraits and genre work. He shared the Pre-Raphaelite admiration for Flaxman and the Nazarenes.

Alfred RANKLEY (1819–72):

He saw himself as a painter on grand historical themes, but these works have now all but disappeared, and it is for his contemporary genre paintings (moralistic as they often are) that he is better remembered.

Louise RAYNER (1832–1924):

Watercolourist who painted many towns and cities, emphasising their Olde Worlde character. Based in Chester, she travelled the country to make her still-collectable pictures. (She can sell today for over £30,000.)

Richard REDGRAVE (1804–88):

A fine painter, now rather overlooked, although two of his paintings are frequently reproduced: *The Emigrants' Last Sight of Home* (1858) and *The Poor Teacher* (1843), a painting he repeated in several forms, and which is also known as *The Governess*. The second of six children, three of whom died before adulthood, and whose mother died of consumption when he was 11, Richard had an unfortunate start for an artist: after a childhood fight, he dislocated his shoulder and had his right arm badly reset. 'Every morning for months I had to carry a heavy tin filled with stones round our garden,' he wrote in his memoir (published posthumously in 1891). 'How well I remember the pain to this day.' Even by Victorian standards his medical treatment was crude – he had, after all, only dislocated his shoulder. 'I could not lift my hand to my mouth, and I gradually became perfectly left-handed. Not that I drew or wrote with my left hand; this, however painful, they forced me to do with my right.'

It is perhaps too easy to interpret Redgrave's paintings as reflecting his sombre childhood. Two of his sisters became governesses, and not only is his most famous painting a poignant study of a lonely, ignored governess living by indulgence in someone else's household and unable to share their happiness, but the theme of an ignored woman recurs in many of his works. 'It is one of my most gratifying feelings,' he wrote in his autobiography, 'that many of my best efforts in art have aimed at calling attention to the trials and struggles of the poor and the oppressed.'

He was no stranger to death. There is a famous and wonderfully Victorian story of his mother, lying on what she must have known would be her deathbed, noticing the candles burn low beside her. If they kept burning, she said, her own life-flame would burn too. But the candles burnt out. Many have commented on the guttering candle Redgrave put into his painting of *The Sempstress* (1844) in which the hard-working lonely sempstress sews in a garret through the night. She is weary and drawn, and the candle is at its end. Outside can be seen the breaking light of dawn – and, as Thackeray noted, in the house opposite another light is burning, where 'you may imagine that another poor shirt-maker is toiling too'. (The painting was first exhibited alongside lines from Thomas Hood's shocking new poem, *The Song of the Shirt*: 'Oh, men with mothers and wives, it is not linen you're wearing out, but human creatures' lives.')

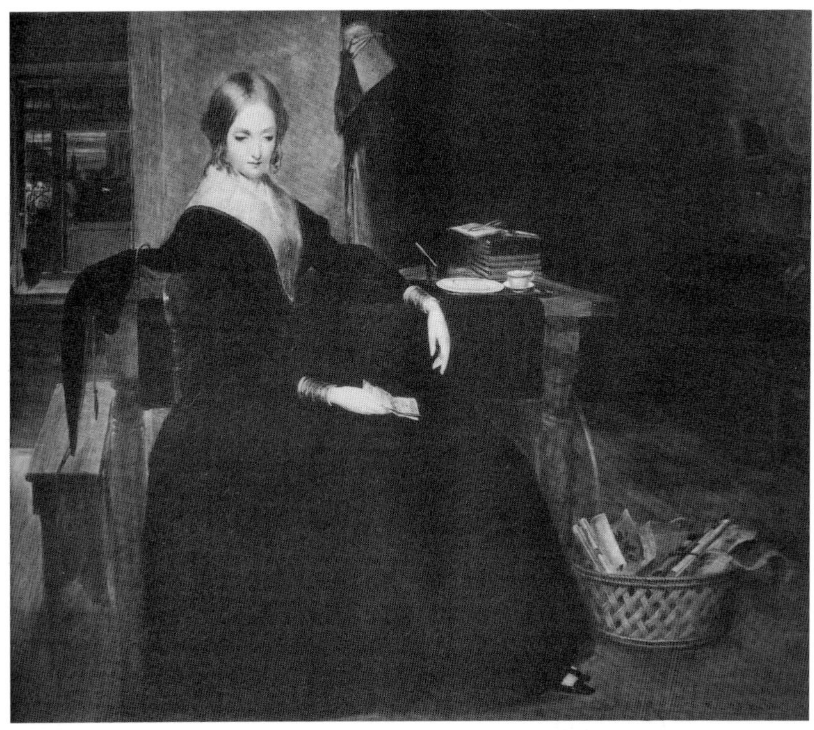

Richard Redgrave's *The Poor Teacher* was produced in several versions from 1843. This engraving was made in 1845

Redgrave's early paintings were moral sermons: *The Reduced Gentleman's Daughter*, *Bad News From Sea*, *The Fortune Hunter*, *The Sempstress*, *Throwing Off Her Weeds*, *The False Lover*, *The Outcast*, and most powerful of all, *The Poor Teacher* or *The Governess*, in which a second look may be necessary to realise that the letter the young woman holds is edged with black, that her dress could be one of mourning (from an earlier death?), and that on her little tea-plate is a single, untouched slice of bread. In his revised version the title of the sheet music is made clear, and it is, of course, 'Home, Sweet Home'. When he painted this picture Redgrave was a drawing master at a private day-school, Mrs Matthew's School in Westbourne Place, where a pupil, then aged 12, later recalled, 'One day Mr Redgrave was giving a lesson to three girls in the back dining-room while I was sitting en penitence in the front one, the folding doors being open. After the lesson the girls told me that Mr R had been sketching me. Within two years after that he painted "The Poor Governess", and her position is that in which I was sitting at the time.'

The 1859 *Art Journal* commented: 'there are few pictures that have called forth so many involuntary sighs as this,' and in recent years, one feels, there are few pictures which have been reused so often on 'period' book jackets. By 1859, though, Redgrave had moved on from moral sermons. His second most famous painting, the quite different *The Emigrants' Last Sight of Home*, had been exhibited the previous year – and note the apostrophe: while the male emigrant waves goodbye, the women and children with him look on more gravely, more aware than he of the difficulties that lie ahead.

Redgrave's later works were a mix of the academic and design. By the time he was elected to the Academy in 1851 he considered himself primarily a landscape painter and his landscapes were as detailed as those of his exciting new contemporaries, the Pre-Raphaelites – but he was never of their band (though Ruskin praised him). Always a meticulous and accurate draughtsman, he had worked as an illustrator and had supplied designs for the Schools of Design; to metalware manufacturers such as Dixon and Sons of Sheffield; to glassware manufacturers like J F Christy of Lambeth and Richardson's of Stourbridge; and to potteries including Minton and Wedgwood. In 1858 he began a twenty-seven-year senior post as an educationalist at the Cambridge School of Art, before the end of which he found himself blighted with cataracts in both eyes (he practically stopped painting in 1878 but managed to submit a final watercolour to the RA exhibition in 1883).

From 1857 Redgrave held the position of Surveyor of Crown Pictures (advising the Queen on her collection) and his comprehensive inventory system is still in use. He is generally reckoned to have been the finest to hold that post. Among other achievements he, together with his older brother Samuel, compiled the useful *A Century of British Painters* in 1866.

WALTER RICHARD SICKERT (1860–1942):

Sickert's very personal style, a kind of Noir French Impressionism, sets him apart from most of his Victorian contemporaries. He was a friend of Whistler who, if equally Impressionistic, had a far less muddy palette, and on his French travels he became a friend of Degas also. Though he had little inclination to follow the French Impressionists *en pleine air* he shared their determination to show the everyday life of ordinary people as it really was – on a bad day. His murky Camden Hill series of gloomy interiors, unlike almost anything done in Britain at that time, gave rise to questions about his mental state and, famously, led American crime writer Patricia Cornwell to write a book naming him as Jack the Ripper! A more cheery view, seen mistily through the glow of subdued gaslight, is found in his paintings of theatre and music hall interiors. It is through these and other paintings that Sickert helped drag Victorian artists into the twentieth century.

ABRAHAM SOLOMON (1824–62):

His life was shortened by an ongoing heart problem and it was on the day of his death, when he was seeking a cure in sunny Biarritz, that he heard the news that he'd been elected to the Royal Academy. During his short life he had become one of the leading genre painters, with works much out of fashion now, in which moral lessons were sentimentally illustrated. *First Class – The Meeting* showed a young couple flirting in a railway carriage while her father slumbered. (A shocked reaction prompted him to make a second version in which the father was awake and the young man wore the uniform of naval officer – which, oddly, was thought to make him more respectable than when he wore civilian clothes.) His follow-up piece was *Second Class – The Parting*. Today we have little appetite for these mawkish tales, but in 1859 his *Waiting for the Verdict* was hailed 'a masterpiece'.

Abraham was elder brother to two other artists, Rebecca and Simeon.

MARCUS STONE (1840–1921):

His career in art began with him helping his father: 'I was not taught, I "picked up",' he wrote later. But if his father lost himself in portraying pretty ladies, Marcus was fortunate enough to be a friend of Dickens, living next door but one to him in Bloomsbury. He had connections through his father and Dickens with famous artists such as Hunt, Egg, Frith and Mulready, and when his father died in 1859 it was Dickens who stepped straight in to help Marcus find work as an illustrator, principally to magazines such as *Cornhill* and *Good Words*, as well as to some of Dickens's own novels in the 'Library Edition'. Stone also provided the first illustrations for *Our Mutual Friend*. He admired Dickens: 'It was his example which was always before me which taught me habits of punctuality, diligence, and the like, and it was his example which saved me from the possibility of becoming an idler or dilettante, of which there are too many in all the arts.'

Though illustration paid the bills, Stone was keen to progress to 'real' art, painting, and throughout the Sixties he struggled to exhibit at the Academy while earning more from drawing woodcuts. (His illustrations for Trollope's *He Knew He Was Right* were notable in being the first photo transfer illustrations for that author.) His Academy paintings were largely historical (*On the Road from Waterloo to Paris* was the best received) but in the Seventies he showed his true colours with sentimental genre studies and 'Regency' figure studies, tasteful enough for a Victorian living room but now very unfashionable: *Rejected*, *Bad News*, *Two's Company, Three's None*, etc. The paintings not only sold but were imitated by less successful artists – so much so that the period has been called 'The Stone Age'.

WILLIAM STRANG (1859–1921):

Strang bridges the Victorian and Edwardian eras with well-observed, sometimes penetrating, portraits and studies of everyday life. They contrast with his more macabre works of Symbolism, often made as etchings or mezzotints, which led to his being one of the few British artists invited to contribute to the first Vienna Secession exhibition in 1898. Strang was a committed socialist (producing works such as his print, *The Socialists*, 1891) and was closely involved with the Art Workers' Guild. In the nineteenth century he was mainly an etcher; in the twentieth he was more a painter. He drew portraits too.

JAMES (JOSEPH JACQUES) TISSOT (1836–1902):

Though French by birth he made his home in England following the Franco-Prussian War of 1870–71 – by which time he was already supplying cartoons to *Vanity Fair* under the pseudonym 'Cöidé'. In France he had worked among the Impressionists but one sees little sign of Impressionism in the work which made him famous here: his sharp and glowing studies of the upper classes. Yet there was another side to this apparently secure sycophant to society: the love of his life, a Mrs

Kathleen Newton, died young of consumption, and the grief-stricken Tissot withdrew from his lucrative career to plunge instead into God and spiritualism. He journeyed to the Holy Land and painted there. But these works, much admired at the time, are now disregarded: it is for his gorgeous genre studies of comfortable affluence that he is remembered (even if they were dismissed by Ruskin as 'mere coloured photographs of vulgar society').

QUEEN VICTORIA (1819–1901):

Though she could never be more than an amateur and though no one would claim she was a great artist, the Princess and Queen was an inveterate artist, filling sketch book after sketch book with lively little landscapes, cartoons and portraits of her family.

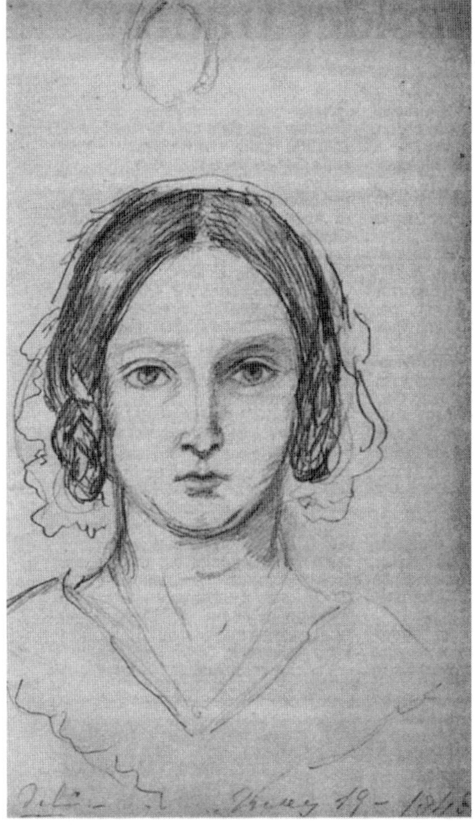

Recently-discovered self-portrait of the young queen, drawn in 1845

Charles Francis Annesley VOYSEY (1857–1941):

Voysey claimed to have become an architect because it was the one profession for which he didn't have to pass an examination – a joke he presumably did not share with those who lived in his houses. Son of a rebel priest who founded the Theistic Church, Voysey learnt his craft in the offices of others before starting his own in 1881, when for his company's first seven years he designed little more than wallpapers (but was as successful at it as are the William Morris or Laura Ashley logos today). He then moved into the design of picturesque, often half-timbered buildings in what swiftly became known as 'the Voysey style'. Though architecture was his business he also made some portraits.

Edward Matthew WARD (1816–79):

Pimlico-based painter of historical and literary subjects, though some of his 'lesser' genre studies are more charming and worth looking at – such as *Hogarth's Studio in 1739* which he painted in 1863. Ward also painted murals in the rebuilt Palace of Westminster. He was married to the portrait and historical painter Henrietta Mary Ada Ward (1832–1924) and father to Leslie, known as 'Spy'.

Edward Arthur WATSON (1860–1922):

A founding member of the Glasgow Boys and a leading Scottish painter of his day, blending continental Impressionism with rural realism. In 1915 he would become President of the Royal Scottish Watercolour Society.

Thomas WEBSTER (1800–86):

One of the less hackneyed genre painters, he headed a colony of artists at Cranbrook in Kent, and produced popular genre works, as well as scenes and characters from popular literature. Many of his works became steel engravings.

Sir David WILKIE (1785–1841):

A leading painter of grand but loosely-painted genre and historical subjects, of the kind that fell out of fashion for a century and a half, though a taste for it has, to some extent, revived. Though his career was largely before Victoria his influence remained considerable – one of the reasons the more progressive of the next generation reviled his work. He'd had a successful career when late in life he took a similar route to Holman Hunt, J F Lewis *et al* through the Middle East and Egypt in search of Bible subjects. His reputation was enough to grant him the chance to paint a portrait of *Muhemed Ali, Pacha of Egypt* (1841) but on his return home from Alexandria he fell ill and died of presumed food poisoning. He was buried at sea. Turner visualised his burial in one of his most powerful paintings, *Peace – Buried at Sea* (1842).

Frederick WILLIAMSON (fl 1856–1900):

A rural genre artist, originally a Londoner, who moved to Surrey and met Foster and Allingham. He was a regular exhibitor from 1856 to 1900.

William Frederick YEAMES (1835–1918):

Though born in Russia, he was the son of the British Consul. In Britain as a young man he joined and was one of the better painters in the St John's Wood Clique, despite which he is remembered as the painter of the wonderfully mawkish *And When Did You Last See Your Father?*

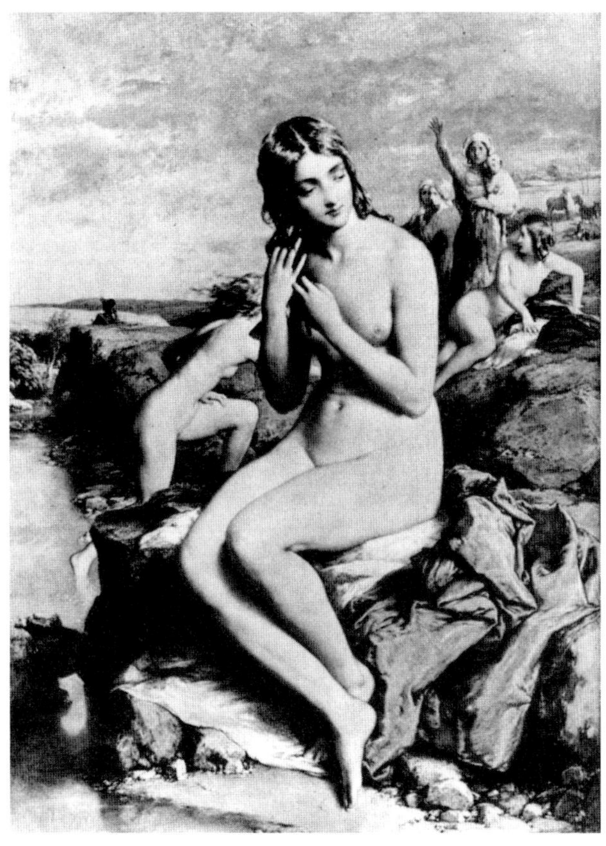

William Mulready's wonderfully Victorian *The Bathers*

Chapter Six

ANIMAL LIFE
The Pretty Baa-Lambs

The depiction of animals was a surprisingly lucrative field. Artists who specialised in it include:

Jacques Laurent AGASSE (1760–1849):

Born in Switzerland, his talent for painting animals led to his being enticed to England to paint for George IV among others, and in the first five decades of the century his paintings were regularly exhibited at the RA. They tend towards a flat yet penetrative style reminiscent of the eighteenth century.

Henry BARRAUD (1811–74):

He and his brother William (1810–50) were skilled painters both of horses and of people. The gentry of the day were as likely to pay for good likenesses of their horses as for ones of themselves or their family. Holman Hunt lambasted Barraud's other métier: 'Chorister Boys, whose forms were those of melted wax with drapery of no tangible texture.'

Thomas BLINKS (1860–1912):

A notable painter of dogs, often in rural settings. His most pricey paintings today are of dogs in country sports. Such oils can fetch up to £30,000.

Joseph CRAWHALL (1861–1913):

A superb and successful painter of genre but mainly animal subjects, not afraid to let the animal and nothing else fill his frame – one hesitates to say 'fill his canvas' as he often painted on quite different fabrics, such as silk and linen, to great effect. His swift painterly style was delicate and almost Japanese at times. From a well-to-do family in Morpeth, Northumberland, the largely self-taught Crawhall moved to Glasgow as a young man and helped found the 'Glasgow Boys' school of painters. His father (1821–96) was an illustrator of the same name.

John EMMS (1844–1912):

Arguably the nineteenth century's best painter of dogs, whose works today could cost you £50,000.

John FERNELEY (1782–1860):

Son of the Duke of Rutland's wheelwright, he became a successful painter of horses and hunting scenes, some of which were wider than a modern living room (which is why they were hung in large country houses). His son, John Ferneley junior (almost always signed thus), was a lesser artist and lived from 1815 to 1862. Another artist son was Claude Lorraine Ferneley (1822–91).

John Frederick HERRING (1795–1865):

Herring senior (1795–1865) was the leading Victorian painter of horses and sporting subjects, and was consequently given royal patronage by George IV and the Queen (and also by the Duke of Orléans). He held the curious post of 'Animal Painter to the Duchess of Kent'. Herring had started life as a stable boy, coachman and sign-painter before his talent was recognised. Later in life he earned enough to own fine horses of his own – some of which became his models. By then he'd broadened his range and was producing fine studies of other animals, domestic and farmyard, painted from life. He is easily confused with his son, John Frederick Herring junior (1820–1907), who painted less well in the same style. Both artists produced a great many sporting prints.

William HUGGINS (1820–84):

One of the best animal painters, though fairly unknown, with a determined preference for bold, at times bizarre, colouring. The earlier William John Huggins (1781–1845) painted naval pictures.

Sir Edwin Henry LANDSEER (1802–73):

Put out of your mind *The Stag at Bay* or *Monarch of the Glen*. To many, these are archetypal Victorian paintings, familiar not so much in themselves as from the many thousands of steel engraved reproductions which, until half a century ago, adorned lower middle-class parlour and staircase walls. Landseer's stags and dogs, indeed all his animals, were brilliantly executed with, for their day, more than photographic realism, though they often combined cruelty (of the hunt) with flashes of sentimentality. So striking are his creatures that the landscapes which sometimes support the animals can be easily overlooked, but they shouldn't be: Landseer was a fine landscape artist too. As a technician, he could not be bettered; even

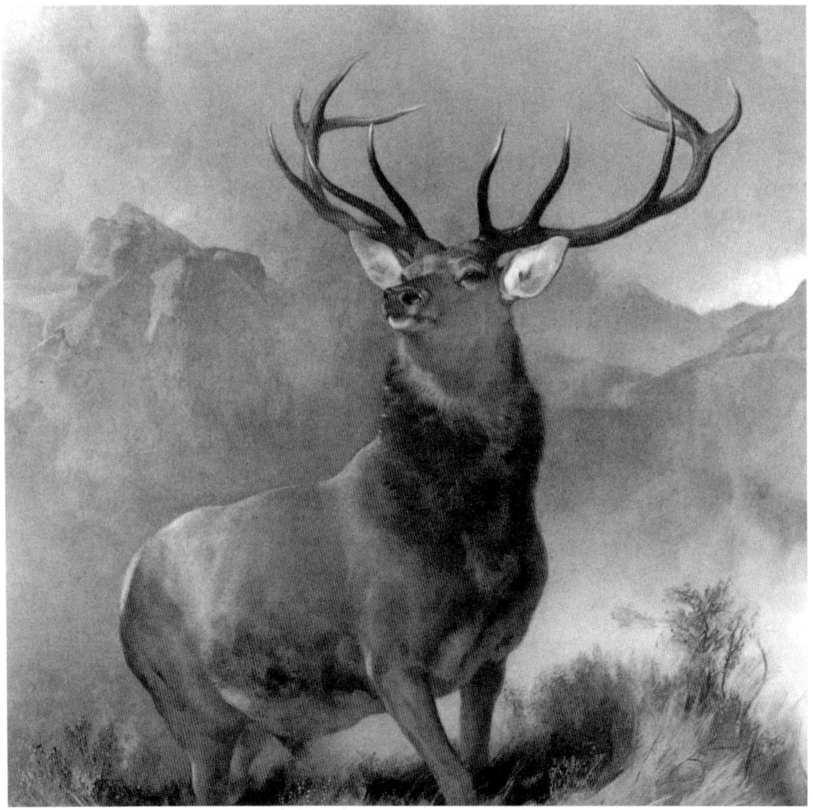

Landseer's *Monarch of the Glen* (1851)

his portraits are superb. But we remember the animals first: the *Stag*, *The Monarch of the Glen*, *Dignity and Impudence* with its winsome dog. We remember also (because how can we forget?) the lions he sculpted for Trafalgar Square.

An indication of Landseer's semi-regal status can be gleaned from his progress on *The Forrester's Family*. The painting was commissioned by Victoria's uncle, Leopold, King of the Belgians, who had admired some frescoes Landseer had made for her at Ardvereike Lodge. Landseer, unfazed by the importance of his client, kept him waiting nearly five years before he finished it and, in the fourth year of waiting, wrote airily to the King's confidential secretary to say, 'If health and good weather continue I will finish the picture in good time.' In *good time*?

Landseer had been a precocious child, making etchings from the age of 7, and exhibiting at the RA when just 13. He was so talented that he even survived tutelage from B H Haydon (the kiss of death for Haydon's other students). By the 1820s he'd become known for his animal studies, and in 1824 made his first trip to the Highlands. Many of his finest pieces date from this decade, before Victoria was Queen. He produced some fine caricatures then, too, of his aristocratic hosts and patrons – caricature remained one of his pastimes. In the year Victoria took the throne, Landseer's *The Old Shepherd's Chief Mourner* was praised by Ruskin as one of the most perfect studies of modern times he'd seen.

By now Landseer was in demand as a portraitist also, and his patrons included cloth manufacturer John Sheepshanks, army contractor Robert Vernon, shipbuilder William Wells – and of course the Queen. He was not as straight-laced as might have been assumed by those who bought engravings of his works; fond of the social whirl, he enjoyed the bohemian pool around Lady Blessington and her presumed lover Count D'Orsay, and his own name was scandalously linked at one time to the Duchess of Bedford. The 1840s were not good for him; he became stressed, suffered a nervous breakdown and depression, and drank too much. (It was said that he'd been jilted by the newly-widowed Duchess of Bedford – but his deterioration was too great to have been merely that.) Through the Fifties and Sixties he was a terrible shadow of the man he had been. For some of the time he was half mad and often he was the worse for drink. But in the public mind, and indeed with many who had known him in happier times, his status demanded that the great man be buried, as he was, in St Paul's Cathedral.

John Frederick LEWIS (1805–76):

He is so well-known for his (early) Spanish and (later) brilliantly detailed Arab paintings that his animal studies are often overlooked, yet in his early years his work was sometimes mistaken for that of his friend and fellow student, Edwin Landseer. Lewis was only 15 when Sir Thomas Lawrence, President of the Royal Academy, employed him to sketch in animals and backgrounds to his portraits. King George IV commissioned animal paintings from him (they are dark and eighteenth-century in style, nothing like Lewis's later, more familiar, work described under Foreign Climes).

Henry Stacy MARKS (1829–98):

A founder member of the St John's Wood Clique, his paintings of birds, often humorously done, are his best works – though he came to these relatively late, having made his name with paintings of scenes from

Shakespeare. His best-known bird picture is *A Select Committee* (1891) depicting a gathering of learned-looking storks, which won unexpected praise from Ruskin. Away from his paintings Marks was renowned for his often irreverent sense of humour.

Beatrix POTTER (1866–1943):

Though her fame came in the twentieth century from her children's books, she was admired for her animal and nature pictures, done mainly in her beloved Lake District, in the late nineteenth. Millais once said, 'Plenty of people can *draw* but *you* have observation.' Her exquisite little works are much sought-after, though they are sometimes cheaper than first editions of her books.

Briton RIVIÈRE (1840–1920):

A capable artist who never quite established himself in the premier league. He began as a follower of Pre-Raphaelite guidelines but soon concentrated his efforts on animal pictures. He produced some decent if sentimental genre paintings also – which more often than not included animals or children.

John MacAllan SWAN (1847–1910):

An animal painter and, at his best, a *wild* animal painter, bringing the beasts of the jungle into Victorian interiors. (Many of his ferocious beasts were, in fact, observed in Regent's Park Zoo.) Swan was well regarded abroad, winning medals in France, Germany and America, and his work was admired by collectors including Mr and Mrs Ionides, both of whose portraits he painted.

Louis WAIN (1860–1939):

Perhaps the most famous of all animal caricaturists (as opposed to painters of animals), he trained at the West London School of Art and from 1883 began drawing his inimitably comic but scarey, anthropomorphic cats. They gained their reputation in the *Illustrated London News* but prowled everywhere, into books and onto postcards, and they reproduced like feral felines. Wain became President of the National Cat Club and worked with other organisations concerned with cat care and reform, but became obsessed and died insane. Many say they can see his insanity in his cats. Given that he'd been drawing them that way since 1883 this seems improbable.

James WARD (1769–1859):

One of the century's best animal painters, specialising in sporting subjects and surprisingly, livestock, who set his beasts in expansive romantic landscapes (in a style indebted, some say, to his uncle-in-law George Morland). Ward's early career was as an engraver of other artists' works but, though he was highly skilled and in great demand, the work didn't please him and he became a painter instead. By the time Victoria came to the throne Ward's career was past its peak; increasingly obsessed by fringe religious beliefs (he expected an imminent Second Coming) and at war with critics, he continued to exhibit but to a variable standard. In his last decade he fell out with Landseer which, for an animal painter, was not a wise career move.

Arthur WARDLE (1864–1949):

One of the greatest and most popular Victorian animal painters, especially successful with dogs and inclined, therefore, to include dead game birds and other country sport appurtenances, which lessens his appeal in the twenty-first century. Wardle was largely self-taught, but exhibited successfully at the Royal Academy and the Royal Society of British Artists from 1880 to 1935. In reproduction his paintings can look like those of Landseer, but Wardle's are considerably smaller – more suitable for the domestic interior. Provided there are no dead birds.

Chapter Seven

HISTORICAL
Great Moments in History

To most of us in the twenty-first century the least interesting Victorian paintings are those in the Historical category. Grandiose, often so unbelievable as to be absurd, populated – whatever their supposed historical period – with obviously Victorian characters in fancy dress, crowded and overblown, large, municipal and at times surprisingly poorly painted, these heavy canvases in their dusty portentous frames are easy to sneer at. Yet their ambitions could be laudable: to celebrate nationhood and great acts of heroism or noble sacrifice. How dare we sneer?

Because they are so Victorian. So Academy.

Yet in their day they celebrated the spirit of the age. Theirs were the themes that enthused Romantic poets and classical composers. Britain was a rising power: having defeated Napoleon early in the century, having subdued the world (we thought) under Nelson and Wellington, having led the world (we thought) with our Industrial Revolution, we were proud of our glorious history. What could make a finer subject? 'When a man says, "Paint me a historical picture," my heart swells towards him,' wrote B R Haydon. 'All my powers rush forth. He seems at once to have turned the key to my cabinet of invention.' He wasn't the only artist thus inspired.

EDWARD ARMITAGE (1817–96):

Though only 20 when Victoria came to the throne and young enough, therefore, to know better, he clung to the Grand Manner style of heavy, dark, mannered historicism. His dutifully worthy style won him a first prize (for *Caesar's Invasion of Britain*) in the notorious competition to find artists to decorate the rebuilt Houses of Parliament in 1840, and Leeds Town Hall may still have his *Retribution* tucked away in a corner.

JERRY BARRETT (1814–1906):

Painter of historical subjects such as *Florence Nightingale Receiving the Wounded at Scutari* and *Elizabeth Fry Reading to the Prisoners at Newgate*.

Sir Charles EASTLAKE (1793–1865):

Very successful then, in the Grand Manner style, and largely confined to remote corners now, Eastlake became a leading arts administrator: he headed the Select Committee to choose artists to decorate the rebuilt Palace of Westminster, and was President of the RA at the time the Pre-Raphaelites first exhibited, thus epitomising the clash of old and new.

William FISK (1796–1872):

Mainly known for his careful if uninspiring historical paintings, he made some portraits also. His son, William Henry (1827–84) was a landscape and historical painter, some of whose Scottish views were bought by the Queen.

William GALE (1823–1909):

Leaving the RA Schools shortly before the Pre-Raphaelites, his work inevitably shows some influences, but most of his output was historical, biblical or mythological. He was born in London and travelled extensively in the Middle East.

Benjamin Robert HAYDON (1786–1846):

The roaring dinosaur of the age, anti-Academy, anti-progress, a severe (though often perceptive) critic and, in his opinion, the country's last great historical painter, his monumental works (which he often failed to sell, despite having worked on each for years) were impressive in a gloomy way, but flawed: he was too ambitious, and he couldn't handle the epic subjects, let alone the epic scale, of his vast visions. He scorned his smaller works, often portraits, never realising that these were far better than his larger ones. Nevertheless he managed to sell to the Queen and several of the nobility (not often enough to save him), he played a large part in securing the Elgin Marbles for the nation, he pushed successfully to have the new Palace of Westminster graced with freshly-commissioned British frescoes, he championed the forgotten poet Keats, and he left one of the greatest sets of diaries (still wonderfully readable and still in print, albeit reduced in scale, unlike his paintings). The diaries end, sadly, with Haydon's suicide.

Edwin LONG (1829–91):

Painter of dramatic scenes from the generally biblical Middle East. His *Babylonian Marriage Market* was a celebrated shocker at the RA in 1875 and is one of a number of similar biblical pieces. Commercially very successful, he extended his range with a notable portrait sequence of twenty paintings entitled *Daughters of Our Empire*, commissioned by Thomas Agnew & Sons to coincide with Queen Victoria's Golden Jubilee year of 1887.

Daniel MACLISE (1806–70):

Irish painter, much at home in London's literary set – a friend of both Dickens and Thackeray – whose work ranges from pretty illustration (often including archetypically winsome ladies) through Historical to massive frescoes (two from the Palace of Westminster competition remain in place; they took him seven years to complete). His 1843 *Girl at the Waterfall at St. Nighton's Kieve* shows Dickens's sister-in-law Georgina Hogarth, and early in his career he produced some attractive fairy pictures (see under Fantasy & Symbolism). When he's good he's good, but . . .

Paul Falconer POOLE (1807–79):

Not an easy artist to categorise: self-taught, his work spans from sentimental genre studies of children and romantic rustics to large historic fantasies and dramatic landscapes haunted by beautiful and mystic characters. It is these latter which made his name; when first exhibited at the Royal Academy they caused a sensation, as well they might. Who, they asked, was this unknown from the provinces (Bristol, actually) whose huge canvas depicting *Solomon Eagle Exhorting the People to Repentance During the Plague of London* was acclaimed officially as Picture of the Year? Was it, as some declared, the greatest history painting produced in English art until that time? Poole was drawn to the dramatic, typified by his *The Visitation and Surrender of Syon Nunnery* (1846), *The Last Scene of Lear* (1858) and, two decades later, *The Vision of Ezekial*. The sheer scale of these works meant that he was able to produce fewer of them than he could of charming genre scenes, but they are the ones that matter. He defies the rule that Small is Beautiful. For his defiance of the rules of Victorian marriage see Francis Danby.

Alfred RANKLEY (1819–72):

He saw himself as a painter on grand historical themes, but his works now have all but disappeared.

David SCOTT (1806–49):

Scottish, like his name (he was born in Edinburgh), he produced in his short life some imaginative and interesting paintings, often on literary or historical themes.

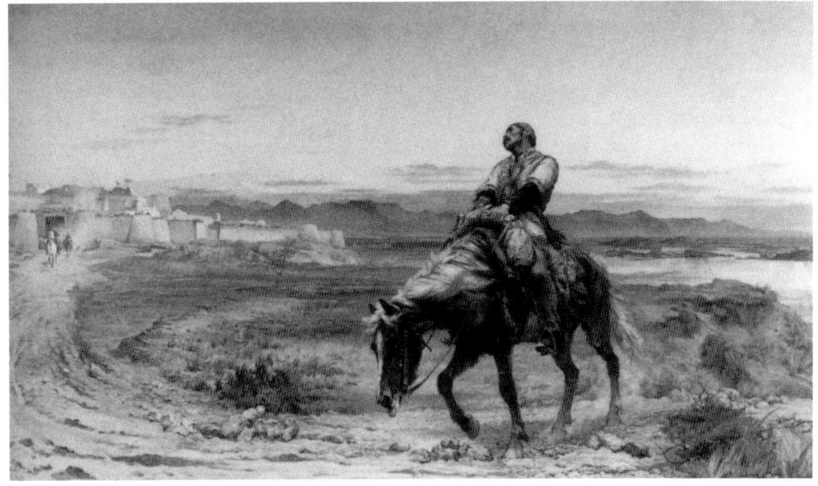

Lady Butler's sobering *The Remnants of an Army* (1879)

Elizabeth THOMPSON (Lady Butler) (1846–1933):

One of the finest military artists – some might say *the* finest – of her day, whose immaculately rendered and scrupulously accurate paintings gave the Victorian public what they wanted to see: the dust of battle, horses and guns, flags and heroes and glorious sacrifice. There was nothing feminine in her paintings, and neither was there squalor. The public loved them, queuing to see them on display and buying them in reproduction. She learnt her craft in Italy, and then, from 1866, at the Female School of Art, South Kensington, where she attended the private 'undraped female' life class. On an 1870 visit to Paris she became interested in military subjects, and on her return to London she exhibited her own first such, *Missing* (1873) at the RA. The following year she showed *Calling the Roll after an Engagement, Crimea*. These led to her sensationalisations of the Crimean and Indian wars, such as *The Return From Inkerman* (1877). Often out of fashion, often ignored in art books, she is an archetypal Victorian artist, magnificent in execution and brilliantly attuned to Victorian taste. Her sister was the leading poet and essayist Alice Meynell.

Edward Matthew WARD (1816–79):

Pimlico-based painter of historical and literary subjects, he also painted murals in the rebuilt Palace of Westminster.

Other artists in this genre include:

Charles West COPE (1811–90), one of the winners in the House of Lords competition that shattered Haydon.

William DYCE (1806–64), whose output included some religious and historical scenes.

John Rogers HERBERT (1810–90) who, like Dyce, painted some religious subjects in historical vein.

Charles Robert LESLIE (1794–1859) painted historical paintings till, late in his career, he switched dramatically to the new Fairy Fantasy genre.

John Seymour LUCAS (1849–1923), whose merry characters in 'period' costume might be considered historical.

Ernest NORMAND (1857–1923), who used Religion and History to justify his paintings of struggling naked maidens.

Solomon Joseph SOLOMON (1860–1927) tried the same excuse as Ernest Normand.

Marcus STONE (1840–1921) is thought of as a genre artist but managed some respectable attempts in the historical mould too.

George Frederick WATTS (1817–1904) produced a number of historical canvases although, in his own words, 'I paint ideas, not things.'

William Frederick YEAMES (1835–1918) was mainly a genre painter, even if he is best remembered for his *And When Did You Last See Your Father?*

Chapter Eight

FOREIGN CLIMES
Religion and Palestine

It is a moot point whether many of the great religious paintings of the nineteenth century aren't better described as topographical, since they can seem inspired as much by the landscape of the Middle East as by religion. But for Victorians there was no more proper theme than the biblical and some artists, in common with many thinking people, were caught up in religious debates and controversy. Holman Hunt, who created the most famous religious image of the century, was in his youth agnostic and it is uncertain whether that painting, *The Light of the World*, was begun as a painting of Christ or of the long-unopened door (a well-worn Victorian metaphor for the long engagement). Did its success inspire him to visit the Holy Land or did he just want to travel? His friend Millais, after all, captured the spirit of the place in *The Carpenter's Shop* without ever setting foot there. Edward Lear, who painted some of the most exquisite Middle Eastern studies, was more interested in landscape than in God, and J F Lewis was taken over by *Mohammedan* life, not Christian.

Notable travellers include:

GEORGE CHINNERY (1774–1852):

This successful portrait artist and miniaturist fled a mountain of debt by setting sail for China. By the time his wife arrived (1829) Chinnery had holed up in a male-only stronghold in Canton, leaving her stuck on the ship where she caught smallpox and died. Chinnery moved as far as Macao (where he had lived before his wife's arrival) and continued with his pleasures, becoming so fat that he needed four bearers to carry his chair around the alleys. Throughout all this time he produced and sent home great numbers of fine sketches, watercolours and oils of China and the Chinese, individual in style, Europeanised and recognisably Chinnery – though some of these were, in fact, produced by local 'assistants', one of whom, Lam Qua, later exhibited at the RA himself.

James HOLLAND (1800–70):

Remembered for his watercolours of foreign scenes, mostly Venice. He began as a flower-painter in the Davenport china factory.

John Frederick LEWIS (1805–76):

He is so well-known for his brilliantly detailed Arab paintings that his early work is forgotten. Beginning as an engraver (in his father's footsteps) he quickly moved on to animal studies, in the footsteps of his friend and fellow student, Edwin Landseer, and their early animal pieces were so alike that their authorship was and still can be confused. Lewis became a full member of the Water-Colour Society in 1829, and in 1832 began his travels with a two-year painting trip to Spain – after which he became

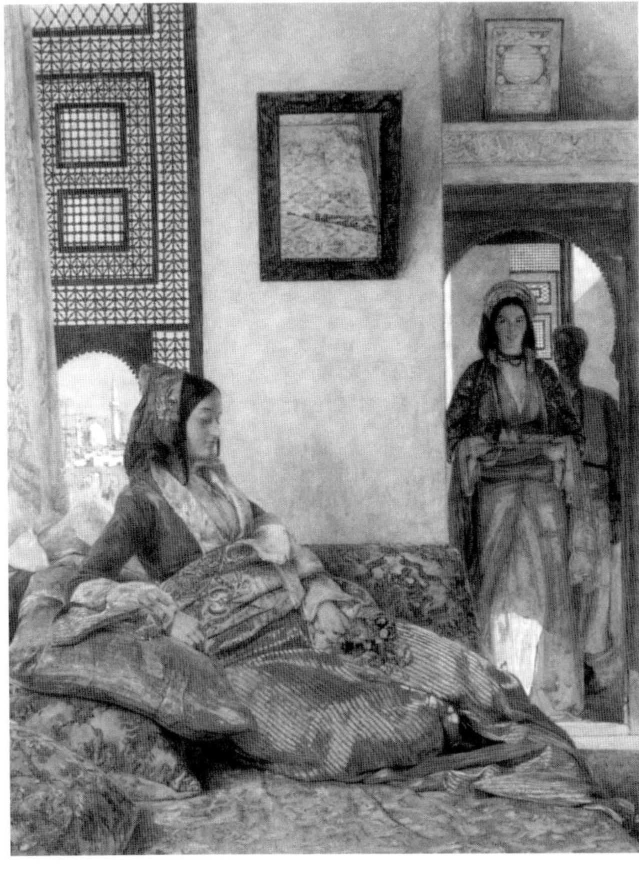

Life in the Hhareem by J F Lewis (1858)

known as 'Spanish Lewis'. He published two volumes of Spanish lithographs.

In the year of Victoria's accession he left England for Europe, then Cairo, and stayed away fourteen years, ten of them in Egypt. When Thackeray met him there, in his 'long, queer, many-windowed, many galleried house', he found the artist ensconced like an exotic minor potentate, full-bearded, in dark blue Arabian costume, well-equipped with local servants: 'Here he lives like a languid lotus-eater – a dreamy, hazy, lazy, tobaccofied life.' Despite appearances, Lewis was working hard, painting and sketching, and collecting materials he could use as backgrounds. When he sent his first work for exhibition at the Old Water Colour Society in 1850 it caused a sensation. The *Art Journal* called *The Hhareem* [sic] 'the most extraordinary production that has ever been executed in watercolour'. It was, the journal continued, 'scarcely possible, without the aid of a glass, even to distinguish all the inimitable elaboration of this picture'. Emphasising the point, the journal added that it was 'unique in the history of watercolour art; such maintenance of finish has never been preserved in any similar production'. The painting sold for £1,000.

When Lewis returned in 1851 (the year of the Great Exhibition) he had married (an English girl, some noted with relief) and had with him trunks of drawings which he worked up into full-scale pictures over the next twenty-five years. Praise continued to fall on him: of his 1855 watercolour, *A Frank Encampment in the Desert of Mount Sinai*, no less a critic than Ruskin enthused: 'If the reader will take a magnifying glass to it, and examine it touch by touch, he will find that literally any four square inches of it contain as much as an ordinary watercolour drawing; nay, he will, perhaps, become aware of refinements in its handling which escape the naked eye altogether.' It was, to Ruskin, 'among the most wonderful pictures in the world'. Few could disagree, for not only was the evidence before their eyes but Ruskin's word was absolute: 'Watercolour can be carried no further; nothing has been left unfinished or untold.' The Redgraves, in their *A Century of Painters of the English School*, agreed: 'his drawing is so exceedingly accurate, and his manual dexterity so great, that he is able to combine the utmost finish without oppressing you with any sense of the labour of execution.'

Ruskin was among several who advised Lewis to turn to oil, and in 1858 he resigned his membership and Presidency (which he'd held since 1855) of the Old Water Colour Society, and was promptly elected to the Royal Academy. During the rest of his life he created a series of truly dazzling oils (which he interspersed with watercolours, reproducing some images in both). An 1852 watercolour, *The Arab Scribe, Cairo*, (the first he exhibited in England after ten years in Egypt) sold for £1.75m at Christie's in 2009 – still short of his record price of £2.2m obtained by Christie's in 2005 for the oil version of *The Mid-Day Meal, Cairo* (1875).

Edwin LONG (1829–91):

Painter of dramatic scenes from the biblical Middle East. His *Babylonian Marriage Market* was a celebrated shocker at the RA in 1875 and is one of a number of similar biblical pieces.

Valentine Cameron PRINSEP (1838–1904):

Prinsep was a more than competent artist, though never a great one, yet he mixed with the greatest and lived as comfortably as the richest. He was born comfortably off, married into money, inherited more, and had all the attributes, therefore, to infuriate his peers – yet was genuinely popular and liked by all. Not because of his money, which he spent lavishly. Not because of his fine house, which he threw open to his friends. Not even because he was a fellow artist. He wasn't of the top rank, and never claimed he was. He was good company, a huge man, strong and jocular, down-to-earth. His name is found in numerous biographies, autobiographies and reminiscences of the time and he always comes out well.

Having a father who had been Chief Secretary to the Government of India and who remained a director of the East India Company till 1874 helped. Val was commissioned to paint the Governor-General, and in 1875 travelled to India, expenses paid, to paint the Durbar (the Indian court and its nobility). On his travels he made hundreds of sketches to work up on his return and, while away, had his house extended to include a second studio large enough to let him work on a 27-foot canvas. The Queen herself perused his sketches (liking the portraits but not the landscapes) and the Prince of Wales (who preferred the portraits of Indian women) bought two. When a number of Val's pictures were hung at the Academy his huge Durbar was poorly received. ('That Eastern monstrosity,' sniffed *Vanity Fair*.) The Queen tucked it away in a distant corner of the Palace.

David ROBERTS (1796–1864):

Despite the grandeur of his more famous paintings, Roberts came from poor beginnings. A Scot, the son of a shoemaker, he undertook a seven-year house-painting apprenticeship before moving (up?) into scene-painting. At Edinburgh's Theatre Royal he met Clarkson Stanfield, and his life changed. In 1822 he and Stanfield moved to London where

Roberts quickly found employment at Drury Lane while, with Stanfield's encouragement, he submitted work to the Academy. He continued working in the theatre, moving to Covent Garden in 1826 but, by the end of the decade, he'd begun a series of European and Middle Eastern tours. Six volumes of his *Views in the Holy Land, Syria, Idumea, Arabia, Egypt and Nubia* were published in the 1840s but, rather than enjoy whatever success they might bring, he shot off again through Europe. Only in the 1860s did he cool his heels a little to paint his series, *London from the River Thames*.

Charles ROBERTSON (1844–91):

Travelled extensively in the Middle East, producing genre studies and large watercolours influenced by Lewis. Good for interior detail, though some of his characters' limbs seem made of plasticene.

Thomas SEDDON (1821–56):

The son of a London cabinetmaker, Seddon began as an artist and designer, and from 1849 switched his attention to landscape. The following year he helped set up an art school for workmen in Camden Town, but within months was struck down with rheumatic fever. Once recovered (a slow process then) his strong Christian faith pushed him to accompany Holman Hunt on his bull-headed excursion around the biblical Middle East in 1853 and '54. Seddon developed a fatal fascination with the area – fatal in that when he went back in 1856 he died there of dysentery. Practically the only paintings of his that remain are from there.

Chapter Nine

NEOCLASSICISM
In the Tepidarium
(Now, That's What I Call a Picture)

The Victorian era was an age of continual progress, but its artists looked backwards – to British history, the Ancient Greeks and the Romans, a Golden Age. And when painting the Antique, anything was permissible – violence, sadism and sex – all three of which sanctioned nudity. A contemporary woman without clothes was naked, not nude, but in a bygone age . . .

Alma-Tadema is the artist most famous for peopling his classical settings with undraped females. He was by no means alone: Leighton, Etty and

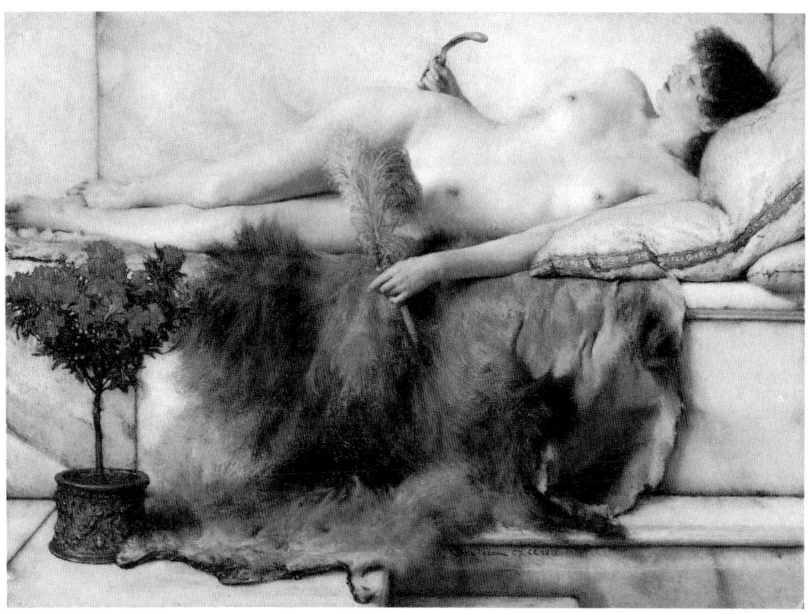

Alma-Tadema's famously erotic *In the Tepidarium* (1881)

Normand came on his heels. Nudes in historical or literary pictures might raise an eyebrow, nudes in Bible pictures more so, but nudes in antiquity were allowed. In fairness, these paintings were not just naked women against a classical backdrop. Settings were carefully researched and painstakingly painted; their artists saw themselves as 'Olympians'. Some, Alma-Tadema and Leighton especially, housed themselves in Olympian residences, grand palaces of art.

Alma-Tadema's first London residence was grand enough, decorated as it was in a bizarre if typically Victorian marriage of styles, but his second, in Grove End Road, St John's Wood, looked like a backdrop to his paintings – as in a sense it was, since he used parts of it over and over again. His studio, with its domed ceiling coated with aluminium paint, cast a silvery white light in the winter like that of Mediterranean sunlight. His furniture appeared often; his Romanesque sofa, for example, features in *Vain Courtship*, *The Baths of Caracalla* and *Comparisons*. Frederic Leighton's residence, Leighton House, Holland Park Road, with its Arab Hall, magnificent staircases and marbled rooms, was so sumptuous that it remains a much-visited museum. Both men, like Watts and other fashionable artists, threw their homes open weekly to admirers. The cream of society came.

The list of Neoclassicists begins, inevitably, with:

Sir Lawrence ALMA-TADEMA (1839–1912):

He was originally Dutch, born Lourens Tadema (though Alma was his middle name), and he trained at the Antwerp Academy. In the 1860s he and his French wife moved to Paris, in which city he lost both her and his son to illness. His success at the RA Exhibition of 1869 encouraged him to move to London the following year (with two surviving daughters), and in 1871 he married his 17-year-old pupil Laura (daughter of a cocoa manufacturer). In 1873 he took British citizenship and, having by then a promising reputation, changed his name to the one we know. (In pronunciation, the emphasis is on the Tad.)

It is said that, because his early pictures failed to sell, his wife gave him an ultimatum: 'brighten them up, make them commercial, because I do not wish to live the rest of my life in penury.' He obeyed. By the mid-Seventies he had become so commercially successful that in 1882 he staged a one-man exhibition of 287 paintings at the Grosvenor Gallery. He and Laura moved to a fine house in St John's Wood (previously the home of Tissot) and Tadema promptly expanded and developed the house into a minor Gothic palace, where he and Laura staged lavish parties. He used Laura (and his children) in a number of his paintings, and had few qualms about showing his wife naked. He occasionally included friends (not naked) such as Sir George and Lillian Henschel who appear in his *Spring* of 1894, and he made frequent use of the glamorous Greek and Italian professional models widely available in London.

After his house was badly damaged from a gunpowder explosion on a barge on the nearby Regent's Canal, Alma-Tadema employed the leading architect Aitchison to entirely remodel it, introducing a Gothic library, a Spanish boudoir and a Japanese painting room. The house now approached the exotic splendour of his paintings, and his rooms became backdrops.

Though in later life much of his income came from society portraits (he painted members of the British and Russian royal families) his speciality was the mock historical – Victorian ladies in classical settings. His paintings were beautifully finished, practically photographic, often smaller than a reproduction suggests and, famously, could be tastefully titillating. The Bishop of Carlisle was shocked by Alma-Tadema's *A Sculptor's Model* of 1877: 'to exhibit a life-size life-like almost photographic representation of a beautiful naked woman strikes my inartistic mind as somewhat if not very mischievous.'

His classical settings were deeply researched and became the model for how Romans (occasionally Greeks, but mainly Romans) lived. Liberty's based costumes and materials on his designs. Well into the twentieth century Alma-Tadema's paintings supplied the template for Hollywood film sets (D W Griffith and Cecil B De Mille were among many who based sets on them). Yet for the first half of that century Alma-Tadema was totally out of fashion, a derided artist whose paintings were sold off by galleries, even in the 1950s, for less than £500. In 1960 *The Roses of Heliogabalus* went for £150, yet by 1973 was auctioned again for £28,000. You couldn't buy it so cheaply today.

His daughter, Laura Theresa Alma-Tadema (1852–1909) became a painter of domestic and genre scenes, often in Dutch seventeenth-century settings.

Lord Frederic LEIGHTON (1830–96):

One of the greatest, perhaps *the* greatest neoclassical artist of the century, whose sweeping landscapes were peopled with heroic males and melting females. The quality of his brushwork and the respectability of his subjects allowed Leighton to fill his canvases with sumptuously desirable women, half-draped or undraped, languorously positioned against imagined backgrounds. With some paintings one can feel heat radiating: think of *The Garden of the Hesperides* (1892) in which three bored but beautiful

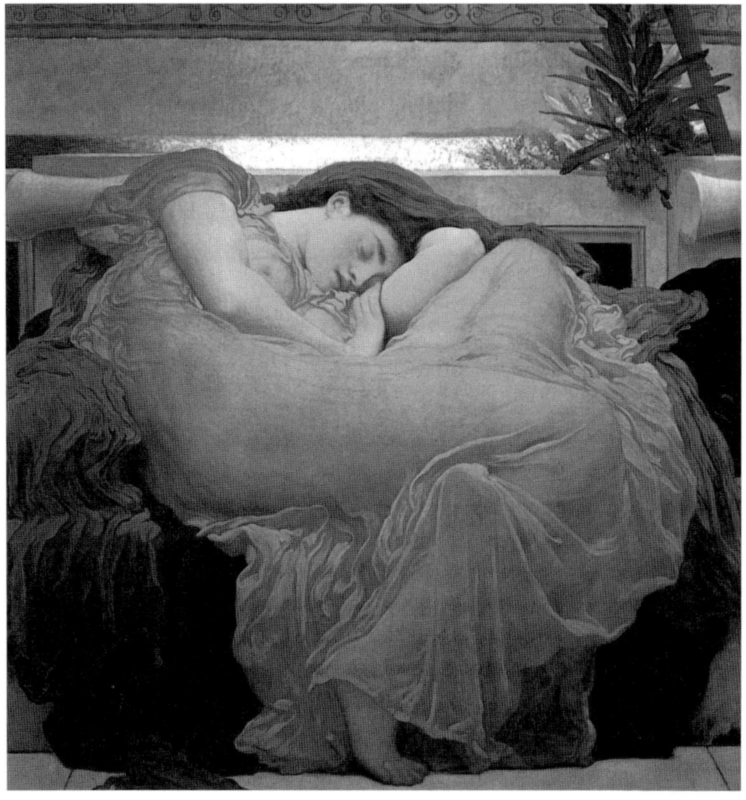

Leighton's *Flaming June*

maidens lie beneath a tree and toy with a giant snake at the seaside, or his late masterpiece *Flaming June* (1895) in which the diaphanous garment accentuates the form of the gorgeous sleeping woman. That such a 'hot' piece could ever have disappeared seems incredible – though disappear it did in the 1960s, only to be discovered, discarded, in a builder's skip.

His first great success was quite different: a stunning 17-foot panoramic *Cimabue's Madonna* (1853) showing the Madonna carried through the streets by a processional crowd. When displayed at the RA Exhibition Leighton casually commented, 'One thing is certain, they can't hang it out of sight.' In the following decade beautiful women dominated his canvases (*Lieder Ohne Worte* being the best) and the paintings, wrote William Rossetti, 'belong to that class of art in which Leighton shines –

the art of luxurious exquisiteness, beauty for beauty's sake, colour, light, form, and choice details for their own sakes, or for beauty's'. His portraits were, unsurprisingly, immaculate likenesses. His 1875 study of Richard Burton is thought to be the finest of this extraordinary man. In preparing for his paintings Leighton often made clay models of his subjects though, despite the fame of his full-size bronze sculpture *Athlete Wrestling with a Python*, he only made two full-size bronzes. (The other was *The Sluggard*.)

The high-born Leighton (Baronet Leighton) was elected to the Royal Academy in 1869, an event he celebrated by extending his already fine house in Holland Park Road. That house, with its stained glass windows, Moorish features and Arab Hall, seems designed more for public viewing than for private comfort. Prize pieces from his travels, carpets, paintings, faience and pottery (he had made a Grand Tour of Europe and the Nile) were displayed alongside his own works and pieces commissioned from leading British artists. Walter Crane, Burne-Jones, Clausen, Caldecott and William de Morgan supplied hundreds of decorated tiles and some mosaic floors. Works from 'advanced' artists such as Beardsley, Ricketts and the disgraced Simeon Solomon were purchased too, to be displayed beside Continental masterpieces. Other artists gave works as gifts: Millais, Alma-Tadema, Singer Sargent, Moore and Watts. The house had domed ceilings, niches, fully tiled walls, panels of stained wood and ivory, tinkling fountains. It was a Victorian fantasy of the East, and Leighton, who never married, threw it open to the public on Sundays and to Society guests at other times for soirées, musical parties, concerts and private views. (It is open to the public today.) Food was supplied by Fortnum and Mason. His patrons came, the royal family came, artists and musicians came to admire.

His manner was lordly, he looked like a god, he was rich and successful: it would have been so easy to hate the man – but he was popular. He was generous to fellow artists, both known and unknown, not all of whom were talented enough to deserve his help. But some did: he commissioned the sculptor Alfred Gilbert, then unknown, to make a work in bronze, and the ensuing *Icarus* (1884) made Gilbert's name. By the time of the Paris exhibition in 1889, when Gilbert exhibited alongside Leighton and other artists, railings were needed to restrain the crowds. On Leighton's death, Gilbert said, 'I can only say that all I know, and all the little I have been able to do as a sculptor, I owe to Leighton.'

Leighton became President of the RA in 1878, and was an efficient, welcoming, reforming leader. He died in January 1896, twenty-four days after having been elevated to the peerage (already a Baronet, he was the first artist to become a peer). He died in pain, having suffered for years from angina pectoris (the disease which killed Burne-Jones) and it is reported that his last words were, 'Give my love to all at the Academy.' Crowds lined the street for his cortège.

Leighton's generosity extended to his models – he supported Dorothy Dene's family for years and left her £10,000 on his death. Among others he helped, mystery surrounds Frederic Mason whose mother, Lily – married, and unknown as a model or artist – was left £1,450 on Leighton's death. Frederic Mason was left a larger sum (£3,420, together with some jewellery) by Leighton's sister. The Mason family had been receiving money since the 1870s, estimated to total £9,000 in all. But who were they? (Another friend of Leighton, George Heming Mason, a minor artist, was not related.) Was Frederic the unacknowledged son of Frederic Leighton? Mason later claimed he was, his family agreed, and it has to be said that he did bear a familial resemblance. Leighton is not known to have had a sexual or romantic relationship with anyone, but Lily perhaps – fifteen years younger than him – could be a love that he concealed. Or Fred could have been the son of Leighton's sister Augusta, farmed out to Mrs Mason at birth – why else would Augusta bequeath £3,420? We will never know.

Albert Joseph MOORE (1841–93):

Moore was a leading light of the Aesthetic school, but his ethereal ladies had to exist somewhere and since the backgrounds – which at times seem no more than exotic wallpaper – were, often as not, neoclassical, I have placed him here.

The Moores were a family of artists: Albert's father William began as a commercial artist painting japanned metalware before becoming a portrait artist, and three of William's sons had artistic careers. The eldest, Col, attended the RA Schools, and the second brother Henry painted seascapes. Albert, like his father, began as a decorative artist, but in the RA Schools relaxed into a less rigid though still meticulous manner. He helped found a sketching club with fellow students Frederick Walker, Marcus Stone, Simeon Solomon, W B Richmond and Henry Holiday, and he continued to work in decoration, particularly with wallpapers and fabric. He worked in several grand country houses, crossing paths from time to time with Morris, Burne-Jones and Philip Webb. His skills in decorative design were evident in his paintings; though he placed graceful ladies (dubbed 'Graeco-West Kensington young women' by his student W Graham Robertson) at the centre of his paintings, he surrounded them with gorgeous fabric.

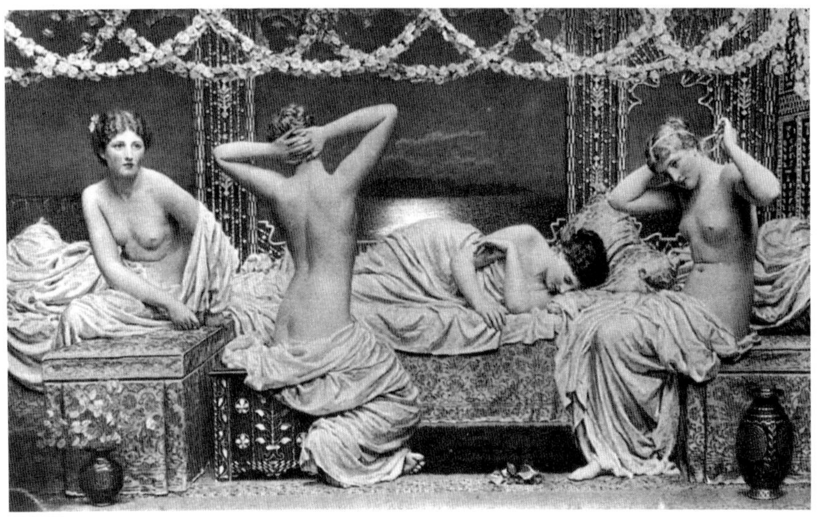

A bevy of Moore's young women in *A Summer Night* (1890)

His works were far more than decorative. The critic Swinburne praised them, as did Whistler. The Aesthetic school loved him (though Rossetti, no Aesthete himself, thought him 'a dull dog'). When Moore moved close to the artistic set around Holland Park, he didn't mix much but remained solitary and individual. Uninterested in historicism, whether accurate or as an excuse for nudity, Moore's sole concern was for aestheticism. Robertson said of Moore's paintings: 'How lovely they were, what clear colour, what perfection of workmanship! The paint was solid, yet light and crumbly as pastel, there seemed to be a delicate bloom on the surface as though they were viewed through a veil of gossamer or pearly mist. They were like flowers; one expected them to smell sweet.'

Moore did not sign his paintings, preferring to incorporate a Greek anthemion as a hidden signature within. (Whistler was inspired by this to adopt the butterfly as his own monogram.) A shy and reclusive man, Moore's talent was not widely recognised in his lifetime, and although Whistler thought him 'the only true great English artist of our day', the public has never fully taken to Albert Moore.

Ernest NORMAND (1857–1923):

The husband of Henrietta Rae shared a studio with her in Holland Park and, while she was criticised for painting chaste and tasteful nudes, he produced any number of flagrantly erotic and exploitative studies which

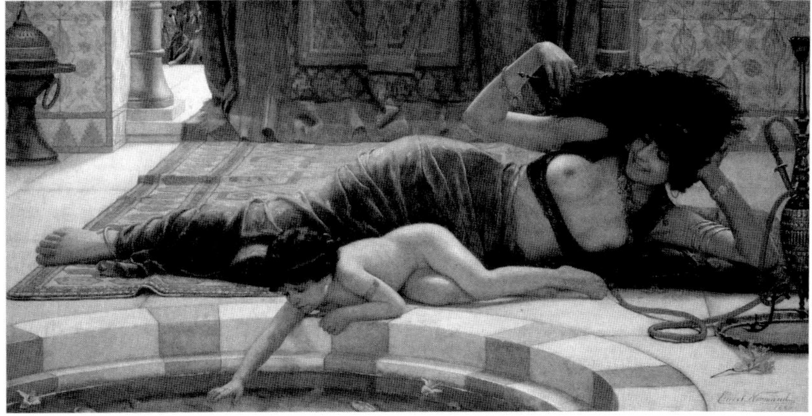

All in the best possible taste: Normand's *Playthings* (1886) is set in an imaginary 'classical' age when life was more relaxed

weren't criticised. His studies of female nudity, bondage (literally: one of his paintings – from 1895 – was called *In Bondage*) and sexual sadism were rendered in glowing colours and praised at the RA. Normand was careful to ensure that none of his naked beauties were of modern times (that *would* have been shocking). They remained exotic insects trapped in amber and preserved from a distant age.

Sir Edward John POYNTER (1836–1919):

One of the century's finest classical artists (he was a painter, sculptor, etcher, muralist and draughtsman), he became the first Slade professor at University College and was President of the RA for twenty-two years. He was made a baronet in 1902. Such a career made it almost inevitable that he'd be anathema to younger progressive artists – and he repaid them with scorn. Poynter was noted for irascibility: 'When he talks to himself,' noted Burne-Jones, 'he always says Yes most amiably, and that's about the only time he does say it.' Graham Robertson, whose hands Poynter painted more than once, found him 'difficult of access' and remote: 'Chronic dyspepsia,' said Robertson, 'is not very improving to the temper.' He had had a lighter period: in the late 1850s he'd been part of the 'Paris Gang', mixing with Whistler, Du Maurier, Leighton *et al* but on his return in the 1860s he buckled down and buttoned up. Typical of his respectable and impressive œuvre is the 10-foot long *Israel in Egypt* (1867) in the Guildhall Art Gallery. Several of his paintings feature the same attractive model; she appears in *Psyche* (1882), *Under The Sea Wall* (1888) and *On The Terrace* (1889).

Solomon Joseph SOLOMON (1860–1927):

Classical and biblical scenes have been adapted freely by numerous artists to make 'respectable' paintings, their subjects allowing them to include massacre, murder, rape, infanticide, nudity and sex – and Solomon's *Ajax and Cassandra* (1886) was reputed to be the most violent rape scene of the nineteenth century. *Niobe* (1888) is a 10-foot high canvas dominated by several bare-breasted maidens, and his portrait of *Samson* (1887) has Delilah bare-breasted as she watches her loved one held down and shorn of hair. As sometimes happens in Hollywood today, body-doubles were used for the female role: Therese Abdullah (a cook's daughter) modelled the head, while an Italian woman, Madeleine Fiorida, modelled the torso. A late venture into the Aesthetic style, *Eve*, in which the voluptuous nude is borne aloft by angels, was sold in 2010 for £600,000.

He was no relation to Simeon or Abraham Solomon.

Apart from these, other artists whose work can at times be considered neoclassical include William ETTY (1787–1849) and Edwin LONG (1829–91).

Chapter Ten

SCULPTURE
Portraits in Stone

Today's art lovers often overlook (or walk straight past) Victorian sculptures as if they'd not been made by some of the century's finest artists. While many works were little more than commemorative, others were more progressive. Frederic Leighton made no more than two important pieces – but what pieces they were, what influence they had! His full-size bronze of muscle and sinew, *Athlete Wrestling with a Python*, astounded almost everyone and was an influence on many painters. His nude athlete, *The Sluggard*, enthralled. These two bronzes, along with his more sentimental child study, *Needless Alarms*, sold rapidly when reissued as smaller, more affordable, statuettes.

Thomas Woolner may seem, at first sight, to have produced nothing more than portrait plaques – but he was a founder of the Pre-Raphaelite Brotherhood. Many people walk past Hamo Thornycroft's public works today with their eyes, it seems, half shut, and should you ever find yourself in Macclesfield Town Hall, look closely at his *Artemis and her Hound* (1880) and remind yourself: someone made that. Some of the finest Symbolist work, too, is found in sculpture; Harry Bates, George Frampton and Alfred Gilbert (whose *St Edward the Confessor* is a portrait of G F Watts). Other names barely remembered outside specialist circles include Henry Armstead, Thomas Brock, Susan Durant, Edward Onslow Ford, William Goscombe John and Frederick William Pomeroy.

In the final two decades of the nineteenth century came a vigorous revival inspired by Symbolists, a move towards bronze instead of marble, exploiting themes of sleep, death, predestination and eroticism. The critic Edmund Gosse, when he coined the phrase 'New Sculpture', welcomed this blast of change. It had rocked the stiff classicism of public statuary, the 'debased and sunken tradition of the Georgian age', as he called it, and introduced themes already current in graphic art, themes of myth and Arthurian romance, found in the canvases of Watts and Burne-Jones. Alfred Gilbert led the way. His *Perseus Arming* (1882) was a hit at the Grosvenor Gallery and his *Kiss of Victory*, exhibited at the RA that year although begun in 1878, inspired Watts's major Symbolist painting *The*

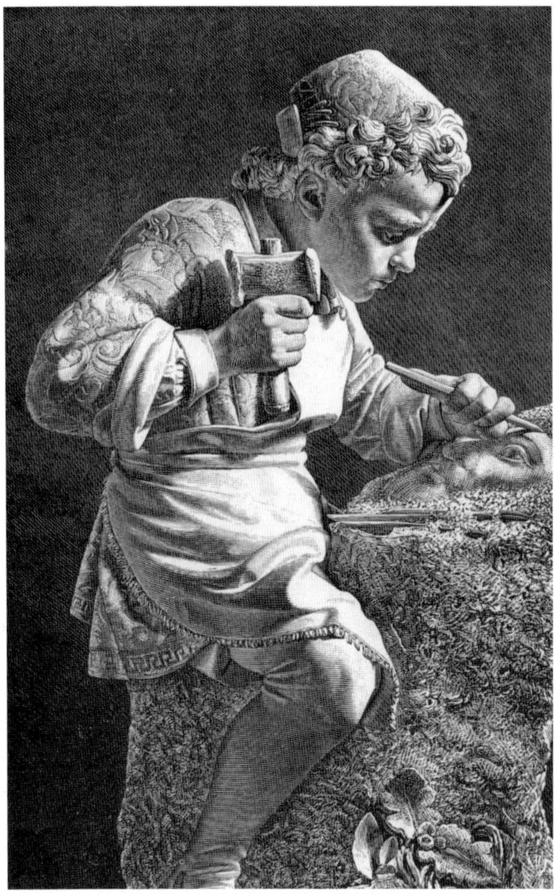

Start 'em young

Happy Warrior. If another Gilbert work, his *Study of a Head* of 1883, seems unremarkable today, one can't deny its enigmatic and sombre beauty. His *Icarus* (1884) remains astounding: a beautiful heroic youth, modelled on Gilbert himself, naked apart from his helmet, gleaming in bronze and irresistible in his bold and doomed ambition.

Sculptors of note include:

John ADAMS-ACTON (1833–1910):

John Adams added the Acton to his name (he was born in Acton) to avoid confusion with an earlier artist of his name. In 1855 the RA awarded him a gold medal for his allegorical sculpture group, *Eve Supplicating Forgiveness at the Feet of Adam* and he went on to become a lifelong portrait sculptor. He sculpted Queen Victoria several times and Edward VII, along with many other notables, some of which are held in the National Portrait Gallery today.

Harry BATES (1850–99):

One of the great names in the 'New Sculpture'. Born in Stevenage, he trained at the RA Schools (earning a Gold Medal in 1883 for *Socrates Teaching the People in the Agora*), then in Paris under Rodin (culminating in his *Aeneid Triptych* of 1885, now in the Glasgow Art Gallery and Museum). He worked at times with Hamo Thornycroft, was involved in the Arts and Crafts movement, sculpted everything from public monuments to doorknockers, and his major works included *Hounds in Leash* (1891), *Pandora* (1891 also), and *Mors Janiae Vitae* (1899). This last work ('Death the Gateway of Life') was exhibited posthumously: recognised in his lifetime as one of the country's leading sculptors, Bates mismanaged his finances and died in poverty.

William BEHNES (1794–1864):

The son of a German piano-maker with an English wife, Behnes was born in London, brought up in Dublin, and trained at the RA Schools. When Victoria came to the throne Behnes was second only to Francis Chantrey as England's most prolific and successful portrait sculptor, but in the 1850s he became increasingly dependent on drink and was declared bankrupt in 1861. But even his late works were of superb quality.

Charles Bell BIRCH (1832–93):

A sculptor of public and civic works, of both single figures and groups (sometimes military), who also designed the bronze griffin on the Temple Bar memorial. He was considered a reliable choice to sculpt public memorials.

Sir Joseph Edgar BOEHM (1834–90):

A sculptor patronised by the rich and famous, all of whom pretended to be unaware of his long-term affair with Princess Louise, who lived with him. A large and overweight man, he was reputed to have died of a heart attack while making love to Louise, who called for help from the palace and had his death certified as from apoplexy. So they say.

William BRODIE (1815–81):

Scottish sculptor whose fascination with phrenology may have helped in his many fine portrait busts and medallions. Though one of the nation's leading sculptors, his best-known work is the smallish kitsch bronze *Greyfriars Bobby* seen on the George IV Bridge in Edinburgh. His brother was the sculptor Alexander Brodie (1829–67).

Joseph DURHAM (1814–77):

Sculptor and portrait artist who, in 1848, achieved public acclaim for his model of Jenny Lind. Many of his later works were of figure groups – genre paintings done in stone. Despite his reasonable success, some say he died of drink. Others say he died of phthisis.

John Henry FOLEY (1818–74):

Influential and important sculptor, a master of public statuary, credited with preparing the way for the 'New Sculpture' of later decades. Born in Dublin, he was the obvious choice to make that city's statue of Daniel O'Connell (still a tourist attraction there). But perhaps his most famous work is on the Albert Memorial; it is said that working there in the open air brought on the pleurisy that killed him.

George FRAMPTON (1860–1928):

A stonemason's son who became one of the country's greatest sculptors, and who lived one of the less troubled lives of artists in these pages. While studying at the RA Schools he made pieces that obeyed the rules sufficiently to win prizes: *Socrates Teaching the People in the Agora* (1884) and *An Act of Mercy* (1887). One of those prizes was a travelling studentship which took him to Paris, where he studied under Antonin Mercié and won a medal at the Salon of 1889 with *Angel of Death*. Back in London he allied himself with the Arts and Crafts movement while, at the inaugural exhibition of the Libre Esthétique in France, he exhibited a new form of work, an arresting bas-relief in polychrome plaster entitled *Mysteriarch* (1892). He continued in this direction with works like the oak-framed bronze relief, *My Thoughts Are My Children* (1894), *Mother and Child* (1895) and *Lamia* (1900). But as the new century dawned Frampton turned to effective but conventional sculptural portraiture, and in 1910 made the *Peter Pan* statue for Kensington Gardens.

Alfred GILBERT (1854–1934):

Born in London, the son of an organist, Gilbert always intended to be a sculptor. He trained at the RA Schools, apprenticed himself to older sculp-

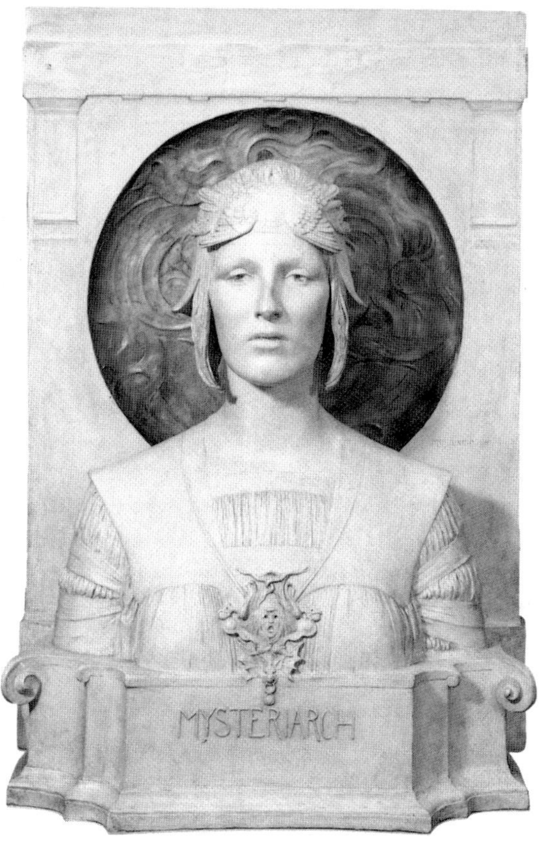

Mysteriarch, an 1892 polychrome plaster by George Frampton

tors in London and Paris, and submitted his works for exhibition in London while in France. *Perseus Arming* (a mere 29 inches tall) was his first work to attract real attention, and he was commissioned by Frederic Leighton to sculpt whatever he wanted. For a young man in his twenties to be recognised in this way by the President of the RA was a career-changing endorsement. Leighton gave him free reign and, where another young artist might have found an open-ended commission frightening, Gilbert said, 'I was very ambitious. Why not "Icarus" with his desire for flight?'

When commissioned to sculpt the Winchester Jubilee Memorial (1887) of Queen Victoria, he ignored tradition and clothed her in a cascade of bronze drapery with a second crown of fronds and lilies – an unexpected and magnificent image, now in the Great Hall of Winchester Castle. He began working in gold and aluminium alloys, and the most famous of his new creations was the Shaftesbury Memorial, *Eros*, unveiled in Piccadilly Circus in 1893. By now he was well-known both as Britain's greatest sculptor and as one of London's notable characters, striding around town in a black cape and sombrero – and spending more than he earned. He overspent on his Maida Vale house, saw his wife suffer a mental breakdown, and in 1901 was bankrupt. For some twenty years afterwards he was a social outcast, and only in his seventies was he received again and hailed as Britain's greatest nineteenth-century sculptor.

John Edward JONES (1806–62):

Dublin-born sculptor and son of the miniature-painter Edward Jones (*c.*1775–1862). Subjects of his many portrait busts included the Queen, Napoleon III, Wellington, Palmerston and Daniel O'Connell.

Richard Cockle LUCAS (1800–83):

A sculptor who learnt his craft as a child by carving knife handles (his uncle was a cutler in Winchester). He was a prolific maker of portrait busts and medallions, many of which are now in the Bethnal Green Museum and the National Portrait Gallery.

Baron Carlo MAROCHETTI (1805–67):

A sculptor and portrait artist whose main claim to fame may be that for some years he allowed his friend Edwin Landseer to share his studio. He designed Prince Albert's tomb for the royal mausoleum at Frogmore.

Alexander MUNRO (1825–71):

Principally a sculptor of portrait medallions. In 1844 the Duchess of Sutherland secured him a post as decorative carver at the Houses of Parliament. Befriended by Rossetti, he dallied with the Pre-Raphaelites, shared a studio with Arthur Hughes in the 1850s, and executed a tympanum relief from a Rossetti design for the Oxford Union. Two of his larger pieces can be seen in London today: the fountain *Nymph* in Berkeley Square and *Boy with Dolphin* in Regent's Park.

Sir W F P NAPIER (1785–1860):

A striking-looking, 6-foot tall man with moustachios and, in later years, white hair and full white beard, Napier was a man of many parts.

Remembered mainly for his successful military career in which he ended as a General, he was a prolific author on military subjects. In his leisure he painted and sculpted, and his statuette of *Alcibiades* earned him honorary membership of the Royal Academy. He also painted portraits.

Matthew NOBLE (1818–76):

Sculptor and monument-maker to the famous, including the Queen. A man of frail health, he was surprisingly prolific – due to his extensive use of assistants (causing rival sculptor Thomas Woolner to sneer that he: 'never touches the work that goes under his name'). Unkind and untrue.

Edgar George PAPWORTH (1809–66):

Portrait artist and sculptor, not to be confused with his eldest son and namesake, Edgar George Papworth (1832–1884), another sculptor.

Patric [sic] PARK (1811–55):

Born in Glasgow, a builder's son, he began as an architectural mason. On reaching his majority he spent time in Rome, and the city inspired him to embark on heroic nude statuary – which was not a success in Scotland. Moving to London in 1835 allowed Park to concentrate on sculpted portraiture, and he won commissions to sculpt famous names. He was over-ambitious, he flouted tradition and, since some of his major projects were not completed and others were rejected (those heroic nudes) he tumbled often into financial difficulty. Over-ambition killed him: one day at Warrington Station he helped an old man staggering along with a large basket of ice, and he haemorrhaged with the strain. He left a widow and five children.

Henry Alfred PEGRAM (1862–1937):

Portrait artist and maker of bronze roundels and reliefs, in the style of Alfred Gilbert but never quite as good.

Sir John Robert STEELL [sic] (1804–91):

Why the name of this successful artist came to be spelt this way has never been explained, but he was Victorian Scotland's greatest sculptor, making statues of the inevitable Burns and Scott as well as contemporary celebrities. He was born in Aberdeen and died in Edinburgh.

Alfred STEVENS (1818–75):

Overlooked both in his lifetime and since, he was a superior sculptor and artist in black and white. From poor beginnings (his father was a sign-painter) this wayward artist studied and worked in Italy as a teenager (supporting himself by selling drawings) before returning to England. Commissions came more from his friends than rich clients, and it's hard to resist the feeling that he was not a lucky man. Nor was he a businessman: for perhaps his most prestigious commission, the Wellington Monument in St Paul's Cathedral, Stevens, on his own initiative, produced a full-scale maquette and overran hopelessly on costs – then failed to complete the work before he died. (It was part-finished by his student, Hugh Stannus in 1878, and completed by John Tweed in 1912.) One project he did complete was making twenty-five lions for the British Museum railings.

William THEED (1804–91):

A sculptor, son of a sculptor father, William Theed the Elder (1764–1817), hence sometimes known as William Theed the Younger. Much of his work was sculpted portraiture – he made the death mask of Prince Albert – and he was exhibited practically annually at the Royal Academy.

Sir William Hamo THORNYCROFT (1850–1925):

In the 1880s Hamo Thornycroft was Britain's leading sculptor, having moved from classicism into new realism. Several of his pieces can be seen in the Leighton House Museum and his finest, *The Mower* (a magnificent example of his realism, made first in 1884, then in bronze in 1894) is in the Walker Gallery, Liverpool. Though he made portrait figures of notables including Gladstone, General Gordon and Cromwell, he was not a traditional 'monumental' artist but a proponent of the 'New Sculpture'. In his later years, perhaps inevitably, he was overtaken by the *avant garde* of the new century and dismissed unfairly as Victorian.

George Edward WADE (1853–1933):

Early patronage from Sir Coutts Lindsay brought him his own studio, where he soon realised that sculpture, rather than portraiture, was his métier. He made portrait busts and monumental statues of the famous.

Henry WEEKES (1807–77):

A notable portrait sculptor (he made the first bust of Victoria after her coronation), he exhibited more than 100 busts and statues at the RA. Fine works include *Resting After a Run* (shown at the 1851 Great Exhibition) of a young girl with a hoop, *Sardanapalus* (memorial to Shelley, 1861) and *Manufactures*, made for Scott's Albert Memorial (1864, finished 1870).

FRANCIS DERWENT WOOD (1871–1926):

Portrait artist and sculptor, urged into his career by his mother, Ann Mary Maw, who had been taught painting by Ruskin. In 1891 he became paid assistant to Alphonse Legros at the Slade School of Fine Art and later, as an RA Schools student, won various prizes including a gold medal for his bronze *Daedalus and Icarus*, a work influenced by Alfred Gilbert. His first RA exhibit was *Circe* in 1895. Many of his public monuments were made in the twentieth century, and in the First World War he used his skills to develop a technique for masking facial disfigurements.

Chapter Eleven

FANTASY & SYMBOLISM
The Fairy Feller's Master-Stroke

FANTASY:

Is there a God? Do fairies exist? Is there another world? Is there something other than this humdrum mechanical existence? Victorians, surrounded by everyday examples of material progress and the industrial revolution, and informed in their reading by the Self-Help morality of Samuel Smiles, Bentham and myriad manuals urging them to do well, get on, work hard and succeed, longed for spiritual escape. If one believed in God, was God enough? And if one did not – as many didn't – then what lay beyond the

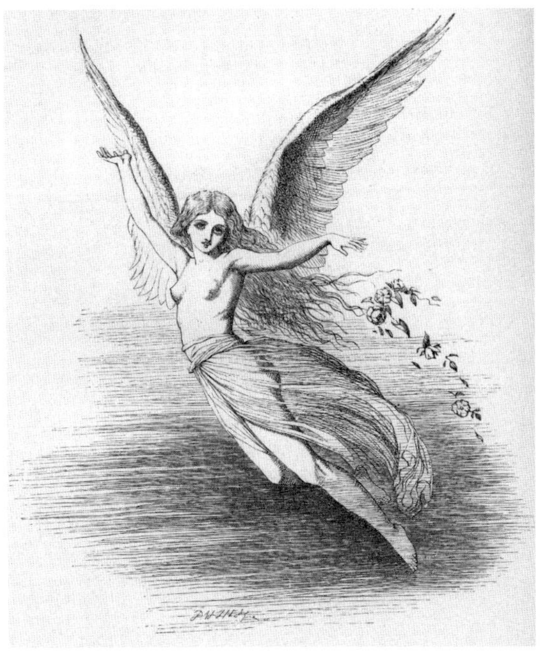

An 'enraptured peri' by Tenniel, from *Lalla Rookh*

material and mundane? Fairies and fantasy, Arthurian legend, myth and magic. To dream thus warmed the soul.

Romantic poets like Keats and Shelley, metaphysical poets like William Blake, prose writers as diverse as Grimm, Hans Christian Andersen, Lewis Carroll and George MacDonald – all helped transform the drudgery of everyday. Shakespeare might have urged the educated reader to sit, 'and let the sounds of music creep in our ears: soft stillness and the night become the touches of sweet harmony' but Victorians couldn't switch on the radio or put on a favourite disc; orchestral concerts weren't heard every day; music was often amateur (or sounded amateur) and spiritual delight came more readily from words and pictures.

Titania: *Hand in hand, with fairy grace,*
Will we sing, and bless this place.
Oberon: *Now, until the break of day,*
Through this house each fairy stray.

Richard DADD (1817–86):

Dadd's fairy paintings are extraordinary enough before we look at his life. A schizophrenic, he was only 26 when he stabbed and killed his father, fled to Europe hoping to murder the Austrian Emperor, was caught, sentenced and locked up for the rest of his life in Bethlem asylum. While there he continued to draw and paint, producing fantasy masterpieces like *Oberon and Titania* and, most famous of all, *The Fairy Feller's Master-Stroke*, which reportedly took him nine years to complete. Fairy paintings like *Titania Sleeping* and *Come Unto These Yellow Sands* come from the early years of his adulthood, and the detailed work in these usually tiny oils is incredible. Later Bethlem works, not of fairies, retain a haunting, surreal air. Dadd's early, pre-Bethlem, works include delicate compelling landscapes. He toured the Middle East, where the excitement and perhaps the sun caused him to write to Francis Frith that he doubted his own sanity. Three months after returning home, he submitted his plea of insanity at the trial: 'I inveigled him, by false pretences, into Cobham Park and slew him with a knife, with which I stabbed him, after having vainly endeavoured to cut his throat.'

John Anster FITZGERALD (1832–1906):

His tiny output includes some of the finest fairy paintings of the nineteenth century, showing fairies and other fantastics interacting with wildlife, and occasionally humans, in mesmerising detail. He is not related to the author and occasional portraitist Edward Fitzgerald (1809–83).

Edward HOPLEY (1816–69):

His output varied between portraits and fairy pictures.

Laurence HOUSMAN (1865–1959):

Long-lived artist and author, associated in the 1890s with various *fin de siècle* movements including Arts & Craft, his influences go back to the Pre-Raphaelites. His illustrative work included some lively and distinctive fairy and fantasy pictures.

Robert HUSKISON (fl 1838–54):

Little is known about Huskison, other than that he was praised for his fairy pictures, that he was of 'low birth', and that he died young.

Charles Robert LESLIE (1794–1859):

The biographer of Constable was himself a painter of historical and literary subjects, though at the end of his life he turned to the current craze, fairy paintings. Leslie was born in London to American parents and brought up in Philadelphia, but his working life was spent here. His son, George Dunlop Leslie (1835–1921), became a member of the St John's Wood Clique.

Daniel MACLISE (1806–70):

Irish painter who worked in several genres (see under Historical) but who, early in his career produced some fairy pictures that, to present-day taste, may be the best things he did. The most famous is *Scene from Undine* (1843) and it's worth noting that his earlier *Pan and the Dancing Fairies*, an oval oil panel in which the cunning Pan looks rather like a caricature of Prince Charles, was sold in 2010 for a quarter of a million pounds.

Sir Joseph Noel PATON (1821–1901):

Scottish fantasy artist, best-known today for his detailed fairy paintings (which can be charmingly erotic or kitsch, depending on your point of view), much influenced by the romance of Celtic legend. Less well-known are the many paintings he made on religious subjects.

William J WEBBE (fl 1850–60):

It is unfortunate that so little is known about Webbe, whose output varied between fairy painting and Pre-Raphaelite naturalism.

SYMBOLISM:

Symbolism had been a European, rather than British, art phenomenon, and its imagery religious more than secular. Medieval paintings had dripped with symbols, and to fully understand their meaning one had to know the language, the code of symbols, just as Victorians knew the Language of Flowers and the generation before them knew the coded

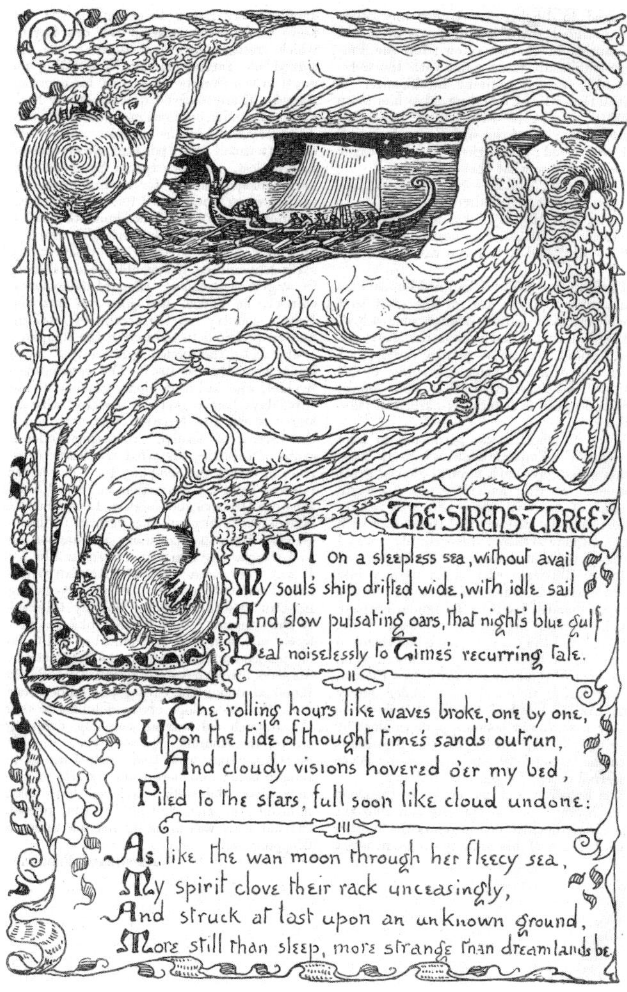

A typical Walter Crane page spread

messages in a lady's fan. Religious symbols were widely recognised: the cross, the fish, the lamb, the lily, ashes, the crown of thorns. Each symbol stood for something and, knowing the symbols, we interpreted the picture. In some early works the symbols were mysterious, either because the true meaning was dangerous and had to be concealed or because the artist, like a poet, prepared an elliptical message that wouldn't give itself up at a glance. Symbolism brought elliptical poetry into art.

In nineteenth-century France, Symbolism began as a literary movement before being taken up in the visual arts. Literature's symbolism was absolutely elliptical: one understood the words, but what did they mean? Perhaps they meant nothing, but merely hinted at a feeling one might interpret as one chose. Was music literal? Why should words be? French authors Rimbaud and Baudelaire led the charge and in 1886, after some thirty years of lonely foraging, a Manifesto of Literary Symbolism was published in Paris. Avant-garde writers were joined by avant-garde artists: Gustave Moreau, Odilon Redon, Puvis de Chavannes and, to a lesser extent, Gauguin, Rodin and Fantin-Latour. Others joined them from around Europe: Klimt, Munch, Ferdinand Hodler, Elihu Vedder, Gustav Vigeland and Fernand Khnopff.

It was not a cause where British artists were left behind – several became lauded on the continent more than they were here. Foremost was G F Watts who, in 1878 at the Exposition Universelle in Paris, amazed the initiated with nine paintings and a sculpture. (One of the paintings was *Love and Death*, 1874–7.) European critics, led by Khnopff, looked with interest at British artists, finding that Watts was not alone. Wasn't Burne-Jones as great a Symbolist? Weren't there wonderful poems in colour from Rossetti? These three were not merely the leading British Symbolists, they joined European figureheads. Symbolism was seen in paintings by Frederic Leighton, Albert Moore, Simeon Solomon and Whistler. In their wake came Cayley Robinson, Beardsley, Crane, Bateman, Richmond, Pickering de Morgan, Sandys, the MacDonald sisters, Ricketts and Shannon, and the sculptors Frampton, Bates, Gilbert and Pegram. For a country thought to be prosaic, hard-nosed and literal, Britain had more Symbolism than its hard-nosed, prosaic people realised.

Robert BATEMAN (1842–1922):

An artist whose private means allowed him to make Symbolic paintings regardless of whether they'd find a market (which they did) while he followed a range of esoteric interests in philosophy and natural sciences. He was prominent among progressives of the Sixties and Seventies exhibiting at the Dudley Gallery.

FREDERICK CAYLEY ROBINSON (1862–1927):

Against the decadent style that swept in towards the end of the century can be set the dreamier though still decorative manner of artists such as Cayley Robinson, who took his lead from, but was not slavishly emulative of, the aesthetic French style typified by Puvis de Chavannes. (Robinson had been educated in France.) Symbols, real or imaginary, abounded in his art, and the best of his pictures are hauntingly beautiful.

FRANCES (1873–1921) and MARGARET (1864–1933) MACDONALD:

The sisters stood out in the *fin de siècle* Glasgow School around Rennie Mackintosh with their beautiful mixed-media creations reflecting Symbolism, Aestheticism and Art Nouveau. They often collaborated, as with their set of four pieces representing the seasons, in which Frances painted *Spring* and *Autumn* while Margaret made *Summer* and *Winter*. They collaborated also on a famous poster advertising the Glasgow Institute of the Fine Arts Exhibition in 1895. Some of Margaret's work can be seen today in the Ingram Street Cafe and the Willow Tea Rooms in Glasgow's Sauchiehall Street. In 1899 Frances married the artist Herbert MacNair; in 1900 Margaret married Rennie Mackintosh; they were dubbed 'The Glasgow Four'. The work of the sisters was so admired by Klimt and others that they were invited to exhibit in Vienna. A tragic epilogue is that, late in life, MacNair destroyed most of his wife's work and much of his own.

EVELYN PICKERING DE MORGAN (1855–1919):

Niece to Spencer Stanhope, she began exhibiting (1877) as Evelyn Pickering, before marrying William De Morgan in 1887. Although often associated with Watts and Burne-Jones, she had a striking Symbolist style of her own. She came from a well-off family, trained at Slade, and lived for two years in Italy where she absorbed influences from Botticelli and the Florentine masters. Watts said, 'I look upon her as the first woman-artist of the day – if not of all time.' As she never needed to sell her paintings, most remained under the De Morgan family and are now within the aegis of the De Morgan Foundation.

SIR WILLIAM BLAKE RICHMOND (1842–1921):

Son of George, grandson of Thomas (and godson of William Blake), the latest in this artistic line was spotted early in life by Ruskin but never fell beneath his spell, perhaps because, through his father, he'd become an associate of Frederic Leighton, and Leighton's lifestyle was more glamorous than Ruskin's. For a while, Richmond shared a studio with Leighton. His finest works were Symbolist, and the most striking was his 8-foot tall oil *Sleep and Death Carrying the Body of Sarpedon into Lycia* (1875/6). Another of his Symbolist works, of similar size but this time 8-foot long rather than tall, is his eerie landscape, *Near Via Reggio, Where Shelley's Body Was Found* (1875).

Despite being (or perhaps because he was) married with six children, Richmond had a long affair with one of his models, Edith Finch, who when not modelling or dallying with Richmond, was no mean musician. Richmond's main income came from portraiture; he painted members of the Stanley, Howard, Stillman and Ionides families, a portrait of Burne-Jones's daughter Margaret, and Val Prinsep's wife Florence. He was also commissioned by the good folk of Kensington to paint Lady Mary Carr-Glyn, wife of their vicar, the Reverend Edward Carr-Glyn. Another of Richmond's models (though not one he had an affair with) was the Italian Gaetano Meo. Richmond's brother Thomas was a good portraitist also.

Henry John STOCK (1853–1930):

One of the later Symbolists, with affinities to Rossetti and Blake. The fact that he, seemingly miraculously, recovered his sight after going blind in childhood may explain his predilection for deeply personal and imaginative subjects, inspired by religion, literature and music.

George Frederick WATTS (1817–1904):

A career to inspire any ambitious artist: from modest beginnings Watts rose to fame and affluence, a fine house and a constant supply of admiring and conveniently wealthy lady patrons. Such patronage began early; in his twenties he spent four years in Italy under the protection of the Hollands, especially Lady Augusta Holland, where he perfected the art of pleasing and tantalising ladies, pleasing himself, and producing the occasional titbit of painting to repay his keep. He was a handsome young man, which helped, and his patrons responded eagerly to his idiosyncrasies and neuroses. He flattered them in his portraits – flattering himself too, sometimes including, sometimes headlining himself in heroic guises. On his return to England he found new patronage from the Prinseps of Little Holland House who provided him with commissions, fresh customers and his own permanent quarters. Mrs Prinsep's famous quote (made without rancour) was that 'he came to stay three days; he stayed thirty years'.

Watts became fully immersed in his role as gifted neurotic genius, sporting a flowing beard and dressing himself in equally flowing robes.

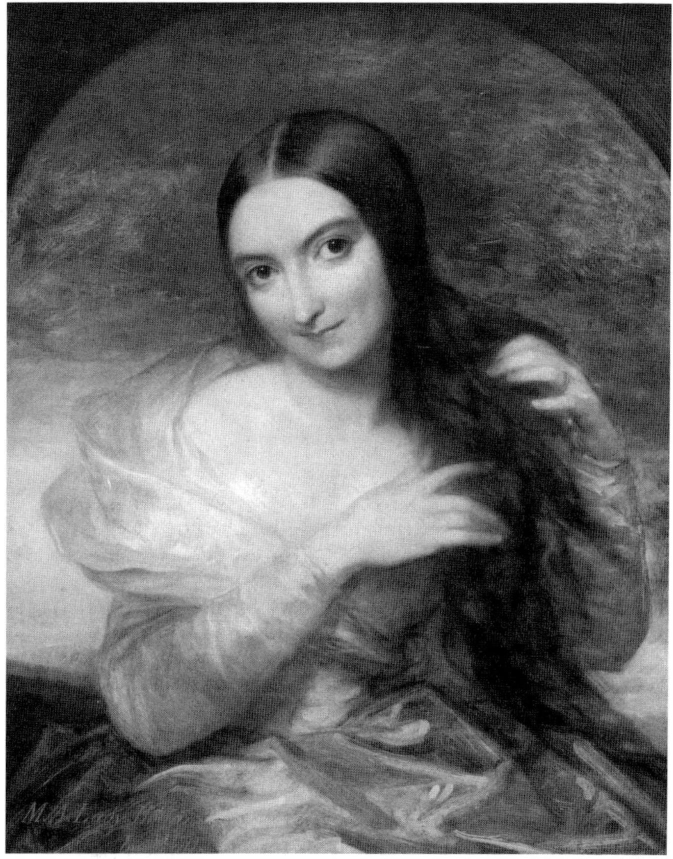

Lady Holland, painted by young Watts in 1844

When people came to call, they hovered in uncertainty as to whether his 'illnesses' would allow him to appear that day or not. Then, in his second decade at Little Holland House, the 47-year-old artist shocked many by suddenly marrying one of his models, the 16-year-old Ellen Terry. Unsurprisingly, the marriage failed, and she left him within the year.

But Watts could do no wrong. He continued court at Little Holland, acknowledging no one – patron or artist – as his superior, and with the money he earned from painting he rebuilt his quarters and studio on a lavish scale. Much later (1886) he married again, this time with success. How did he manage it?

Through painting. Though his behaviour may strike us as outrageously phony, we can't deny the man could paint. His portraits flattered but they also – as in the famous case of his painting of Carlyle – revealed the person behind the oil paint. Portraiture may have been secondary to his first love, the allegorical, but portraiture paid the rent (he made over 300 portraits and by the 1890s was charging 500 guineas a pop). Chesterton wrote of him that 'He scarcely ever paints a man without making him five times as magnificent as he really looks.' Henry James called him 'the first portrait

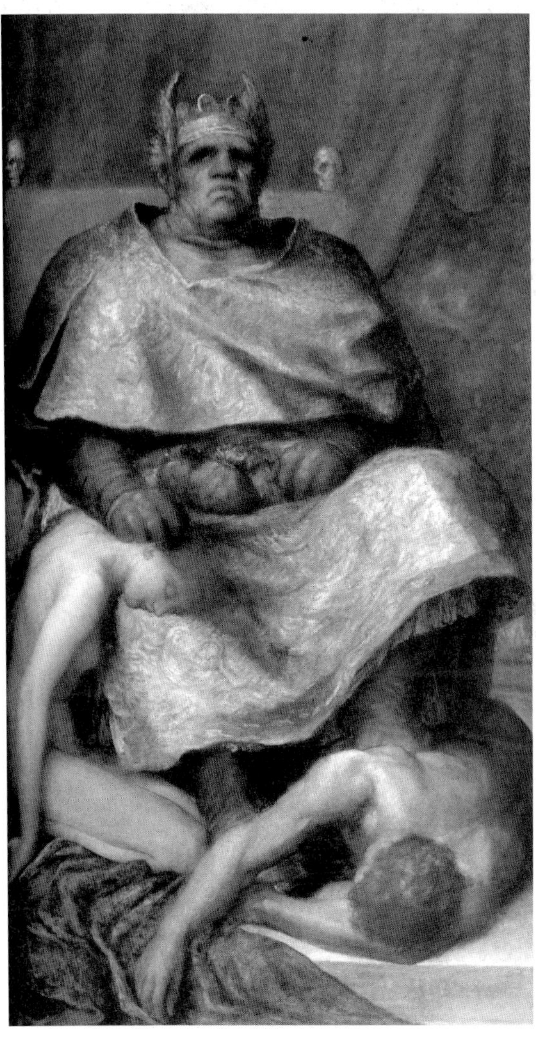

Mammon by Watts has a message for us today

painter in England'. Watts didn't disagree: a portrait, he said, 'is a summary of the life of a person, not the record of accidental position or arrangement of light and shadows'. Watts's high-minded confidence raised not only his own prestige but that of fellow artists: no longer were they artisans dependent on patrons' whims; they bequeathed their talent and had their own whims.

It is debatable whether Watts was principally a portrait painter or a Symbolist (on the continent they had no hesitation in placing him among the finest Symbolists). Striking among those works are *Love and Death* (1874–7) – shown to acclaim at the 1877 opening of the Grosvenor Gallery and the following year in Paris – and *Hope* (1886). Of his disturbing *Mammon: Dedicated to his Worshippers* (1884–5) Watts wrote, 'Material prosperity has become our real god, but we are surprised to find that the worship of this visible deity does not make us happy.' *Plus ça change . . .*

His second wife, Mary Fraser Tytler [sic], was actively interested in alternative religions and cults, and in 1884 Watts became an Honorary Associate Member of the Society for Physical Research, though he may have been more interested than convinced. What he learned there may have inspired some of his visionary works like *The Happy Warrior* (1884) or *The Dweller in the Innermost* (1885). He preferred to show, he said, 'The infinite looming large behind the finite – that is the impression which great art alone can convey.' Among other Symbolist works are *Time, Death and Judgement* (completed 1886), *She Shall Be Called Woman* (several versions, *circa* 1892), and *The All-Pervading* (completed 1893).

Watts presented many of his paintings to the nation. He knew his worth, and wanted succeeding generations to know it too. He began donating pictures from 1897 to the National Gallery, where they were displayed in the Watts Room, and when he donated to the Tate he wrote: 'I cannot tell you what satisfaction it gives me to think that the objects of my life's work should find a resting place during my lifetime. Of course it is not for me to make conditions & I do not presume to do so, but I hope as they embody a single idea & have reference to one & the same object they will be placed together, I feel also it would be a fine thing to have one room made magnificent in itself by means of a splendid colour say the deepest & noblest red that can be got!'

Chapter Twelve

DECORATIVE & AESTHETIC
Fin de Siècle, Still Life, Nudes

THE AESTHETIC MOVEMENT:

It is understandable that some confuse the *fin de siècle* fashions of the last decade of the century with the Aesthetic movement. Certainly aestheticism was a feature of that decade (actually a decade and a half, from around 1885 to 1900) but, if the main proponent of Aestheticism in art was Whistler, then we must remember that much of his impact came in the 1860s. Pater's influential promotion of 'art for art's sake' came in 1873 (he'd picked it up from the French philosopher Victor Cousin, who died in 1867). Aestheticism rejected the Victorian love of realism and accountability, and put in their place colour and tone, line and pattern. As the poet Swinburne said, 'Its meaning is beauty; and its reason for being is to be.'

With many movements in art, it is debatable who was a member – Whistler certainly, and Albert Moore (though I have called him Neoclassical), Burne-Jones (who with some reluctance I have placed with the Pre-Raphaelites), and Simeon Solomon ditto. Rossetti and Arthur Hughes are Pre-Raphaelites also and the impossible-to-classify Watts I have called a Symbolist. Aubrey Beardsley, that quintessentially *fin de siècle* figure, is under Illustrators. In truth, artists overlap – most are little concerned with which 'movement' they are ascribed to – and Aestheticism was more an influence than a movement.

James Abbot McNeill **WHISTLER** (1834–1903) is the one artist who can be placed in no other category. He was one of the most important, certainly one of the most individual, artists of the age. American by birth, influenced by French and Japanese art, he carried art from realism to aesthetic impressionism – and he began this shift in the 1860s, when almost everyone else was still coming to terms with Pre-Raphaelitism and the slow demise of the old-fashioned Academy. Whistler was two steps ahead, overlaying the delicacy of Japanese art onto the translucency of French Impressionism. He began titling his works as 'Nocturnes',

'Symphonies' and 'Arrangements' rather than give descriptive names. Many of his works were essays in colour, rather than reproductions of actual scenes or people and, as with most things new, they confused and irritated – most famously in the case of Ruskin. Poor Ruskin. In 1878, late in life and with his mind clouding, the ailing critic, unable to bring any of his normal armoury to bear, stared at Whistler's *A Falling Rocket* bemused. It was 'flinging a pot of paint in the public's face' he wrote – and Whistler sued. Ruskin, as confused in court as when confronted by the picture, was found to have libelled Whistler. But a court, like Ruskin, supports the status quo, and it awarded Whistler one farthing's damages. A Pyrrhic victory. In fighting the case Whistler lost a considerable sum of money and had to file for bankruptcy – though he'd won the moral

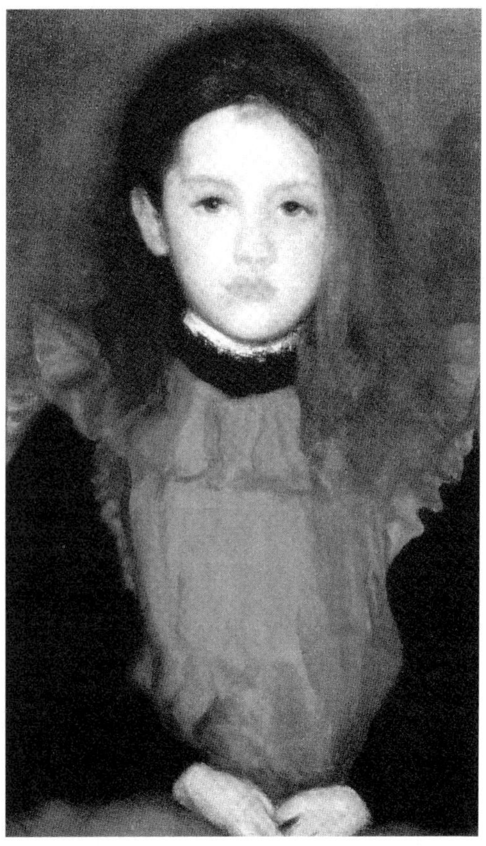

Little Rose of Lyme Regis (1895)

victory. (Or had he? Artists thought so but many of the public, happier then as now with the familiar, agreed with Ruskin that Whistler's piece was just a daub and splatter of paint; a fraud and cheat, which 'my child could have done'.) To us, more than a century later, *A Falling Rocket* is one of Whistler's most evocative paintings and places him with Turner, earlier in the century, and Monet, sojourning here from France among Britain's finest Thamesmen. These three alone might reassure artists who feared the camera might replace paint.

Whistler also painted people, and his portraits were a long way from photographic likenesses – as he emphasised in his titles. One of his most famous works, popularly but wrongly known as *Whistler's Mother* is actually *Arrangement in Grey and Black No 1* – because to Whistler the arrangement of tone and colour was the basis, the purpose, of the painting. (His *Arrangement in Grey and Black No 2* is the contentious Carlyle portrait, showing the great cynic sitting for his portrait weary and disbelieving.) Whistler's portraits are far from abstract exercises: his mother is old and tenderly painted, Carlyle exposed. His women are real and beautiful; his children ethereal but in no way mawkish: *Little Rose of Lyme Regis*, as she stands patiently before the artist, looks lovely but we know that, once released, she'll scoot off to play.

An artist associated with Whistler, an artist who, were it not for that connection, would be entirely forgotten today, is Walter **GREAVES** (1846–1930). A curious figure, he and his brother Henry were discovered by Whistler while working as Chelsea boatmen. They were taught to paint by him and, in time, Walter learnt to paint in a Whistler-like manner. In return, he taught Whistler to row. When Whistler decorated the Peacock Room for his patron Leyland, the Greaves brothers helped, in a minor way. Walter Greaves painted in a naive style – he also made some caricatures of his teacher, and one of Carlyle – but their ways parted and the Greaves brothers died in penury. They had made the mistake of giving up river work for art.

FIN DE SIÈCLE:

Victoria's Jubilee was in 1887, when the century had forsaken its youthful vigour to grow solid and mature. Many of its revolutionary artists had become pillars of the establishment and were disdained by the new generation as much as the one-time revolutionaries had disdained the Academy. In literature and art the dominant new trend was Aestheticism, expounded by Walter Pater and seized upon: 'Art for art's sake' was the cry; away with narrative and utility. The pursuit of beauty took artists down differing paths: some sought the spiritual and ephemeral, others the wild and decadent. Some combined the two.

It was nothing new for artists to seek things spiritual and ephemeral, and in Victorian England they'd had the example of Whistler to guide them for two decades; his Nocturnes and Symphonies were abstract poetry. Albert Moore had sacrificed meaning for beauty since the 1860s.

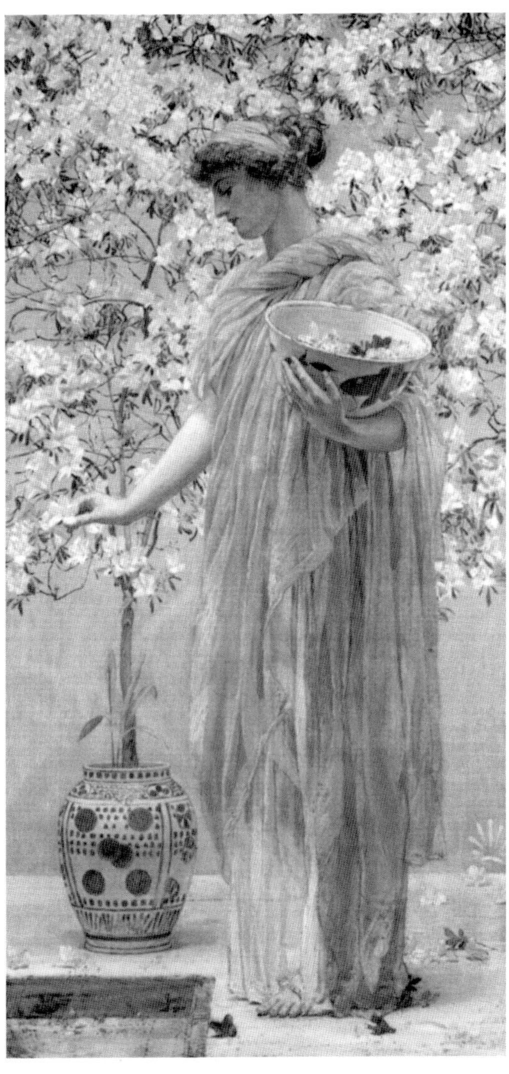

Azaleas by Albert Moore (1868)

Twenty years since its inception the Pre-Raphaelite artists had moved from Ruskin's 'absolute, uncompromising truth' to romantic dreamlike mysticism – the *un*realism of Burne-Jones and his followers.

A sign of things to come appeared in 1868 with Moore's *Azaleas*, a shimmering canvas in which a young woman in a yellowish toga picks flower-heads from an azalea tree in a painted pot. There's no symbolism, no hidden message. The painting was not the first of his classical dreams, but its exhibition at the Royal Academy spurred Swinburne into writing a defence of the cult of beauty. He linked the painting with Watts's *The Wife of Pygmalion* from that year: in these, he said, 'The melody of colour, the symphony of form, is complete: one more beautiful thing is achieved, one more delight is born into the world; and its meaning is beauty; and its reason for being is to be.'

Watts, Whistler, Burne-Jones, Moore – their works needed no more than to be beautiful. What they were not, and what was about to come snapping at their heels, was shocking, offensive and outrageous. In the parallel world of literature one man in particular, one notorious example, stepped publicly from the path of beauty onto the dangerous side-road that led – or hinted it might lead – to depravity, sin and decadence. That man was Oscar Wilde, whose early works exuded scents of beauty, whose middle period strayed into paradox, but whose late works seemed to many Victorian souls to be ripe with odours of corruption. *Fin de siècle* poets and essayists skipped nervously along his path, combining with new-wave artists to make works that seemed indecent (for the time) but which stretched boundaries. *The Yellow Book* was their most famous magazine and, of all the literary and graphic artists who contributed, none summed up the new direction more sensationally than did the consumptive, ferociously talented *enfant terrible*, Aubrey Beardsley.

Apart from *fin de siècle* artists in other chapters, there are these:

Charles CONDER (1868–1909):

Conder reached his peak in the last two decades of his life – not as a shocking *fin de siècle* artist (he was far from shocking), but as an exponent of the beautifully aesthetic. In delicate, Impressionistic paintwork he conjured fragile nudes, dreamlike landscapes, coastal studies and decorative genre scenes. Some of his work, especially his watercolours on silk, seems too fragile to survive.

Charles RICKETTS (1866–1931):

A central figure in the *fin de siècle* aesthetic movement, whose own delicate studies and drawings were almost eclipsed by his tireless promotion of art ('for art's sake') in publishing and exhibition. Together with his lifelong companion Charles Shannon he launched the high-minded but doomed *Dial* magazine and formed and ran the Vale Press, a company devoted to the production of simple but beautiful books, exquisitely printed and illustrated but, sadly, produced in such small editions that they are forbiddingly expensive. Ricketts was generally admired, indeed loved, by fellow artists and eventually became Director of the National Gallery.

Charles SHANNON (1863–1937):

The close companion and oft-times collaborator with Charles Ricketts in their publishing enterprises was both a lithographer and an accomplished artist, varying between idyllic and aesthetic works and well-made portraits – notably of other artists, such as *Lucien Pissarro* (1895), *Alphonse Legros* (1896) and *Thomas Sturge Moore* (1896).

Joseph SOUTHALL (1861–1944):

Born in Nottingham and a student at the Birmingham School of Art, Southall was a turn-of-the-century painter (mainly outside our period) who combined elements of the Aesthetic, the Symbolic and the Arts and Crafts movement. Egg tempera painting was a speciality of his, and in 1901 he became a founder member of the Society of Painters in Tempera. His first Royal Academy hanging was a watercolour, *Cinderella* (1895), and his most important nineteenth-century work was an egg tempera mythographic work, *Beauty Receiving the White Rose from her Father* (1898–9).

STILL LIFE:

In Britain, among professional artists, still-life painting has never been predominant. Prized as it is among buyers (it's respectable and looks nice on the wall), with tutors (as an easily set and managed exercise that can be done indoors), and by amateurs (for much the same reasons schools and tutors like it), still life fails to inspire most British artists. When it is approached by modern artists from any country (modern being after 1900, let us say) it is usually only to be subverted. Picasso and the Cubists painted still lifes. Abstract artists, they say, do too. Among Victorian artists there are relatively few who put still life first.

Hercules Brabazon BRABAZON (1821–1906):

An extremely competent, to some degree overlooked painter, who continued with meticulous still lifes and flower studies into the last years of his life, when other artists had turned to more challenging, though not always more rewarding, subjects.

William Henry HUNT (1790–1864):

His early talent earned him a place at the RA exhibition when he was just 17, and in his twenties he progressed from exquisite and innovative water-colours of still-life and figure studies (a number of which show the same boy model) to the unlikely works for which he became famous: birds' nest studies, of which 'Bird's-nest Hunt' would show more than 800 in exhibitions of the Society of Painters in Water-Colours. A number of Victorian painters followed his lead, but none could truly match him. His output is all the more extraordinary when one remembers that he was infirm and that for any but the shortest journeys he had to be conveyed in a wheelbarrow by his gardener.

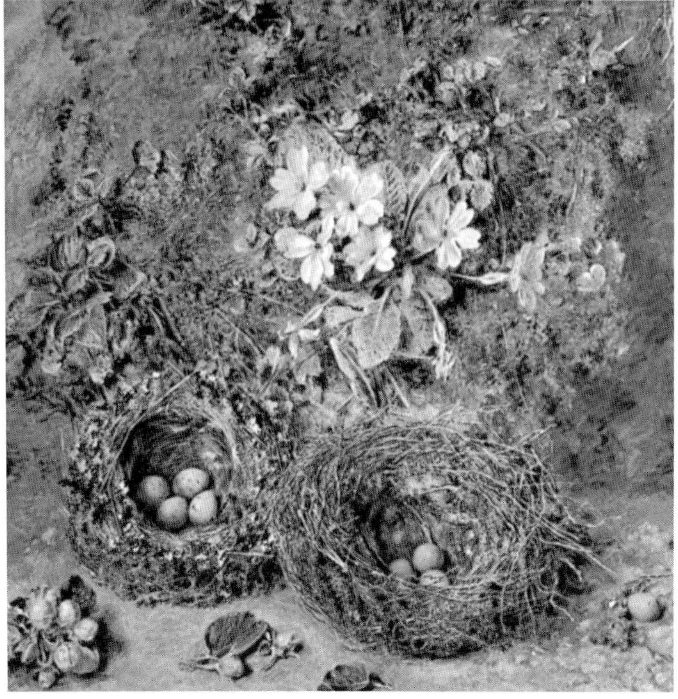

Primroses with Bird's Nest – a typically realistic still-life watercolour by W H Hunt

GEORGE LANCE (1802–64):

A still-life painter whose meticulous Dutch-inspired style seemed out of date even in his day – though the *Art Journal* in 1857 said his paintings of fruit: 'which are his speciality, have never been surpassed in luxuriance and richness of colour, in truth, and in effective and most harmonious grouping.' The V&A and the National Portrait Gallery have self-portraits.

THE VICTORIAN NUDE:

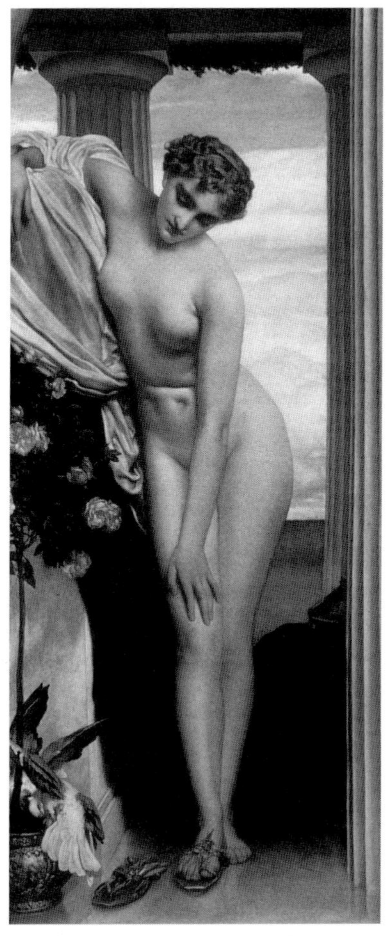

Leighton's *Venus Disrobing for the Bath* (1866–7)

Victorian artists learnt and practised life-painting from nude models. Clothes got in the way; it was only when clothes were removed that one could study and render properly the body and how it lay. Many a Victorian life study, however respectable it might finally appear, was first drafted from a nude model. Only when the form was right were clothes draped over it.

But did those lovely young ladies – the pulchritudinous young ladies straining against the ropes and chains of Edward Normand's paintings, for example – did they really just get dressed and go home again in the evenings? Almost certainly yes, if his wife had anything to do with it. Normand's wife, Henrietta Rae, had on a number of occasions to explain why she painted beautiful though tastefully nude young ladies. But was it acceptable, people wondered, for *women* artists (Rae and Ethel Walker) to paint nudes? What artistic justification could there be for William Etty's blossoming beauties? Nudes were permissible 'in their place' – and their place was in classical antiquity. Or in the Bible. Normand posed his maidens as early Christians thrown to the lions (who presumably did not like the taste of cloth) and Solomon Solomon, when painting his *Samson*, had Delilah unaccountably bare-breasted as she watched her loved one held down and shorn of hair. Victorians, for all their apparent prudishness, splattered the walls of public buildings with voluptuous nudes. Rich men – rich married men – displayed nudes in their houses, in their halls and dining rooms, where they could gaze down at paterfamilias as he said grace.

'Venus herself,' maintained George du Maurier in 1895, 'as she drops her garments and steps on to the model-throne, leaves behind her on the floor every weapon in her armoury by which she can pierce to the grosser passions of man. The more perfect her unveiled beauty, the more keenly it appeals to his higher instincts.' (Discuss.)

Many artists appealed to those higher instincts, including:

Edward CALVERT (1799–1883):

His private income may explain his small output – small but exquisite. In his thirties he produced a dozen beautiful woodcuts in the dreamy style of Blake, and in his forties he painted some ethereal nudes in classical style, inspired this time by his friend Etty. Other works were less inspired and less interesting.

William ETTY (1787–1849):

It is extraordinary to think how respectable this prolific painter of nude women was. Many of his nudes were simply nudes, with no 'classical' reference or justification. He sent one of his female models to Constable with the note: 'All in front memorably fine.' Lusciously painted, often romantic, sometimes erotic (Thackeray wrote that 'some of these pictures would not be suitable to hang up everywhere – in a young ladies' school, for instance'), they graced the walls of galleries up and down the land. Some still do, others are regularly reproduced, but rarer are his portraits and occasional landscapes.

Etty hailed from a modest and deeply religious family in York but showed signs of what was to come with his *Cleopatra's Arrival in Cilicia* (1821) which raised eyebrows at the RA Exhibition. An accompanying study for *Youth on the Prow and Pleasure at the Helm* (a painting finally exhibited in 1832) provoked *The Times* critic to write: 'Naked figures, when painted with the purity of Raphael, may be endured: but nakedness without purity is offensive and indecent, and in Mr Etty's canvas is mere dirty flesh.' Perhaps this criticism spurred Etty into the production of bare-breasted Amazons, nymphs and martyred maidens.

Etty died of asthma, uttering the extraordinary observation, 'wonderful, wonderful, this death'. The city of York gave him a civic funeral.

Alfred Joseph WOOLMER (1805–92):

A painter of literary and genre subjects, best-known now for his 'arty' nudes, sometimes transplanted into imaginary sub-Turner landscapes. Though his output was prolific (over 350 works exhibited at the Society of British Artists) his private life was just that – private. Who were his parents? What was his wife's name? No one knows.

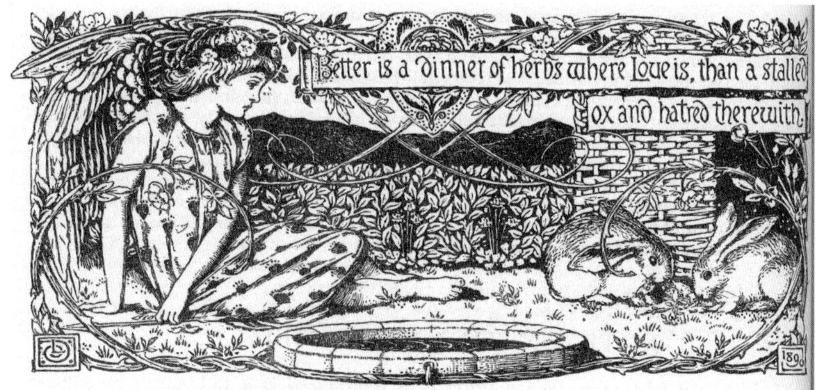

Chapter Thirteen

A CENTURY OF BLACK & WHITE
Printmakers, Engravers & Caricaturists

In the nineteenth century, artists experimented eagerly with new colour, using new pigments from their colourmen and new colour reproduction techniques from their printers. Colours we now take for granted had been freshly created: cadmium yellow in 1817, chrome yellow in 1820, cobalt yellow in 1861. Perkin's Mauve, a new rich purple dye created in 1856, inspired a craze led by the Queen herself: she wore it and the Pre-Raphaelites painted with it. (Holman Hunt led a fierce campaign against some of the less reliable new colours when he found they faded and were impermanent. Turner, a keen experimenter, triumphed with new yellows but fell foul of a new iodine scarlet that faded to brown.) Artists relied upon their colourmen: the tills rang at Rowney & Co., founded by Thomas and Richard Rowney in 1789, and at Winsor & Newton, founded in 1832. Printing in colour improved dramatically – and profitably – with technological breakthroughs at colour printers Ackermann, Baxter, Edmund

Evans, Vizetelly and Kronheim. It was George Baxter who introduced colour to wood and steel engravings, Thomas de la Rue who invented chromolithography.

Yet at the same time a great deal of superb work was produced in black and white: etchings and mezzotints; pen and ink studies; caricatures and cartoons; illustrations for books and magazines; engraved copies of art originals. While Illustration has a chapter to itself, here we look at some notable black and white engravers, caricaturists and cartoonists.

ENGRAVERS AND PRINTMAKERS:

Thomas Oldham BARLOW (1824–89):

An etcher and engraver of the highest quality, who engraved works by saleable artists such as John Phillip, his first major commission, for whom he would become executor. Millais appreciated Barlow's reproduction of his paintings and twice portrayed him, notably in *A Ruling Passion* (1885). Barlow went on to engrave Landseer, Ansdell, Turner and others.

George BAXTER (1804–67):

One of the leading Victorian colour printers, whose innovatory technique combined a metal plate with an astonishing number of up to twenty additional wooden blocks, each printed a different colour. His excellent prints were cheap and could be produced in vast numbers. But over-ambition told for him and he died bankrupt and embittered.

Samuel BELLIN (1799–1893):

A notable printmaker and engraver who learnt much of his craft in Rome (meeting artists such as Turner there). After his return to London in 1834 he began reproducing and publishing the work of leading artists of the day, from Hunt to Landseer. Throughout his life he was renowned for his good nature and charity, especially towards less fortunate artists.

Samuel COUSINS (1801–87):

One of the century's great engravers and printmakers whose talent emerged early: he sold his first drawings from a shop window when only 10, and was taken on as apprentice to the mezzotint engraver Samuel William Reynolds (1774–1835) at 13. The quality of his engraving was such that he was sought-after by print publishers and major artists seeking the best person to make commercial copies of their works.

Francis CROLL (1827–54):

A skilled Scottish engraver whose life was cut short by serious heart disease.

William (1787–1852) and Edward Francis (1791–1857) FINDEN:

The brothers became renowned for their magnificent and archetypal steel engravings for single plates or, more often, expensive drawing-room books. Their work included portraits, landscapes and careful copies of fine paintings, including works by Turner and Landseer.

Samuel FREEMAN (1773–1857):

Engraver and charter member (i.e. joint founder) of the Artists' Benevolent Fund. His steel engravings ranged from copies of old and contemporary masters to his own compositions on religious subjects.

Sir Francis Seymour HADEN (1818–1910):

A noted etcher and surgeon (good with the knife) who published excellent treatises on both; in 1880 he was the obvious choice to be made President of the Society of Painter-Etchers, and he remained so till his death. He was a practising and leading surgeon, and he campaigned vigorously against cremation, advocating a natural 'earth to earth' burial instead, and for which he invented a papier-mâché coffin.

William Henry MOTE (1803–71):

An engraver and portrait artist, not to be confused with George William Mote.

William NICHOLSON (1872–1949):

A major portrait and still-life artist whose main work came in the twentieth century. He trained at Herkomer's academy but was expelled for posing a nude model with an umbrella; whether Herkomer objected to the nude or the umbrella is unclear. In 1894 he and his brother-in-law, James Pryde, combined under the name J. & W. Beggarstaff to produce a famous series of posters, issued in large and now collectable volumes as *London Types, An Almanac of Twelve Sports* and *An Alphabet*. Following Victoria's Jubilee they also produced two sets of *Twelve Portraits* (1899 and 1902). These fine print-works, though, are secondary to his painting. Nicholson's son was the twentieth-century abstract artist Ben Nicholson.

Josiah **WHYMPER** (1813–1903) and his brother Ebenezzar [sic] founded the Whymper firm of engravers. Josiah's son Edward Whymper (1840–1911) became an engraver also, and took over his father's business in the 1890s. His first major commission as an artist came from his real passion, mountaineering, when Longman had him draw the Alps. It can only have fuelled his passion, as Edward went on to make a number of great ascents, including the Matterhorn, a climb on which four of his companions fell to their deaths.

Other engravers of note include: Charles BAUGNIET (1814–86), Auguste Thomas Marie BLANCHARD (1819–98), the HOLL family (Francis, William and Charles), Richard James LANE (1800–72), Charles George LEWIS (1808–80) and his father, Frederick Christian LEWIS (1779–1856), Henry Duff LINTON (1816–99), Thomas Herbert MAGUIRE (1821–95), Henry Thomas RYALL (1811–67), James THOMSON (1787–1850), Charles TURNER (1774–1857), William WALKER (1791–1867) and his wife Elizabeth (1800–76).

CARICATURISTS:

Four notable caricaturists described in the Illustration chapter are Alfred CROWQUILL (aka A H Forrester), George CRUIKSHANK, Harry FURNISS and Louis WAIN. Two others of note are the following:

'APE' (CARLO PELLEGRINI) (1839–89):

One of the century's great caricaturists, he was born in Italy, and when he first arrived in London in the winter of 1864 (having fought in Italy for Garibaldi) he was so poor he had to sleep in doorways of the West End. Despite having had no formal training he was soon resident caricaturist for *Vanity Fair*. As such he became hugely popular – and influential, in that, for the many readers who had never met the celebrities, his images *were* those people. (His first *Vanity Fair* caricatures were signed *Signe*, before the more famous *Ape*.)

'Ape' was practically a caricature himself: 5 feet 2 inches tall, with a huge head and tiny feet, he wore immaculate white spats and highly polished boots, and had long Mandarin-like fingernails. He never walked when he could ride. Kind and generous, speaking fractured English and flaunting his homosexuality, his various whims included bringing macaroni dishes to elegant dinner parties, refusing invitations to country houses for fear of strange beds, and keeping a cigar in his mouth as he slept. He was much loved, and there was great sadness when he died of tuberculosis.

'SPY' (SIR LESLIE WARD) (1851–1922):

The son of the history painter E M Ward, he was educated at Eton and had no formal artistic training until entering the RA Schools in 1871. Via Millais, a family friend who had seen his caricatures, Ward was introduced in 1873 to the editor of *Vanity Fair* who had just fallen out with his magazine's main caricaturist, 'Ape'. For some years the two shared top billing in *Vanity Fair*, until 'Ape' died and 'Spy' carried on alone, producing his final cartoon in June 1911. He continued to paint portraits.

CARTOONISTS:

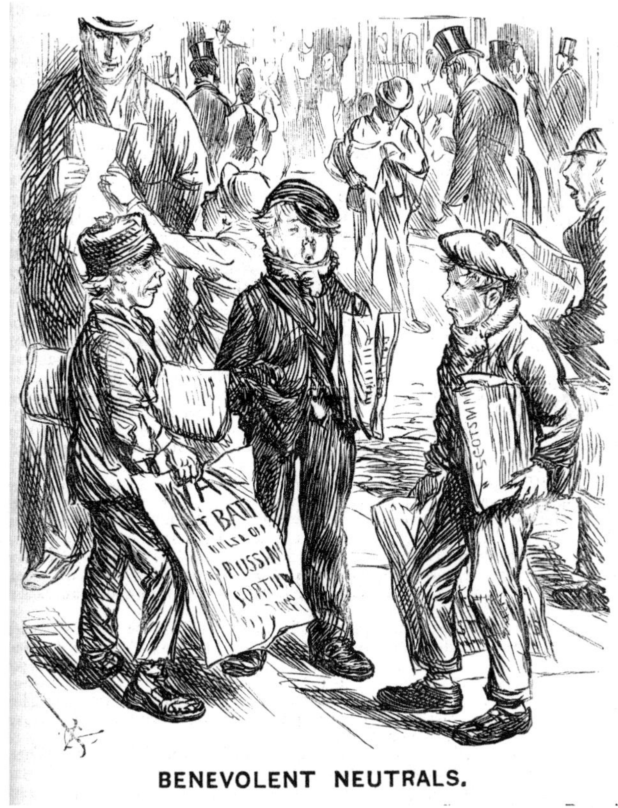

BENEVOLENT NEUTRALS.

A Charles Keene study of London life for *Punch* December 1870

The Illustration chapter has details on Richard DOYLE, George DU MAURIER, Kenny MEADOWS, Leonard RAVEN-HILL, Linley SAMBOURNE, James Frank SULLIVAN, John TENNIEL and William Makepeace THACKERAY. Other cartoonists of the period include:

Charles Samuel KEENE (1823–91):

One of the century's best-loved and more prolific black and white artists, though he did also produce some oils. He is known for his sharp observation of Victorian 'types'. Keene began as an engraver producing book illustrations for the Whymper brothers – a useful grounding – and by the Fifties was contributing to *Punch* and the *Illustrated London News*. His first real breakthrough came in 1864 on the death of John Leech, who he succeeded as chief social cartoonist for *Punch*. His work for that magazine was notable for the excellence of its line-work more than for its humour, and a volume of his pieces, *Our People* was published in 1881.

Keene the man had a more eccentric appearance than did many of his creations: he was a tall, shabby, gangly, bearded bachelor, housing himself in a succession of dreary lodgings. His heavy smoking and dismal diet were said to have hastened his death – though he did live to 68, no bad age in those days – and when his will was read he was found to have left over £30,000, no bad legacy then either.

John LEECH (1817–64):

One of the great black and white illustrators and cartoonists of everyday life, famed for his work in *Punch* and other periodicals and for his illustrations to Surtees's tales of Mr Jorrocks. The young Leech's father ran the London Coffee House on Ludgate Hill, which must have provided many subjects for the lad's life-studies and cartoons (though when the coffee-house business failed, the relationship between father and son failed too). Among many books illustrated by him, Dickens's *A Christmas Carol* must be the best-known, though Leech would have preferred to be remembered for his own collections, such as the *Pictures of Life and Character* (issued in volumes between 1854 and '69). Though a handsome and apparently athletic man, he died of angina and general ill-health.

Phil MAY (1864–1903):

Popular late Victorian cartoonist much reproduced on Edwardian postcards, who died young, almost certainly because of – and certainly helped by – his addiction to drink. May was born in Leeds, began a succession of jobs at the age of 13, failed as an actor, and found himself reduced to sleeping rough and begging in London until his skill as a cartoonist began to bring in an income. The 1890s were his heyday.

Chapter Fourteen

ILLUSTRATION
Art for the Millions

Many Victorian artists earned more from illustration and reproduction of their pictures than they did from paintings. The nineteenth century saw an explosion in cheap print, and publishers knew that words sold faster if accompanied by pictures. Books and magazines were a hungry market. In the early decades, the reproduction of illustrations was mainly via metal plate (usually steel), but from the mid-century the preferred medium became the woodblock. Steel plates had to be printed separately from the text (either as a separate run or on a separate page) but woodblocks were printed in the same run, so the pictures could be easily integrated into text. Generally, engravers either copied the artist's work onto a wooden block or engraved from a drawing the artist made directly onto the wood. Woodblock engraving was suitable for all kinds of drawing, whether it be cartoons for *Punch*, actuality pictures for the *Illustrated London News*, illustrations to stories in *Household Words*, *Once a Week*, *Cornhill*, *Good Words*, *The Quiver* et cetera, or 'art pictures' for the Victorian equivalent of coffee-table books. Millais wrote to his wife in 1861 that 'if I will do one drawing a week for *Once A Week* they will give me £600 per annum', and that he might expect to make as much as £5,000 from illustration that year. He could have lived on the income from illustration alone, before earning a penny from his paintings.

An artist could easily earn in excess of £20 for a magazine or book illustration, though the engraver, who worked on the piece much longer, earned a good deal less. £20 was a low but acceptable monthly wage. Contrasted with these workaday fees were the profits to be made from reproduction rights to original paintings, where often the money made from engravings outweighed the price of the original painting. When the dealer Gambart paid a record-breaking price (quoted as £5,000, though perhaps a little less) for Hunt's *Finding the Saviour in the Temple* he earned back his outlay several times over, first by exhibiting the painting itself in Bond Street for several months, before sending it on tour around the country for nearly four years. Meanwhile he took subscriptions for the engraved versions (early editions being more expensive than ordinary

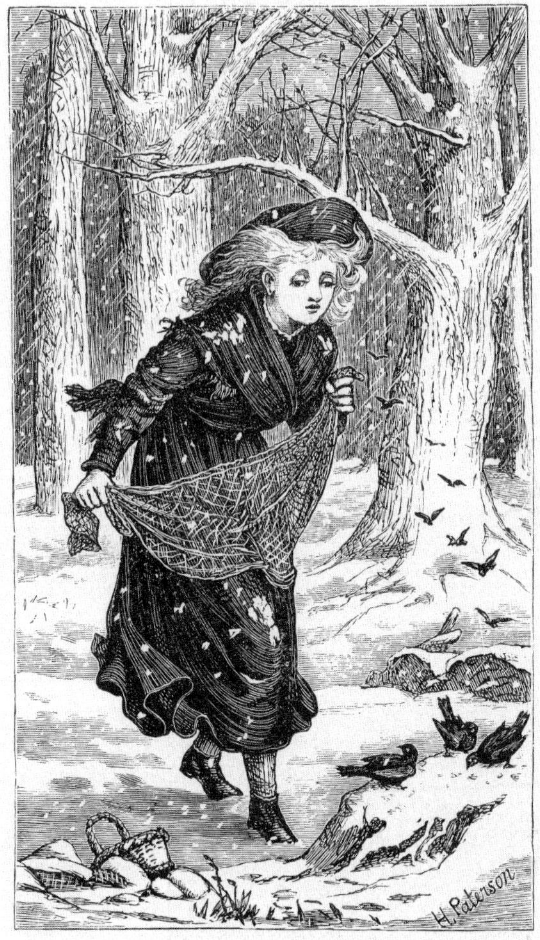

Illustration to *The Quiver* by Helen Allingham (Miss Paterson before marriage)

ones later). He almost lost his investment, however, when a flaring gas light set fire to the Bond Street gallery – a fire extinguished at the last moment when it was smothered with a lady's shawl.

Had he listened to Hunt's friend Millais he would never have bought the painting. Millais wrote to his wife in April 1859 that 'it will be like sinking his money in a gutter, for I never saw such a sad, sad failure'. A few days later Millais was still of this mind: 'I will engage to say that Hunt's picture will not be worth 300 after the four years' work. The proportion and drawing is absolutely *execrable*, but enough of this. I have not said this openly as it would be put down to jealousy.' Indeed.

While top artists could earn mouthwatering fees, those with lesser reputations did not, *but* illustration work paid reasonable bread-and-butter money. Many artists began in illustration and some – Millais included – continued in it while their paintings fetched massive sums. Few artists scorn bread-and-butter money. (Think of Millais and his £600 per annum.) Lower on the pecking order came the engravers, many of whom were artists too, or hoped to become so. Artists who developed national reputations had been engravers in their formative years. Walter Crane began in the engraving workshops of the radical Chartist Linton – one of the leading firms – though Linton recognised Crane's talent early on and quickly set him drawing original works rather than merely making cuts from others' sketches. Artists supplied their pictures either on paper (less desirable, as the pictures had to be copied before they were cut) or on the same whitened boxwood blocks the engraver worked upon. For an engraver it was mind-numbing, eye-straining work to carefully cut out all the white in an artist's work and leave the black to receive ink. In Crane's *Reminiscences* he describes the Linton workshop:

> *A row of engravers at work at a fixed bench covered with green baize running the whole length of the room under the windows with eyeglass stands and rows of gravers. And for night-work, a round table with a gas lamp in the centre, surrounded with a circle of large clear glass globes filled with water to magnify the light and concentrate it on the blocks upon which the engravers (or 'peckers', or 'woodpeckers' as they were commonly called) worked, resting them upon small circular leather bags or cushions filled with sand.*

Artists considered principally as illustrators include:

Aubrey BEARDSLEY (1872–98):

One of the finest and most shocking artists of the nineteenth century, whose work epitomises the decadence of the *fin de siècle*. In the final years of a century during which advances in print technology and mass circulation made black and white illustration a commonplace, Beardsley took the form to a new dimension, forsaking cross-hatching and tonal shading for stark contrasts of sheer black and white, creating impact through immaculate design. The technical brilliance of his work can be – and was at the time – eclipsed by the shocking subjects he depicted. His nudes were flagrant, carnal and sexually explicit (though beautifully stylised) – horrifying the public far more than did the fleshy nudes adorning the walls of public halls (and not a few domestic interiors).

Robert Anning BELL (1863–1933):

The son of a London cheesemonger, Bell began as an architect and sculptor (sharing a studio with George Frampton) before finding his feet in the Arts and Crafts movement. Life was best for him in the 1890s; the new *Studio* magazine favoured him and from 1895–99 he held regular employment as an instructor at Liverpool University School of Architecture. He branched out at the newly-established Della Robbia pottery in Birkenhead, for whom he designed its trademark galleon motif and many ceramic relief panels. By then he was also in demand as a book illustrator: his stand-alone editions of Shakespeare's *The Tempest* and *Midsummer Night's Dream* are particularly fine creations. In works such as these he allowed his fascination for fantasy and mysticism a freer rein.

Randolph CALDECOTT (1846–86):

Illustrator and watercolourist. The son of a Chester accountant, he began as a bank clerk and submitted sketches to local periodicals until some were accepted for *London Society* in 1871, after which he rapidly found success as an illustrator of children's books (mainly for Edmund Evans). In the Seventies he was second only to Kate Greenaway in popularity, though his subjects ranged wider, into the jollities of country and often sporting life.

George CATTERMOLE (1800–68):

Born comfortably off in a village near Diss in Norfolk, his natural affability and independent means helped him move in artistic and society circles in London, where he befriended Dickens, Lytton, Thackeray, Disraeli, Browning, Landseer and many more. He saw himself as a watercolourist, even if today he is better remembered as an illustrator: Dickens engaged him to illustrate *The Old Curiosity Shop* (1840–41) and *Barnaby Rudge* (1841), and many of his early works were architectural and historical illustrations to fine books. Cattermole exhibited well over 100 watercolours, of which the last was the much-praised *The Unwelcome Return* (1846).

Walter CRANE (1845–1915):

A follower of Burne-Jones, though their work together was not always successful. Despite Burne-Jones's criticism of Crane's work for the Howards at Number 1 Palace Green, Rosalind Howard commissioned

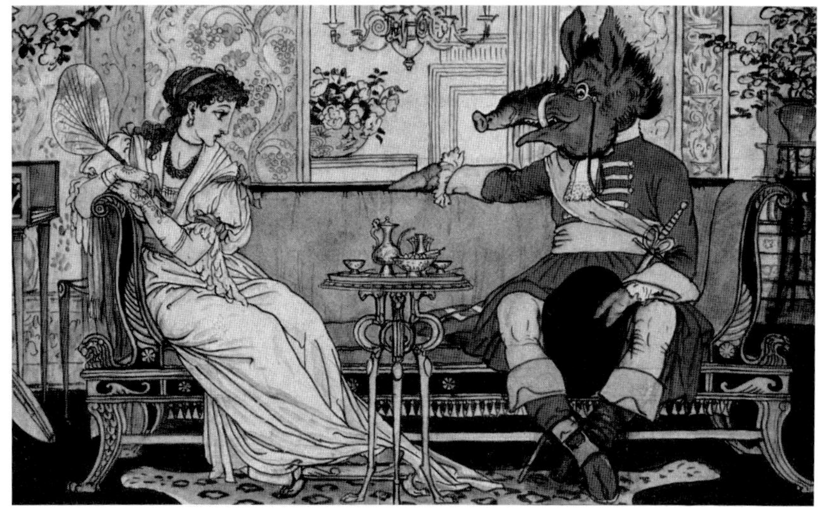

One of Walter Crane's illustrations to *Beauty and the Beast*

Crane to supply works for her boudoir, including *Mere in Cheshire* and *Hunting Moon*. They were hung alongside some sketches by Burne-Jones and Crane's large painting *The Annunciation* in which Julia Stephen was the model. Despite these grand commissions Crane was a strong socialist (along with Morris) and produced a number of cartoons and a banner for the cause.

Alfred CROWQUILL (aka A H Forrester) (1805–72):

Illustrator and writer who, together with his brother Charles Forrester (1803–50) collaborated as the caricaturist Crowquill, producing squibs for early editions of *Punch* and other comic magazines. After around 1860 Alfred's work shifted into illustration for children's books. Both brothers suffered from and eventually died of heart disease.

George CRUIKSHANK (1792–1878):

One of the century's best and most prolific illustrators – of Dickens, of Grimm's Fairy Tales, of his own Comic Almanacs, and of much, much more – his spidery yet vigorous caricatures are instantly recognisable. Irascible, at times impossible to work with, he fell out with Dickens when he claimed that the author wrote tales to fit his (Cruikshank's) pictures rather than the other way round. Later in life he became violently teetotal and produced many drawings and tracts in support of the anti-drink cause. It was a disastrous and sad distraction for a man previously loved for his wild comic imagination.

DALZIEL Brothers:

Though the Dalziels are famed mostly as book engravers (theirs was the largest such firm, responsible for many of the mid-century's finest illustrated books) the brothers were illustrative artists in their own right. The four were George (1815–1902), Edward (1817–1905), John (1822–1869) and Thomas (the better artist, 1823–1908).

Richard DOYLE (1824–83):

Much-loved cartoonist, satirist and fairy illustrator, the designer for *Punch* of its longest-lasting cover (Punch and Toby). An obviously talented child (his teenage illustrated *Dick Doyle's Journal* is still in print), he joined the staff of *Punch* in 1843 but eventually fell out with fellow-satirists over their attitude to Roman Catholics. From 1851 he worked mainly in illustration, and his fairy pictures are still much reproduced. First editions of books such as *Fairyland* and *The King of the Golden River* are sought after, and show that he was equally at home in black and white (cartoons and squibs) as in colour (all those fairies). A number of his colour works can be seen today in galleries. Doyle was one of seven children, and his brother Charles (1832–93, father to Sir Arthur Conan Doyle) also painted fairy pictures.

George DU MAURIER (1834–96):

In his day, Du Maurier was one of the country's most famous artists – largely through his illustrations to *Punch* but also through illustrations elsewhere. He was more a wry social commentator than a laugh-out-loud cartoonist; a book of selected Du Maurier illustrations could serve as a detailed guide to Victorian manners, modes and attitudes. He commented even on fellow artists, as when in his best-known book, *Trilby*, he used fellow members of the 'Paris Gang' as models for his characters. He was grandfather to the author Daphne du Maurier.

Harry FURNISS (1854–1925):

In *Punch* from 1880 to '94 he was one of the most effective and prolific caricaturists, many of his sketches revealing more of their subject than do official portraits. In his cartoon for Pears soap a tramp declared, 'I used your soap two years ago, since when I have used no other.' As an illustrator he worked for numerous magazines and newspapers, as well as providing superb accompaniments to books including Carroll's *Sylvie and*

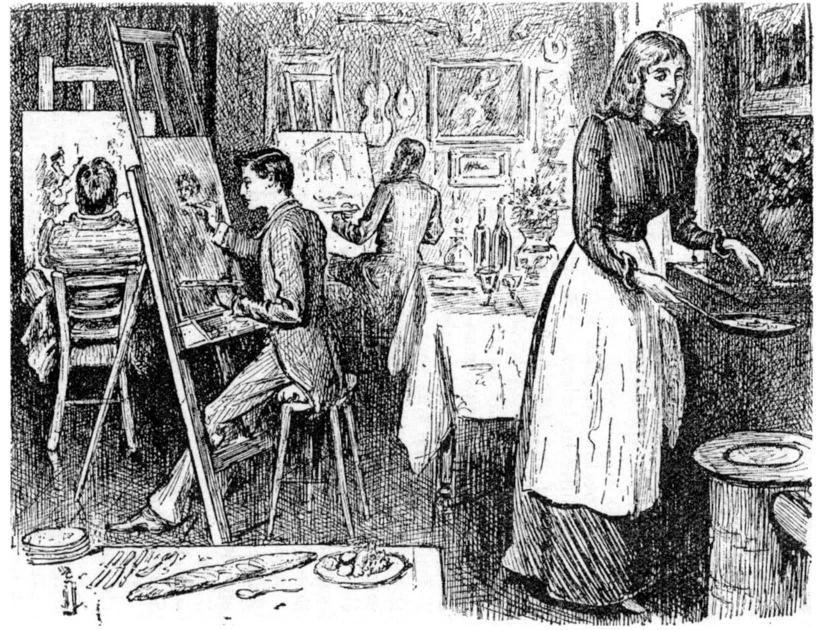

A Du Maurier illustration for his novel *Trilby*, 1894

Bruno and *Sylvie and Bruno Concluded*, and other books for children and adults. His own children acted as models, and Dorothy (later a decent artist herself) became his archetypal little girl. He wrote and illustrated forty books of his own (eighteen in the Victorian period) and illustrated the complete works of Thackeray and Dickens in the Edwardian. He was also successful on the lecture circuit, with magic lantern. In his long-running feud with the Royal Academy (which spurned black and white artists) he produced four volumes of cartoons and caricatures of their exhibits.

Sir John GILBERT (1817–97):

His knighthood shows the regard in which he was held. A painter of historical and literary subjects, he also illustrated a number of important books, including a landmark Shakespeare (or Shakspeare as it was titled) which is still in print with all his pictures. Yet Gilbert, born in Blackheath, failed to be accepted by the RA Schools and was in consequence largely self-taught. He applied his attention to the Old Water Colour Society and became an Associate in 1852, a Full Member in 1854, and its President in 1871. Despite his love of watercolour he earned much of his money from illustration, with which he was most comfortable. To every editor's delight, Gilbert could compose and draw any subject directly on the woodblock, with no preliminary sketches, in about an hour while a messenger waited. In 1893 he presented a collection of his pictures to the nation, and the gift was divided between the municipal galleries of London, Birmingham, Liverpool and Manchester. Gilbert was given the freedom of the City of London, the first artist to be so honoured.

KATE GREENAWAY (1846–1901):

One of the most beloved illustrators, mainly of and for children, selling well then and selling even more today. Her father was an engraver to the *Illustrated London News* and she studied art at the Slade. In 1877 she exhibited at the RA and began to provide book illustrations for Edmund Evans. Simple as her pictures were, they appealed to the Victorian public (as they do to today's nostalgic public, who should beware of the many fakes) and were appreciated by the magisterial John Ruskin.

HENRY HOLIDAY (1839–1927):

A fine artist who worked mainly in stained glass, though he is also remembered for his delightfully grotesque illustrations to Carroll's *The Hunting of the Snark* and, to specialists, as editor of *Aglaia*, the journal of the Healthy and Artistic Dress Union. His rather formal *Dante and Beatrice* was much reproduced in its day.

ARTHUR BOYD HOUGHTON (1836–75):

A promising artist and illustrator whose life was cut sadly short. One of the greatest illustrators of the 1860s, his *Arabian Nights* remains a landmark, and he was a notable contributor to *The Graphic* in its early days. Some of his paintings were engraved for magazines, an example being his *Interior with Children at Play* reproduced in the magazine *Good Words* of 1863 as *Childhood*, shown on page 168.

ARTHUR HUGHES (1832–1915):

An important figure in both Illustration and the Pre-Raphaelite movement (see more details in that chapter) his book illustrations, notably to the novels of George MacDonald, are unsurpassable, and he supplied fine accompaniments to works by Thomas Hughes (he made the originals for *Tom Brown's Schooldays*) and Christina Rossetti (*Sing Song*). Illustrations to the MacDonald stories – *At the Back of the North Wind*, the Curdie books, *Phantastes*, et cetera – are among the most exquisite in Victorian book illustration.

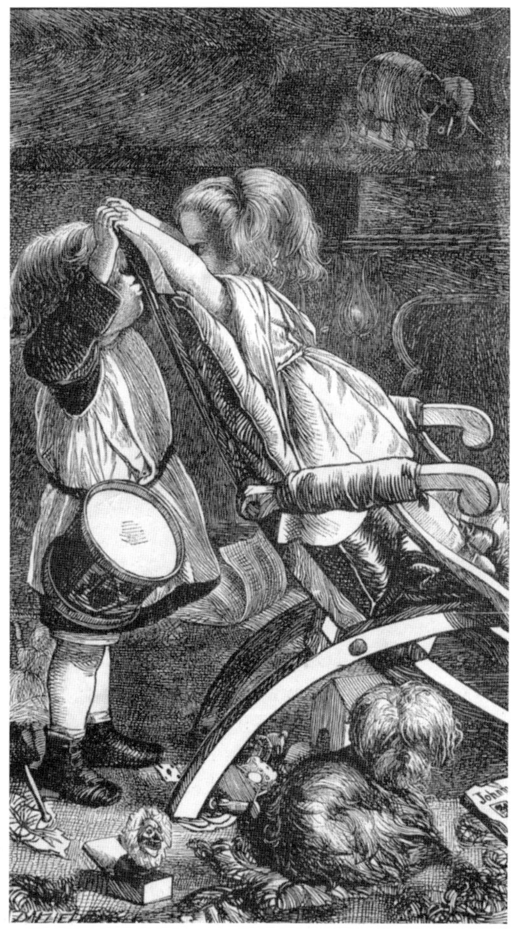

Houghton's *Childhood*

KENNY MEADOWS (1790–1874):

A popular illustrator and cartoonist born to a poor ex-Navy family in Cardigan and brought up in a lighthouse, he moved to London in 1823 and made his living there. His proficiency found him plenty of work with book and magazine publishers (especially in the early years of *Punch* and, later, the *Illustrated London News*, for which he often worked in colour), although to him his greatest artistic success was his three-volume illustrated Shakespeare issued in 1843. Among other books he illustrated, *Granny's Wonderful Chair* stands out.

John William NORTH (1842–1924):

Best known for his illustrations in black and white to various magazines and books, he was a fine and, to a degree, underrated watercolourist also – though figure drawing was not his strong point: despite the meticulous care he took with landscape, the human interest was sometimes added by fellow artists. His watercolours progressed in his lifetime from the clearly-drawn illustrative to a freer, more dreamlike style.

Marianne NORTH (1830–90):

One of the century's finest botanical illustrators. Barely out of her teens she began specialising in painting flowers and, fortunate to have an MP for a father, she made herself known to the directors at Kew's Royal Botanical Gardens. They recognised her obvious talent and encouraged her to travel in search of botanical subjects to Canada, the United States, Jamaica, Brazil, Japan, Borneo, Java, Ceylon and India. She was a lone, intrepid traveller, eccentric in garb and behaviour, but above all a superb artist. Later in life she presented her collection to Kew, to be shown in a gallery designed and financed by her. It opened in 1882, while she continued to travel. She died a spinster.

Sidney PAGET (1861–1908):

Prolific and versatile illustrator, much used in the *Strand* and similar magazines, famed for his version of what Sherlock Holmes looked like (the image was *not* based on Paget's brother Walter, as some claimed). A number of his paintings were exhibited at the RA.

'PHIZ' (Hablot Knight Browne) (1815–82):

One of the most famous Victorian illustrators, notably though by no means exclusively of Dickens. Like the clown who wants to play Hamlet, Phiz wanted to be a 'proper' painter, but his lack of formal training stood against him and, eventually, he resigned himself to what he did best, illustration. After suffering a stroke in 1867 which left him partially paralysed he continued to work (some oil paintings, and a number of illustration projects) but his disability marred his output and, were it not that he needed the money, it would have been kinder had these later pieces not been published.

George John PINWELL (1842–75):

Known mainly for his illustrative work – he was one of the better black and white artists – he produced some attractive genre watercolours also, before succumbing to an early death from lung disease. Coming from a poor background, never well-off and having to work for his living, he made plenty of illustrations.

Arthur RACKHAM (1867–1939):

Perhaps the most famous Victorian illustrator – although, in truth, his best-known work dates from the Edwardian decade. He studied art at the Lambeth School (and was initially influenced by fellow student Charles Ricketts) and he joined *The Westminster Budget* in 1892 as a commercial artist. But it was his illustrative work elsewhere that made his name. Although *Peter Pan* was Edwardian, in the Nineties Rackham illustrated works of Defoe, Shakespeare, Grimm and numerous novels, and contributed to magazines. The originals of these illustrations are much collected.

Leonard RAVEN-HILL (1867–1942):

At his peak between 1890 and the First World War, Raven-Hill was a prolific cartoonist with a vigorous sense of line. Confining himself to pen and ink he worked with confidence and verve, adding class to the publications for which he drew. He became Art Editor for one of them, *Pick-Me-Up*, in 1890, and he helped found the more artistic but poorer-selling *Butterfly* in 1893, while selling work to *Punch*, *The Idler*, *Black & White*, *Windsor* and *Pall Mall Magazine*. He worked for *Punch* till around the Second World War.

Charles ROBINSON (1870–1937):

Brother of W Heath Robinson and a much-loved illustrator in his own right, especially for children. His are the best illustrations to Stevenson's *A Child's Garden of Verses*. Charles had probably the most decorative style among the three brothers (Thomas being the third), making great use of flowing black lines and bold white space.

William Heath ROBINSON (1872–1944):

The most famous of the Robinson brothers whose drawings of deliberately ludicrous labour-saving inventions have bequeathed us the term 'Heath Robinson' for any form of bizarre contraption. These famous pictures (first appearing during the First World War) have unfairly eclipsed his other illustrative work.

Linley SAMBOURNE (1845–1910):

An inventive and prolific illustrator and artist, he provided the best (though not the first) accompaniments to the often illustrated *Water*

Babies, where he made the grotesque seem amusing. He was frequently seen in *Punch* and other magazines, working at the former for forty-three years. His house in Kensington, decorated in the aesthetic style but crammed with pictures and photographs, was open to hordes of visitors and is now the Linley Sambourne Museum.

Edmund Joseph (1869–1933) and James Frank (1853–1936) SULLIVAN:

Edmund was a watercolourist and illustrator, contributing to *The Graphic* and various magazines of the Nineties, and a more than capable portraitist: he made a fine study of Sarah Bernhardt and a series of Gloucestershire portraits now housed in the British Museum. His older brother James was a topical cartoonist and caricaturist, especially on *Fun*, in which he illustrated for twenty-four years, and to which he contributed a long-running cartoon featuring 'The British Working Man'.

John TENNIEL (1820–1914):

Best known for his illustrations to Lewis Carroll's *Alice* books, Tenniel was a household name as one of *Punch*'s chief political cartoonists. His

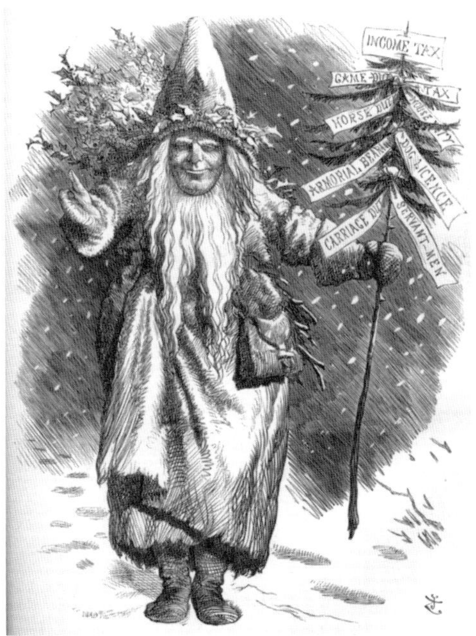

A Tenniel *Punch* cartoon heralding New Year 1870

full-page studies – caricatures more than jokes, appearing every week – were the backbone of the magazine, and took up a great deal of his time. *Punch* would suggest a subject on Wednesday. Tenniel would spend all Thursday thinking how to interpret it as a cartoon, spend Friday drawing it, and on Saturday would take the finished work and carefully transfer it to a woodblock for engraving. Three days (two and a half in a good week) to prepare a single cartoon. He was also a top-rate non-humorous illustrator (see his drawings for *Lallah Rookh* and others) and, later in life, an accomplished fairy artist.

William Makepeace THACKERAY (1811–63):

One of the century's most famous authors, Thackeray started out as an artist cum illustrator embellishing his writings with his sketches. Given that many of his early 'squibs' were for magazines such as *Punch* (he was on the board), his cartoon-like drawings enhanced his pieces. When the articles were collected into book form his pictures went with them. But for novels he found he hadn't the technical skill for 'proper' illustration. Certainly his figures could be wooden and his young ladies anaemic, but Thackeray was a caricaturist, his drawings were cartoons and they presented an author's view of his texts. *Vanity Fair* should never be read without his illustrations, any more than *Alice* should be read – at least the first time – without Tenniel's. His later books were illustrated by others – better artists, certainly, yet one can't help feeling something was missing: if only he'd had the time to work on his sketches, rather than dash them off.

Hugh THOMSON (1860–1920):

Prolific and able watercolourist and illustrator, who set too many of his subjects in Regency costume. He was born in Coleraine and moved to London in 1883, where he found work with Macmillan the publishers, illustrating books and popular series including Austen, Dickens, Shakespeare and Thackeray. A fine collection of his work can be seen in Coleraine Museum.

Frederick WALKER (1840–75):

In his short life he accomplished much. Small, shy and never robust, he was popular and respected by fellow artists. Much of his income came from illustration, and he was chosen by Thackeray to illustrate *Lovell the Widower* when his own sketches were not up to scratch. In the Sixties he branched out into genre painting – oils and watercolour – and if his subjects were conventional his use of media was not: he outraged some members of the Watercolour Society with his unrestricted use of body colour and, according to his painter friend J W North, was happy to paint in unnecessary detail 'to be afterwards carefully worn away, so that a suggestiveness and softness resulted – not emptiness, but veiled detail'. Walker put it more simply: 'It's astonishing how much I have rubbed out in order to keep it simple.' He died of consumption.

John Dawson WATSON (1832–92):

Born in Sedburgh, trained in Manchester, his paintings were a blend of not too sentimental genre and Pre-Raphaelite clarity, though he initially earned a good deal of his bread-and-butter income through magazine illustration. As the Sixties progressed he began to paint more freely in oils and watercolour. His sister married Birket Foster.

Major illustrative artists described elsewhere include Myles Birket FOSTER, Sir Hubert von HERKOMER, Henry HOLIDAY, Frank HOLL, John LEECH, Daniel MACLISE, Phil MAY, Sir John Everett MILLAIS, William MULREADY, Charles RICKETTS, Dante Gabriel ROSSETTI, Frederick SANDYS, Charles SHANNON, Dorothy TENNANT and Louis WAIN.

Chapter Fifteen

ARTISTS AND MODELS
Close Relationships

There are few periods other than the Victorian where artists' models have become almost as well-known as the artists themselves. Best known are those associated with the Pre-Raphaelites – Lizzie Siddal, Fanny Cornforth, Annie Miller and Alexa Wilding. Lizzie Siddal's story is the most famous; it includes her being discovered in a hat shop, her romance with Rossetti, her ordeal in a cold bathtub for *Ophelia*, her growing dependence on laudanum and drugs, her early death and her subsequent exhumation. When we look at the many images of this wan, listless anaemic girl we wonder: what did they see in her? They – the artists, the critics and everyone associated with that circle – treated her with the kind of awe which we today might show towards a film star. She had, one feels, the same otherness, the same remoteness of someone outside our world.

Her companions in that circle were far from ethereal: before Rossetti took her up, Fanny Cornforth had almost certainly been a prostitute – the only question is whether she'd been amateur or professional – and Annie Miller is described to us as one of the earthiest and filthiest creatures they had seen. Fanny's relationship with Rossetti is better documented than is Lizzie's; it lasted longer (until his death) and is illuminated by many letters still available to us in volume form. Annie's relationship with him was slight, though almost certainly sexual, but the doomed Pygmalion-like affair she had with Holman Hunt is a racy read – with a splendid ending, at least for her. Alexa Wilding remains unknown to us: the most beautiful of the Pre-Raphaelite models, and one Rossetti failed to bed – she was 'the most retiring and least self-asserting of creatures,' he wrote to his mother, 'quite ladylike, only not gifted or amusing.' Beauty, for Alexa, was enough.

His fellow Pre-Raphaelite Holman Hunt was a fool with Annie, while the third of the great trio, Millais, plunged into one of the century's most talked-about and scandalous romances when he fell for the wife of its greatest art critic. Ruskin's wife Effie posed for Millais both when she was Effie Ruskin and when she became Mrs Millais. Equally scandalous, though known to a smaller circle, was the tempestuous affair at the end of the following decade between Burne-Jones and the glamorous Maria Zambaco. For many years there were whispers and raised eyebrows about G F Watts and the succession of female patrons who doted on him, indulged him, gave every appearance of being infatuated with him – and who at times doubled as his models. But hadn't one of Frederic Leighton's wealthiest patrons, Eustacia Smith, posed in the nude for the handsome artist?

Victorian artists were trained to paint from life. Any person, adult or child, real or imaginary, shown in a picture should be drawn from a live model. Practically every *thing* in a picture, every building, every piece of furniture, every item worn, every animal, every tree, should be taken from a true example, they'd been taught. Hence the Victorian studio was cluttered with 'useful' objects which could be incorporated into their works. Hence it was common for the portrait and commemorative artist to ask for the loan of jewellery and clothes worn by their subjects. Hence, throughout the century, models plied for hire.

A minimum rate of a shilling an hour might seem risible today – but it was more than a shop-girl earned, and the work was easier (provided one was willing to take one's clothes off). Shop-girls, barmaids, servant girls and actresses were joined by jobbing actors, labourers, soldiers and jacks of all trades, together with professional children, such as the Dene children, Connie Gilchrist and Bessie Keene. Often, artists used their own children. Modelling paid enough to attract good-looking foreigners to London. Greeks and Italians were most numerous; leading Italian models included Alessandro di Marco, Colorossi, Gaetano Meo, Antonia Caiva, Madeleine Fiorida and Antonia Cura. But the two most famous Greek models were far from professional. Marie Spartali was the daughter of the Greek Consul-General; she wanted to be an artist but as soon as she strayed into the art world she was snapped up and used as a model by Rossetti, Burne-Jones and others. Maria Zambaco was rich and beautiful – and, as Burne-Jones was to discover, she was tempestuously Greek.

When Rossetti married Lizzie Siddal he was having a long on-and-off affair with Fanny Cornforth and pursuing his ex-model Jane Burden, now Mrs Janie Morris, who he effectively stole from her husband. William Morris fell for Georgiana Burne-Jones who, troubled by her own marriage, held Morris off. Her husband dallied for several years with Maria Zambaco. George Howard, late in a long and apparently successful marriage to Rosalind, eventually betrayed her with her sister-in-law, Maisie Stanley (also married: she was Lady Sheffield). Rosalind, meanwhile, had to resist overtures from serial philanderer Scawen Blunt.

Several artists 'married beneath them', both in age and social class. Not

Rossetti – he was the son of an immigrant political refugee and Lizzie Siddal the daughter of a lower middle-class cutlery trader. For years he conducted a sexual relationship with Fanny Cornforth, a barely-reformed prostitute who he regarded as a whore with a heart of gold. Even his later love, Janie Morris, née Jane Burden before she married middle-class William, was an Oxford porter's daughter. Madox Brown married his young uneducated cockney model, Emma Hill. F G Stephens married Clara Charles, a barely literate widow he'd had educated, as did Frederick Shields, who at 42 married a lass of 16 who he then sent to school. Hunt's long infatuation and off-on engagement to Annie Miller was explicable only in terms of sex; she was the dirtiest, most common and worst brought up of all the Pre-Raphaelite models – bright enough to drop Hunt eventually and marry into the upper middle classes.

Romantic passion wasn't the only problem an artist had with models. For the central figures in *Derby Day* Frith engaged an acrobat and son from the Drury Lane pantomime. Before he could be induced to pose, the child spent most of the first session tumbling and performing somersaults. When he finally settled down his father, unaccustomed to remaining still, felt faint and had to stroll around the garden. Frith gave up, borrowed their costumes, and hired a professional man called Bishop – who was fond of drink and soon vanished for six weeks. When he finally reappeared he said he'd been in prison. He'd got into a fight in Palace Gardens, he said. The fight had been stopped by a policeman who Bishop hit, and the following morning, he continued:

> *I was took before the beak. The policeman swore as I assaulted him in the execution of his dooty. I told him it was a lie, and was giving him a little more of my mind, when the magistrate says: 'Silence, man!' he says. 'Go to prison for three weeks.' That made me wild and I up and says, 'You call yourself a beak?' I says. 'Why, you ain't up to the situation; and I'll tell you what, I'm a artist's model, and I sits for them as draws for* Punch*; and I'll have you took and put in* Punch*, you just see if I don't.' The beak opened his mouth at that. He ain't often spoke to like that, you bet, sir; and after a bit he says: 'Now you will go to prison for six,' and that's where I've been, sir.*

Frith, who had sold his *Ramsgate Sands* to the Queen in 1854, was commissioned for several royal portraits, including a commemoration of the wedding of the Prince of Wales. Not only did he have to persuade the foreign royals to stand still and pose (some refused) but he had to crave loans of clothes they'd worn on the day (some refused again). So he painted some royals from photographs. For the King of Greece Frith had to accept his elder brother, Prince Frederick, as substitute. Frith painted him in the same session in which he painted the Crown Prince of Prussia:

> *The two never ceased talking – in a language I did not understand – for an hour and a half at least. When the sitting was over, a difficulty took place at the door of the Rubens room – my temporary studio – as to which of the two young men should take precedence; there they stood, each refusing to go first, till at last the Crown Prince of Prussia cut the knot by backing through the doorway, the Dane following face to face.*
>
> *The Danish Prince left immediately for his college; and when he next found himself face to face with the Prince of Prussia, it was on one of the battlefields in Schleswig-Holstein.*

Perhaps an artist was wiser to select models from members of his family.

THE MODELS THEMSELVES:

EMMA MADOX BROWN, née EMMA HILL:

She was Brown's model before and after their marriage, her earliest appearance being as Cordelia in *King Lear*. She was in his *Chaucer* and a lovely early pastel and watercolour, *Oure Ladye of Good Children*, but the most famous image is as the emigrant in *The Last of England*. In his curiously-lit *The Pretty Baa-Lambs* he gave Emma a Madonna-style makeover and she carried their baby daughter Kate. (The sheep were brought to his studio every morning from Clapham Common in a truck.) Another haunting image comes in the unfinished *Take Your Son, Sir* of 1851. (Their son Arthur is the baby.) Emma was a semi-literate teenager when he met her, and in true Professor Higgins style he had the waif transformed and taught in secret before revealing her to his friends. Their eventual marriage was a success, though Emma liked a tipple.

LUCY MADOX BROWN:

His daughter by his first wife Elizabeth features in a number of his works, both as herself in portrait studies and as a necessary child (in *Chaucer* and *The Last of England*, for example, as well as the *Oure Ladye of Good Children*). Rossetti used her while working with Brown; she can be seen in his *Cherub Angels Watching the Crown of Thorns* (1848). An arresting

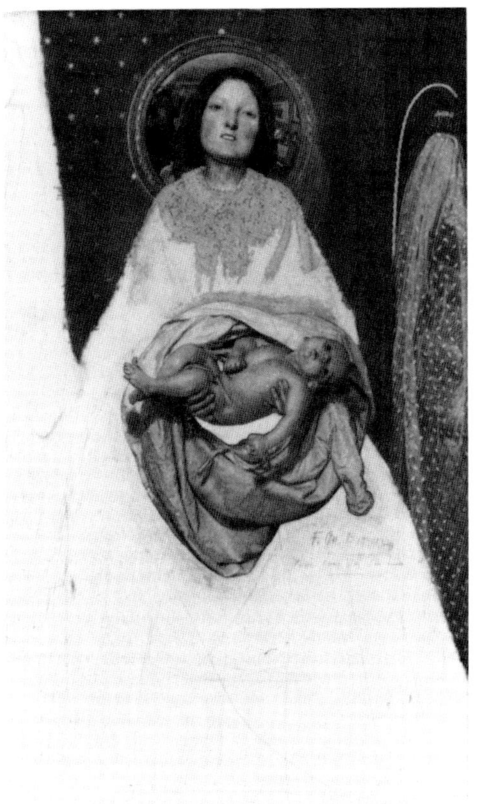

Emma confronts the father with his child: *Take Your Son, Sir* (unfinished)

child (born 1843), she painted in her father's studio, exhibited in her twenties, but gave up painting professionally when she married William Michael Rossetti in 1874. He had known her since childhood. They had twenty years of happy marriage until her death in 1894.

Georgiana BURNE-JONES (née Georgie MacDonald):

Long-suffering wife of the artist, she sat for her husband and for George Howard and for Edward Poynter. Seen at her most striking in *Clara von Bork*, the virtuous companion-piece to Burne-Jones's *Sidonia von Bork* (modelled by the less virtuous Fanny Cornforth). Their daughter Margaret is at the top of his *The Golden Stairs* (1876–80.)

Antonia CAIVA:

A professional and striking Italian model who sat for Poynter, Leighton and Burne-Jones (*The Golden Stairs*) etc.

COLOROSSI:

Model to Burne-Jones in the 1860s, shared at times with his pupil George Howard.

Fanny CORNFORTH:

A larger-than-life character, rivalling Annie Miller as the most exuberant Pre-Raphaelite model. Born Sarah Cox, a blacksmith's daughter from Steyning in Sussex in 1824, she changed her name when she moved to London, taking Cornforth from a grandmother and Fanny, perhaps, as a popular name for a woman of her calling. She had a room in Dean Street, Soho. That her calling was prostitution has never been in much doubt: Rossetti's friends and family grumbled for decades about her hold on him, and William Bell Scott (who did not like Fanny) said that when Rossetti first met her in the Strand (in 1858) she 'was cracking nuts with her teeth, and throwing the shells about. Seeing Rossetti staring at her, she threw some at him.' Fanny's more sanitised account, given much later to Samuel Bancroft junior, had Rossetti (together with Madox Brown and Burne-Jones) pass her at a fair: 'They were especially attracted by the great beauty of this country girl, and especially by her great wealth of magnificent golden hair; and one of them, "accidentally on purpose", in passing behind her, gave it a touch with his fingers so that it all fell down her back.'

Rossetti used Fanny in *Bocca Baciata* (1859), a portrait commissioned by Boyce (according to Boyce's diary for a mere £40) and completed with more attention to detail than were many Rossetti portraits. The title comes from a Boccaccio sonnet, *Bocca baciata non perde ventura* (The mouth that was kissed does not lose its freshness) – and his fellow artist Arthur Hughes, in a letter to William Allingham extolled its 'most beautiful head . . . such a superb thing, so awfully lovely'. He continued: 'Boyce has bought it, and will I expect kiss the dear thing's lips away before you come over to see it.' Given that Fanny was fond of Boyce and almost certainly extended her favours to him, Hughes may have been deliberately ambiguous.

Other notable pictures of Fanny Cornforth include *Fazio's Mistress*,

Lady Lilith and *The Blue Bower*, and the last substantial portrait Rossetti made of her was his crayon drawing, *Lady With a Fan* (1870). One of the most famous paintings is the unfinished *Found* ('The calf picture,' as Fanny called it) in which she portrayed a fallen woman come to town from the country and now 'found' by the farm boy who once loved her. Rossetti began this work in 1853 for MacCracken, started it again in '59 for Leathart, began again in both '69 and '79, then left it still with the background only sketched upon his death. It was then acquired by William Graham. (Both this lovely sketch of her head and, I think, the initial full drawing, are more beautiful than the painting.)

Fanny was part of Rossetti's life longer than any other model. Initially she modelled for him and other artists, and she slept with other artists too. Early in their relationship, in 1859, she married a man called Timothy

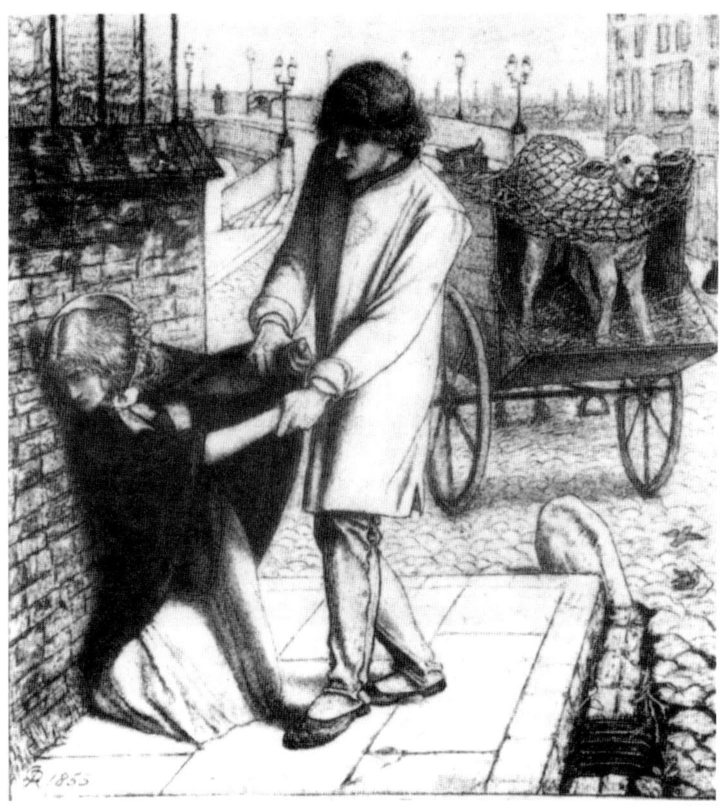

Rossetti's first drawing for *Found* (1853)

Hughes, about whom little is known other than that he died in 1872. He played little part in her life, and why she married him is unknown, although Fanny did claim that Rossetti used her husband as a model for David in the triptych altar-piece he made for Llandaff Cathedral. She lived for years either with Rossetti or supported by him, and there is no doubt they were deeply attached to each other – despite everything his family tried to break them apart. One wonders how Christina Rossetti reacted to his using Fanny as model to the illustrations he made for Christina's first book, *Goblin Market* (1862). Among portraits of Fanny by other hands critics still argue as to whether she is *Sidonia von Bork* in Burne-Jones's stunning water-colour of that name (1860); she certainly sat for him in 1858.

Antonia CURA:

Italian model for Burne-Jones.

Alessandro DE (or DI) MARCO:

Model to Burne-Jones in the 1860s, and shared at times with his pupil George Howard. Described by Graham Robertson as 'a fine, upstanding slip of a boy', his lithe and rather feminine body was used at times by various artists, including Burne-Jones and Walter Crane, to serve for a woman. Crane's wife (daughter of the philandering Frederick Sandys) had decided from experience that her husband must not use female models, so to him the androgynous Alessandro was a godsend – to model Venus, for example, in *The Renaissance of Venus* (1877). When Frederic Leighton saw the finished picture he recognised the body instantly: 'My dear fellow, that is not Aphrodite – that's Alessandro.'

Dorothy DENE and her sisters:

Frederic Leighton's favourite model was born Ada Alice Pullan (she adopted the name Dorothy Dene for the stage) and was twenty-nine years younger than him. He discovered her when she began her career as an actress, spotting 'a young girl with a lovely white face', according to his biographer Emilia Barrington, as she stood at the door to one of the Holland Park studios – probably that of Herbert Schmaltz, an artist who could have been named after the sentimental style of his paintings. Dorothy said she'd lost her mother and her father had run off, leaving her and her elder brother to look after the other five. Whether this account is true is uncertain. Dorothy's youngest sister Isabel (calling herself Lena, or Lina, and only 13 at the time) first posed for Leighton in 1880, the same year Dorothy appeared in his (respectable) *Light of the Harem*, and appears also in a pair of Leighton's studies: *Bianca* and *Viola*, of 1881.

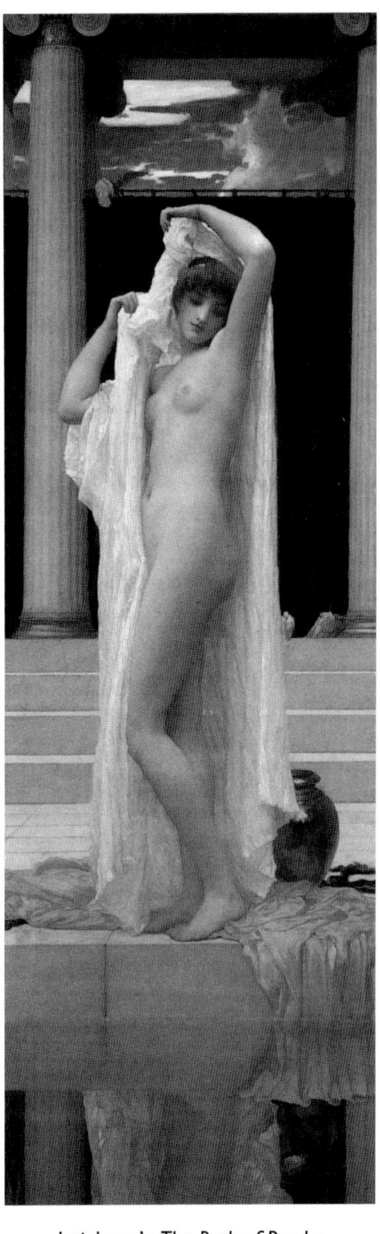

Leighton's *The Bath of Psyche* (1890), with Dorothy Dene as the model

Two years later another sister, Henrietta (or as she preferred, 'Hetty Dene') posed for his *Farewell*, and young Edith sat for *Memories* (1883). In 1884 Lina posed as *Letty* (a portrait much admired by Ruskin, always a soft touch for young girls) and continued to sit for Leighton through the 1880s; his 1888 *Captive Andromache* features both Lina and Dorothy. By this time he was supporting the entire family. When he died he left Dorothy £5,000 outright and another £5,000 in trust.

Dorothy was the most blatantly nude of all his models – more naked than nude, to some reviewers. In *The Bath of Psyche* (1890) where she 'displays her charms for the admiration of mankind,' as the critic Harlaw put it in 1913, 'Psyche's contour is perfect and her form is deliciously rounded.' Harlaw couldn't tear his eyes away: 'The exquisite pearly fairness of the skin must ever make this rendering of the amorous deity the standard of colour as of modelling.' Watts, too, admired her 'splendid growth and form such as an ancient Greek never saw'. Leighton was assumed to be having an affair with Dorothy, but he denied it, telling his sisters, 'If you hear these rumours again, meet them with a flat, ungarnished denial.' Dorothy had little success as an actress, but was immortalised in his paintings – most famously in *Flaming June* (1895) but also in *The Last Watch of Hero* (1887), *Perseus and Andromeda* (1891) and *The Garden of the Hesperides* (1892).

Dorothy continued to model after Leighton's death, and was one of the hottest models in town. Watts rhapsodised about her complexion having 'a clouded pallor, with a hint somewhere of a lovely shell-like pink'. Her sister Edith married the artist Herbert Schmaltz, and Dorothy modelled for him too – notably for one shocking painting, *Love is Blind* (1898), in which, blindfolded, she crawls towards a masked but lustful satyr. Schmaltz painted him with his own face, giving the work the ironic legend: 'Maidenhood, blindfolded by innocence, knows not that beneath the godlike mask there lurks the soul of a satyr.' Schmaltz must have had a sense of humour. (It has been said that he slept with Dorothy, who sadly died the following year, 1899, of pelvic peritonitis and other conditions which, put together, might suggest a botched abortion.)

Edith DENE:

The younger sister of the famous Dorothy modelled both for Leighton and for his near neighbour, the lesser artist Herbert Schmaltz. For Schmaltz she posed for *Dream of Yesterday* and in the same year (1889) she married him.

Walter DEVERELL:

One of the inner band of Pre-Raphaelites, he sat for his friends in several paintings. He was Thomas Woodstock in Madox Brown's *Chaucer*, he is the leftmost character in Millais's *Isabella*, and Claudio in Hunt's *Claudio and Isabella* (1850–3). He was Orsino in his own *Twelfth Night*.

Adrian DI CASTELLO:

Professional model who supplied the body but not the head of the graceful young soldier at the left of Hunt's *Rienzi* (1848–9). Millais was substituted as the head.

Kate DICKENS:

The author's daughter modelled for Millais as the troubled young lady in *The Black Brunswicker* (1860) – sadly not one of his best paintings, though the likeness was said to be good. Millais's son and biographer reassures us that, while they posed, Kate and the male model never made physical contact!

Marie FORD:

A professional model whose most famous appearance must surely be in Rossetti's *The Beloved* (1864), in which she portrays the bride (for whom Fanny Cornforth is sometimes wrongly identified).

MARGARET FREEBODY:

Born Margaret Kennedy, she married John Freebody, a sea captain friend of the artist Tissot who painted her in a number of works in and around 1873 – often on board ships that Freebody captained. Margaret's brother, Captain Lumley Kennedy, appears in some of these. They are both, for example, in *The Last Evening* (1873).

CONNIE GILCHRIST:

A popular child model, she posed for Leighton's *Daphneporia* (1874–6), modelling all the young women in the chorus. She was in *The Music Lesson* (1877), his *Study: At A Reading Desk* (1877) and other works, until her final appearance for him in *Winding the Skein* (1878), a painting in which she looks a very mature 13. She posed for Whistler in *Harmony in Yellow and Gold*, as well as for Frank Holl and other artists of the period. She was also one of the comely children photographed by Lewis Carroll. A few years later she became a 'skipping-rope dancer' at the Westminster Aquarium and the Gaiety, and a few years later she married the Earl of Orkney. Good looks took her far.

FRANCES GRAHAM (later FRANCES, LADY HORNER):

Daughter of the patron William Graham, Frances appears (with cymbals) in Burne-Jones's *The Golden Stairs* (1876–80) and in his *The Arming of Perseus* (1885–8). Her relationship with the artist, which was certainly close, gave rise to speculation, especially as she was married. (She first posed for him in *The King's Wedding* of 1870 when she was a mere 11.) Another Graham daughter, Amy, was painted – without scandal – by Rossetti as *Il Ramoscello* (originally *Belle e Buona*) in 1865.

MRS JAMES HANNAY:

The wife of one of his friends, she sat for the watercolour version of Rossetti's *Dante's Dream* (1871, now in Liverpool's Walker Art Gallery).

JACK HARRIS:

Dominates Millais's *Isabella* as the man kicking the dog.

RUTH HERBERT:

Actress and occasional model to the Pre-Raphaelites who called herself 'Mrs Crabbe' offstage, but no one ever met 'Mr Crabbe' or was sure that he existed. Renowned for her succession of wealthy lovers, she posed as Mary Magdalene in Rossetti's *Mary Magdalene at the Door of Simon the Pharisee* (1853–9), a painting in which Burne-Jones modelled for Christ.

Rossetti was much smitten by her, though was not rich enough to bed her, it is said. He made a watercolour *for* and possibly *of* her (the model's identity is uncertain) during the time he was infatuated; that painting is *Writing on the Sand* (1858–9). The model in that picture, presumably Miss Herbert, reappears wistfully in his lovely *Morning Music* (1864). Ellen Terry described Ruth in her autobiography: 'Very tall, with pale gold hair and the spiritual, ethereal look which the aesthetic movement loved. When mother wanted to flatter me very highly, she said that I looked like Miss Herbert!'

Jo HIFFERNAN:

Irish mistress and muse to Whistler. She appeared in his *Symphony in White No. 1* (1862) and *No. 2* (1864) among others, but was perhaps

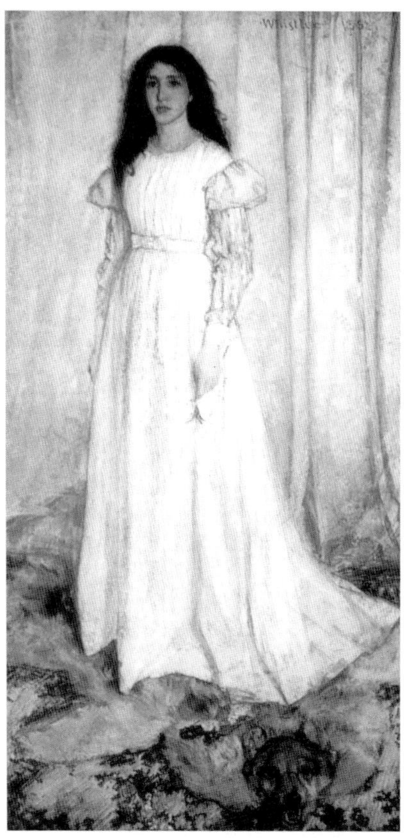

Symphony in White No. 1 (The White Girl)

never more wonderfully captured than in Gustave Courbet's *Jo, the Beautiful Irish Girl* of 1865–6, a painting Courbet kept until he died. Courbet used her again in *Sleep* and, it is said, the pornographic *Origin of the World*.

Mary HODGKINSON:

Most famous as the Virgin Mary in Millais's *Christ in the House of His Parents* (1850) and as the more beautiful *Isabella* (1848). She was married to his half-brother Henry.

Lady Augusta HOLLAND:

Mary Augusta and Henry Fox Holland married in 1833 at the start of his diplomatic career. In the 1840s at Casa Feroni in Florence they created a notable diplomatic and artistic salon, the prize of which was their artist in residence, the young, handsome, extravagant G F Watts. He painted Augusta a number of times, sometimes in dishabille and, as it was rumoured she was bored with her husband, the rumours made much of her relationship with the young artist.

Noel HUMPHREYS:

Son of the book illustrator of the same name, young Humphreys portrayed Christ in Millais's controversial *Carpenter's Shop* (1849–50).

Henry IRVING:

Actors, being famous, were often models, wittingly or not, and few had their image captured more often than Henry Irving. But an actor's interest tends to be in himself, not the artist – as illustrated by the Graham Robertson story of Irving's telling Ellen Terry that he had bought a painting:

> *'As I was passing a frame-shop I saw that thing that Whistler did of me – Philip of Spain – do you remember it.'*
>
> *'I should think I did. Well?'*
>
> *'Well, I thought I'd ask the price and the man said a hundred pounds.'*
>
> *'A hundred pounds?'*
>
> *'Yes. Was that too much?'*
>
> *'A hundred pounds! There weren't any other Whistler pictures in the shop, were there?'*
>
> *'O yes, lots. I didn't look at 'em – I only wanted the portrait.'*
>
> *All the next day Ellen Terry was hopelessly busy but on the day*

after she flew to the frame-shop: not a Whistler canvas was to be seen – the great chance was lost.

And they say, 'Vanity, thy name is woman.'

Willie JAMES:

The little boy in *Bubbles* (1886), though he appeared in other paintings such as *The Ruling Passion* (1885) in which he can be seen with his brother George. He was Millais's 5-year-old grandson. The inspiration for *Bubbles*, it is said, came when Millais saw the boy blowing soap bubbles. Millais had a sphere of glass made to model the bubble, and he painted the boy in the famous green velvet suit and frilly collar. Thinking, perhaps, that it was no more than a charming childhood study, Millais sold the painting and its copyright to the *Illustrated London News*, which in turn resold the copyright to Pears Soap. The *Illustrated London News* used it first, in their 1887 Christmas number, before the adapted version floated out by the million to advertise soap.

Millais seems to have been sanguine about this 'misuse' of his art. His son's biography claimed that a 'furious' Millais protested in vain, but evidence from the Pears company suggests he thought the re-use 'magnificent' and that he offered to paint as many pictures as they wanted for advertisements and to write a commendation on the way they'd handled his work. A letter in *The Times* in 1889 quoted Millais as saying, 'It is an admirable reproduction and is a credit to Messrs Pears, and to my picture.'

Mary Emma JONES:

The common-law wife to Frederick Sandys was, as an actress, known as 'Miss Clive'. The two met in 1862 when she modelled for *The Magdalen*. Despite his man-about-town reputation the couple had a happier relationship than did many married couples, living together under the name of Neville. Ten of their children survived him. Mary was the original inspiration for his sultry *Proud Maisie* (1867, V&A), a painting of which he made around a dozen replicas.

Mrs KEENE, and Elizabeth (Bessie) KEENE:

Mrs Keene was one of Rossetti's favourite models, sitting also several times for Burne-Jones. She appeared in Burne-Jones's *The Days of Creation* and *Vivien and Merlin* among others, and is one of the models used for *The Golden Stairs* (1876–80). Bessie was her daughter, a model since childhood. A mischievous child, she modelled several of Jones's beatific cherubim and angels, as well as a lovely portrait, *Vespertina Quies*.

KEOMI:

A gypsy model discovered by Sandys in Norfolk and brought to London to model a number of paintings, including his *Medea* (1866–8). She is believed to have been his mistress. Rossetti included her as the rightmost figure in his *The Beloved* (1865–6).

LILLIE LANGTRY:

'Jersey Lily' was so called from the island where she was born (as Emilie Le Breton, in 1853). Of her arrival in London in 1876 Graham Robertson wrote, 'It was the first and only time in my life I beheld perfect beauty.' Famous later as mistress to the Prince of Wales (King Edward VII), Lillie

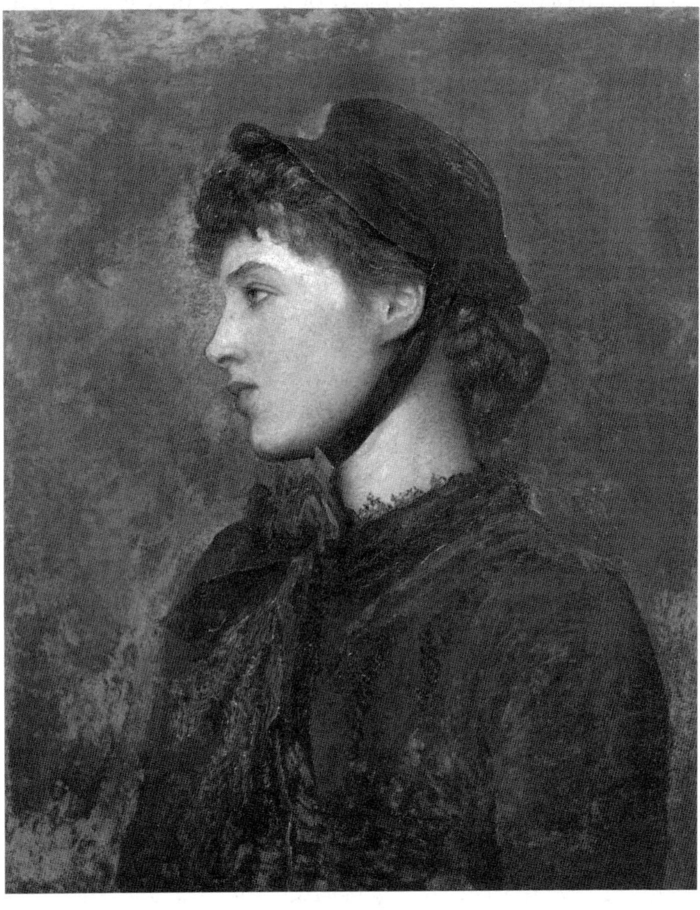

Lillie Langtry as *The Dean's Daughter* (Watts, 1879)

was an actress and occasional model. She bares a nipple in Leighton's *Idyll* of 1880–1 and can be seen more chastely in his (rather dull) *Wedded* of 1881–2. She is utterly respectable in Millais's *Effie Deans* (1877) and his portrait of her as *A Jersey Lily* (1878). Burne-Jones included her in his processional *The Golden Stairs* (1872–80). Watts painted her as *The Dean's Daughter* in 1879/80. She wrote, 'I spent hours and hours posing without experiencing strain or fatigue. Sometimes scarcely a stroke of work was done in the studio. Watts would ring for tea, ignore the sitting and, instead, entertain me with lengthy dissertations on art.' That was the life.

LONG MARY:

Several of Watts's paintings and many of his chalk drawings from the later 1860s show a tall young woman whose 'noble form' he said, had 'flexibility of movement as well as magnificence of line'. We know her as 'Long Mary' and she can be seen in his *The Three Goddesses* on which he worked from 1865 to 1872.

MAITLAND:

A favourite model of Ford Madox Brown, sitting for two figures in his early masterpiece, *Chaucer* (broadly 1851 but completed in January 1868); Maitland is both Gower and the Black Prince. In *Wycliffe* he is Gower again, as well as John of Gaunt and 'Catholic Faith'. In *King Lear* (1848–9) he models both soldiers at the right.

GAETANO MEO:

Italian model used by a number of major artists, including Leighton (*The Arts of War*, his fresco for the South Kensington Museum); Luke Fildes (the man in the boat in *Fair Quiet and Sweet Rest*); Burne-Jones (*Love Among the Ruins* and the face of God in *Dies Domini*) and Hamo Thornycroft (*The Mower*). Meo became an assistant in W B Richmond's studio, set up as a painter on his own, and led a team of workmen laying mosaics in St Paul's Cathedral, a project which took around ten years. Meo's daughter, Elena Fortuna Meo, a 22-year-old violinist, ran off to live with the mercurial theatre designer Edward Gordon Craig (son of Ellen Terry and her lover Edward Godwin). She and Craig had three children, before he left her for the dancer Isadora Duncan (by whom he had two more).

EFFIE MILLAIS:

While still married to her first husband, Effie Ruskin, as she then was, posed for Millais in *The Order of Release*. After she and Millais married, she continued to pose for him – as Madeleine, for example, undressing

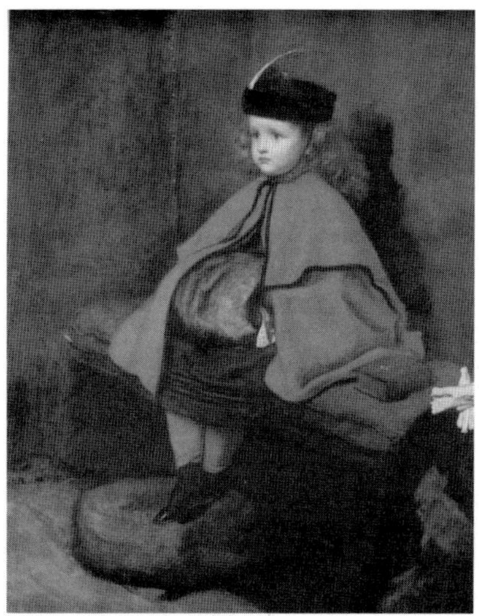
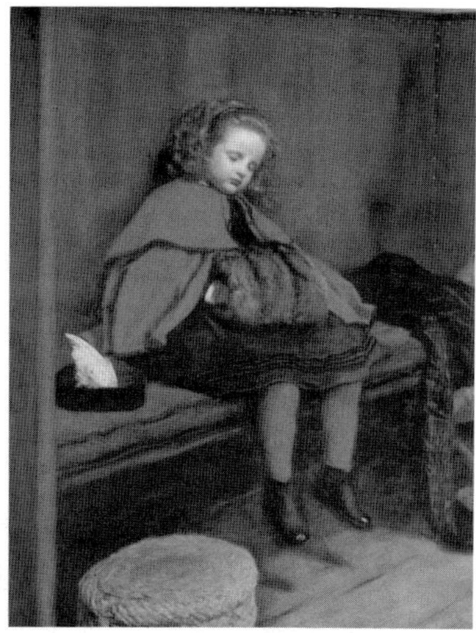

My First Sermon and *My Second Sermon*

in her chamber for his *Eve of St Agnes* (1863), a full-scale, detailed painting which the efficient Millais completed in five and a half days. (This was after he'd abandoned Pre-Raphaelite punctiliousness.) Some blame the famously spendthrift Effie for leading her husband into increasing lucrative commissions. His letters suggest he was as keen to change as she.

That same year (1863) saw Millais's sentimental and enormously popular *My First Sermon*, for which the model was again Effie Millais – but this time the 5-year-old Effie, their daughter. The success of that portrait, for which engravings sold in vast numbers, hastened Millais towards a succession of child pictures. He'd put children into earlier works, but the public's eagerness for *My First Sermon* (soon to be followed by *My Second Sermon*, 1864) predicted a profitable line. Millais's son reported that his efficient father made an oil copy of *My First Sermon* in two days flat, and that the copy was as good as the original. Not every subsequent child picture featured Effie: *Sleeping* (1867) was of his third daughter Alice, and in his *Boyhood of Raleigh* (1870) the two attentive boys were his sons Everett and George. The grown-up daughter Effie's son William modelled in Millais's later success, *Bubbles*.

Annie MILLER:

Few professional models came from polite backgrounds, and Annie Miller came from the grubbiest of them all. She was a charwoman's daughter (though her mother died when Annie was a child) and she lived with her invalid ex-soldier father, his brother and his wife and the various children, together with four young working men (three were chimney sweeps), all crammed together in a cellar. Holman Hunt came across her when she was working as an 18-year-old, flirtatious if foul-mouthed barmaid, and she agreed to pose for him – often in the nude, which didn't worry Annie one single jot. Hunt was soon wildly infatuated, but his strict morality forbade him to touch her – though Annie, it seems, would have had few qualms. One solution would have been for him to marry her – but to Hunt she appeared wildly lower-class, physically dirty, and frighteningly animal. Little of this earthy vitality shines through in the paintings – indeed, she is a convincing penitent in his *Morning Prayers* (1860). Her

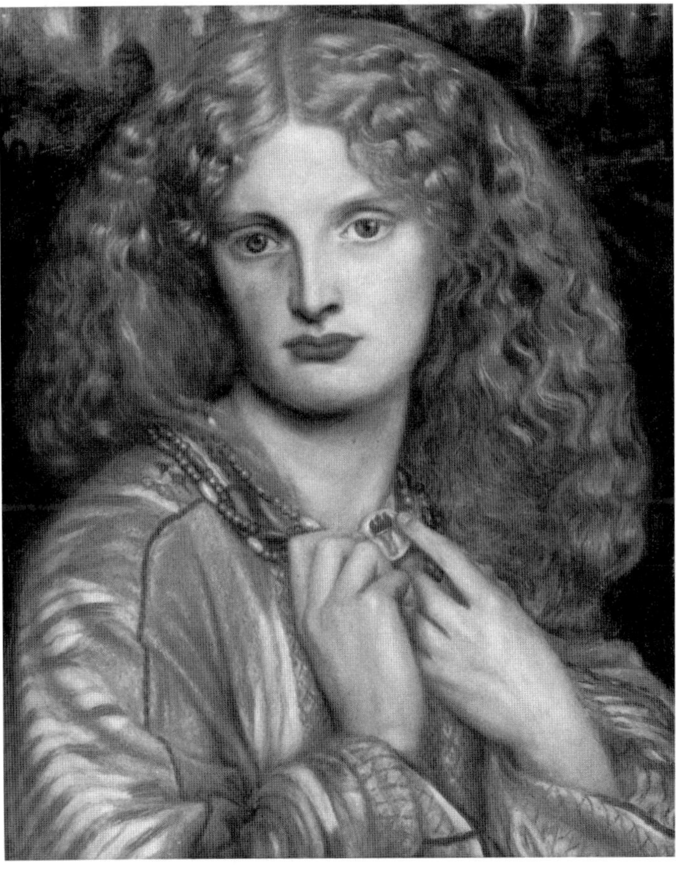

Rossetti's depiction of Annie as *Helen of Troy*

most famous appearance was in his startling 1853 *The Awakening Conscience*, although in the version we have now her face has been overpainted. (The expression he originally gave her attracted criticism and bewilderment, so Hunt repainted it.)

Annie was Hunt's great youthful folly (not that he was so young then) but if he was to marry her, he decided, he must have her educated – and he must get her clean: she was a notoriously grubby girl, with matted hair and filthy fingernails. He arranged for Annie to be taught to read and write and, more ambitiously, to be taught deportment and elocution. Much of this would take place while he exiled himself in the Holy Land – and, to oversee the transformation while he was away, he enlisted the aid of his friend Frederic Stephens. Fred should visit, check on progress and pay the bills. (Hunt placed £200 – a year's income then for an office worker – in a special bank account.)

Annie tried, the women teaching her tried (to an extent), but real life is not *My Fair Lady*. Although Hunt had given both her and Stephens strict instructions forbidding it, she began to sit for Rossetti – and the inevitable happened. (She was the model for Rossetti's *Helen of Troy*, 1864, and he presented her less flatteringly in his 1860 portrait, *Annie Miller*.) Stephens did his best to pull them apart, but neither Annie nor Rossetti took much notice – and Annie, before long, found herself an even better catch, the seventh Viscount Ranelagh, a notorious if good-natured rake. Annie knew she was supposed to marry the absent Hunt and, while not forsaking fun, continued with her lessons. When Hunt finally returned (after two years) he found her clean, with unmatted hair, and able (just about) to speak nicely.

But he didn't propose. At this distance it's hard to tell whether Hunt realised their marriage would go wrong, or whether, as seems equally possible, he couldn't summon up the nerve to ask her. He claimed he had to sell his latest painting (*The Scapegoat*) so he could afford to marry. Time dragged by. Annie was puzzled, then disenchanted. Did he want to marry her – what *did* he want? Hunt heard whispers of her behaviour while he'd been away. Marriage began to look unlikely – and Annie thought it unfair: she may have had some fun, but hadn't she done what he'd demanded? She'd cleaned herself up, taken lessons, learnt to behave properly – what more did he want? They didn't break off their unofficial engagement – yet. Hunt vacillated between thinking her unworthy and wanting her in his bed (as far as one can tell, he never slept with her), while Annie alternated between berating him and ploughing on with lessons in the hope that they would marry. Stephens remained their go-between. (There were rumours that he'd dallied with Annie himself.)

Hunt considered a more suitable marriage to someone else – but to whom? He had no one in mind, though he did ask his friends whether they knew anyone who might prove suitable. His love for Annie blew hot and cold – and he continued to use her as a model: a notable portrait from those days is *Il Dolce Far Niente* (Sweet Idleness). She even posed as Lady Godiva – and how he resisted the obvious temptation is anyone's guess.

Things got worse. Annie heard he was looking elsewhere for a bride, and she hit back with something close to blackmail: she had his letters, she could prove he'd been supporting her – and, if they weren't going to marry, he must pay her off. Hunt hit back with bluster. Annie asked advice from Viscount Ranelagh, who advised her to tell Hunt she'd sell his letters to the gutter press. Hunt was desperate: she could ruin his reputation. But he was determined not to give in.

The resolution came when Annie met, fell for and captured Viscount Ranelagh's cousin, the wealthy Thomas Ranelagh Thomson, who lived alone and needed a wife to run his fine house in Mayfair. Annie married Mr Thomson and lived comfortably and happily ever after, as far as we know, among the upper middle classes. In the immediate aftermath, Hunt painted over her face in the most famous painting he'd made of her. When we look today at his *The Awakened Conscience* we see a different woman and a different expression from the one that originally caused such a stir.

JANE MORRIS (née BURDEN):

People disagreed then as they do now as to whether Jane was beautiful or merely striking. Rossetti, in his poem 'Genius in Beauty' ('Beauty like hers is genius,' he wrote), rhapsodised her 'sovereign face, whose love-spell breathes even from its shadowed contour on the wall'. But when Rosalind Howard first met her in 1868 she was unimpressed: 'she has a fine head with remarkable eyes but is an invalid & seems uninteresting & does not talk enthusiastically on any of Morris' topics of interest.' (Jane at that time was deep in the troubled triangle with her husband and Rossetti.) But W Graham Robertson, who met her when she was past her youth, said she 'required to be seen to be believed, and even then she seemed dreamlike . . . When I first saw her, the dusky wonder of her hair was threaded with grey, but the face seemed to change hardly at all: it was as if cast in pale bronze, the lines of the low brow and the carven lips remaining firm and sharp.' He, too, noticed Janie's sadness: 'I fancy that her mystic beauty must sometimes have weighed rather heavily upon her. Her mind was not formed upon the same tragic lines as her face; she was very simple and could have enjoyed simple pleasures with simple people,

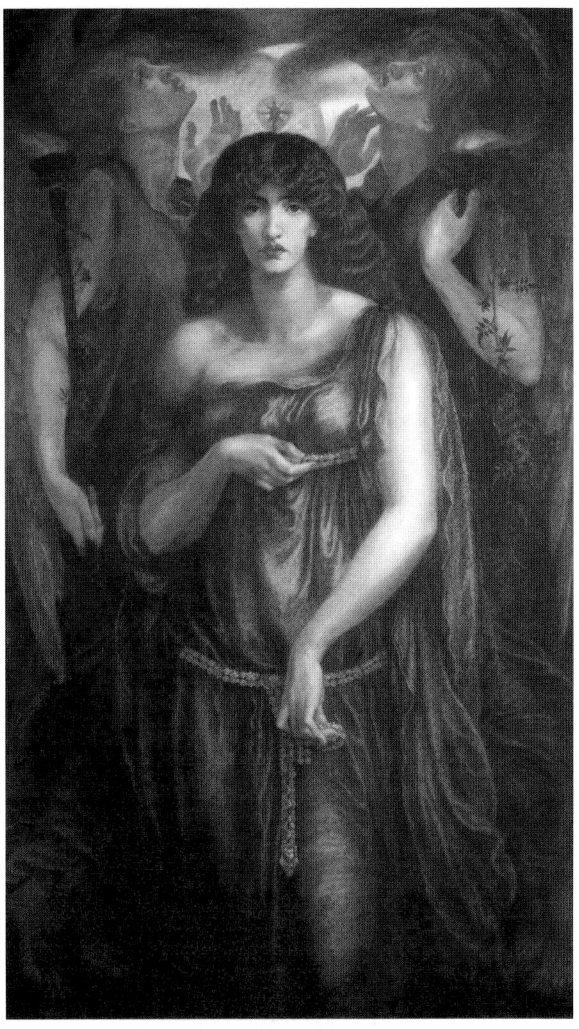

Rossetti's largest portrait of Jane Morris: *Astarte Syriaca* (1877)

but such delights were not for her. She looked like the Delphic Sybil and had to behave as such.'

'Imagine,' invited Henry James, 'a tall lean woman in a dress of some dead purple stuff, guiltless of hoops (or of anything else I should say) with a mass of crisp black hair, heaped into great wavy projections on each of her temples, a thin pale face, great thick black oblique brows, joined in the middle and tucking themselves away under her hair, a mouth like the "Oriana" in our illustrated Tennyson, a long neck, without any collar, and in lieu thereof some dozen strings of outlandish beads. In fine complete.'

Men, it seems, could not resist describing or painting her.

There is one painting of her by her husband: his *La Belle Iseult*, the laborious and not wholly successful painting which taught Morris he was not cut out to be a Pre-Raphaelite painter. She was the subject of Rossetti's *Water Willow*, *Prosperine*, *Pandora* (several versions), *Astarte Syriaca*, *Mariana*, *La Pia de Tolomei* (done in his characteristically slow manner, between 1868 to '80) and was his Beatrice in *Dante's Dream*.

MAY MORRIS:

Daughter of Jane and William, used as a model in a number of paintings, including Rossetti's *La Ghirlandata* (1873, May is both the angels) and

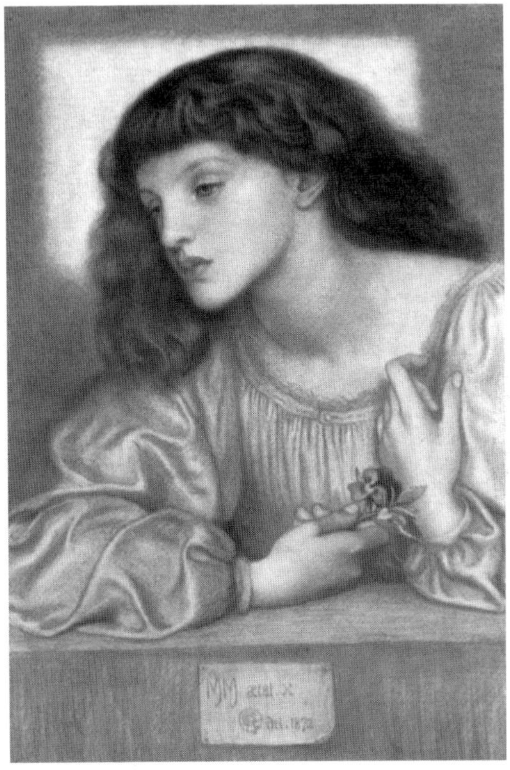

The 10-year-old May Morris painted by Rossetti

his second version of *Rosa Triplex* (1873). She is one of the more prominent women in Burne-Jones's *The Golden Stairs* (1876–80.)

Kathleen NEWTON:

The hidden love of Tissot's life and the attractive woman in many of his paintings after 1876 – often referred to as *la mystérieuse*. She was born Kathleen Kelly, married Isaac Newton (a surgeon in the Indian Civil Service), was divorced by him for adultery, and by the time she met Tissot she had two children (who feature in a number of his paintings). She and Tissot lived together – despite a deal of social ostracism – for six years before she died of TB in 1882. So grief-stricken was Tissot that he could not remain in the house they'd shared; he sold it to Alma-Tadema.

'OLD COULTON':

A relatively elderly professional model of the mid-century who carved himself a useful niche. Madox Brown used him several times – for example, as Wycliffe in the painting of that name and as *King Lear*.

Helen PETRIE:

Sat for one of Millais's loveliest studies, *Only a Lock of Hair* (1859).

Hetty PETTIGREW:

Harriet Selina Pettigrew, daughter of a Hampshire cork-cutter, and her two sisters (Rose and Lilian) modelled for Hunt, Leighton, Millais, Poynter, Sargent, Sickert, Steer, Tweed and Whistler. Whistler preferred Hetty, delighting in her wit and acuity. When he dithered over payments she told him point blank that she never posed without payment and that her minimum was half a guinea a day. 'Oh, Hetty dear, that's much too much,' Whistler tried. 'I'm so sorry,' she sneered. 'I'd quite forgotten you were one of the seven and sixpenny men.'

Julia PRINSEP:

Niece of the patron Sara Prinsep, in 1879 she modelled for Burne-Jones in *The Annunciation*, though the resultant face looks more like that of his wife Georgiana (see his *King Cophetua* for example). Julia had just married the obsessively industrious writer Leslie Stephen (which might explain her serious and resigned expression) and was, at the time, pregnant with her first child Vanessa, later to become the artist Vanessa Bell, elder sister to Virginia Woolf.

MATILDA PROUDFOOT and ISABELLA NICOL:

Two girls from Perth, immortalised by Millais in his *Autumn Leaves* and *The Blind Girl* before he moved away from Pre-Raphaelitism. (Sophie and Alice Millais were the other two girls in *Autumn Leaves*. Sophie drops leaves into the basket held by Alice.) The youngest girl, Isabella, may have been the model for his *L'enfant du Régiment* painted around the same time.

EDIE RAMAGE:

The pretty little girl in Millais's big-seller, *Cherry Ripe* (1879). *The Graphic* paid 1,000 guineas for it, printed a special colour supplement and sold 600,000 copies. (It is said they could have sold a million.) Edie was the niece of the editor of *The Graphic* and the costume was one she'd worn to a fancy dress ball (impersonating the girl in Sir Joshua Reynolds's *Penelope Boothby*).

ANNA OR NANNA RISI ('LA NANNA'):

Gorgeous Italian model, painted several times by Leighton, most notably in *Pavonia* (1858–9). Her pose, in which she gazes back at us across her shoulder, puzzled some viewers at the time. Today we are struck by her melancholy beauty, not her pose. In later life she became the mistress of the German artist, Anselm Feuerbach.

CHRISTINA ROSSETTI:

Used inevitably by her brother. She was Mary in his first major oil picture, *The Girlhood of Mary Virgin* (1848–9) in which her mother provided the head of St Anne. It had long been rumoured, and was finally admitted by Holman Hunt, that Christina helped model the head for Christ in his *The Light of the World*. Hunt wrote in a letter to Edward Clodd that the head was a composite formed from various male sitters (to give the head a masculine aspect) and that he used Christina for 'growth of eyebrows and eyelashes, the solemn expression, when the face was quiescent . . . I had only one sitting, and in spite of my general plan then of relying upon one painting for my final effect, I did later retouch the head from a variety of men, one political refugee from Paris lodging above me, for his beard, being among the number.' It seems typical of Hunt's fanatical attention to detail that he should use a series of people to model one head.

DANTE GABRIEL ROSSETTI:

With his striking Italianate looks it's not surprising that the artist featured in a number of his friends' works, most characteristically perhaps in Hunt's

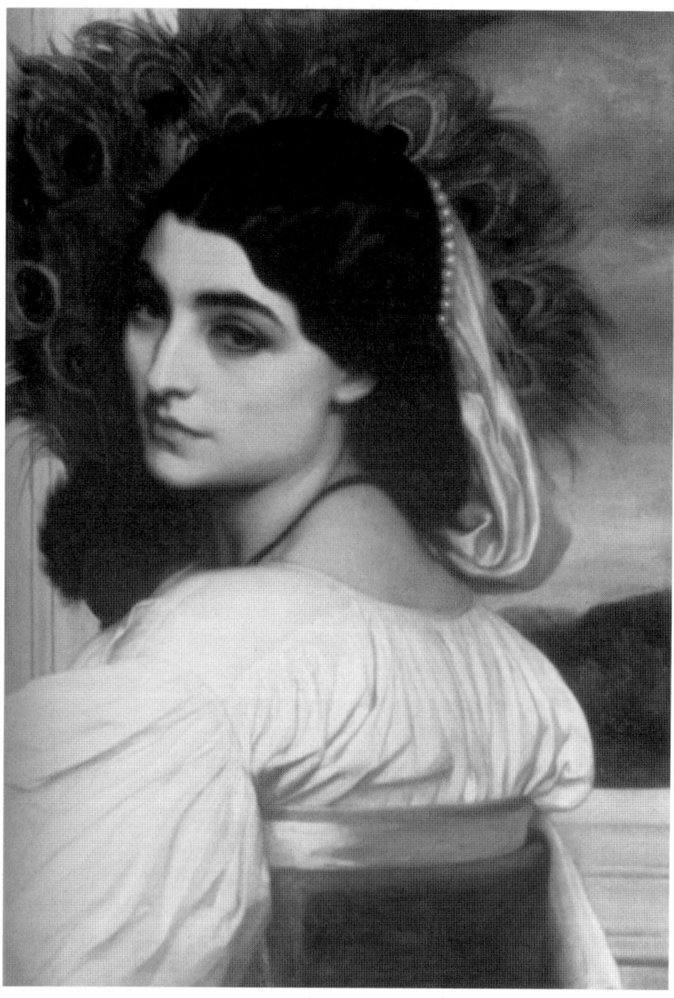

Pavonia (Anna Risi painted in 1858–9 by Leighton)

Rienzi (1848–9). He was Chaucer in Brown's painting, and was a late addition as the jester in Brown's *King Lear* (1848–9). He was Feste in Deverell's *Twelfth Night*. In Millais's *Isabella* he can be seen ignoring the action while knocking back his glass of wine. (His father sits four along from him, wiping his lips with a napkin, and his brother William is Lorenzo. Rossetti senior was also Joseph in Millais's *Carpenter's Shop*.)

William Michael ROSSETTI:

The loyal William was most useful as critic and archivist to the movement but also served as an occasional model; his face had just the right quality of saintly sacrifice, even in the straightforward but fine portrait of him painted by Madox Brown in 1856. In Hunt's massive *Converted British Family* he took the starring role, one might say, as the sheltered missionary.

Anne RYAN:

A famous beauty, we're told, though this is not especially obvious from her portrayal in Millais's *A Huguenot* (1851–2). It is tempting, though almost certainly fallacious, to ascribe her agonised expression to the fact that she was waiting to have an operation on her throat ('something to be cut away,' Millais wrote to Mrs Combe). In this painting Millais painted Anne's dark hair as blonde. He tinted it correctly in his *The Proscribed Royalist* (1852–3), a painting which was originally to have shown Effie Ruskin. (Effie replaced Anne in *The Order of Release*.)

Elizabeth SIDDAL:

Her first known appearance was as Viola in Deverell's *Twelfth Night* – perhaps fittingly, as Deverell was said to have discovered her, working in Mrs Tozer's hat shop. Hunt, in his memoirs, said that Deverell used his mother to persuade 'the miraculous creature' to sit for him, but that he found the work difficult. Hunt suggests that Rossetti helped him with the hair; this would be when Rossetti and Siddal met. She first modelled for Rossetti in *The First Anniversary of the Death of Beatrice* (1853–4); in this picture she is merely looking on and does not take the dominant position she would assume in later works. The two had a long on-off affair (mainly on) through the whole of the 1850s, despite his infidelities and reluctance to marry her. Only when she was ailing did he relent, and they married in May of 1860. By then the original passion had faded and they became as near as they ever would to a normal marriage. Lizzie became pregnant but the child was stillborn.

Lizzie's own death is a matter of conjecture: she was never well and had become increasingly dependent on laudanum; she may have killed herself or she may have accidentally overdosed. Rossetti was hysterical with grief (and almost certainly with guilt) and, in a flamboyant gesture, insisted that the manuscripts to all his poems should be buried with her in the coffin. Some years later he relented and had the coffin dug up and the manuscript recovered. Legend has it that her hair was still a flaming red.

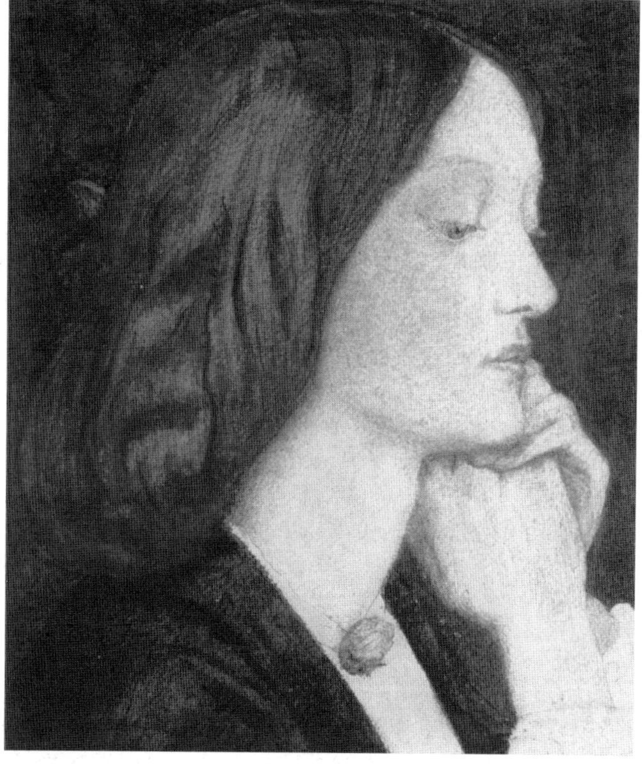

Elizabeth Siddal by Rossetti (1854)

Lizzie's original surname had been spelt Siddall but Rossetti persuaded her to drop the last letter to make the name seem less lower-class. From early in their relationship he taught and encouraged her – making great claims for her genius (that she was a better painter than he, etc.) and insisting that his listeners concur. She was, in fact, a competent but naive artist, very much in his style – and derivative, to be frank. She continued to model for him while working at her own paintings, and in 1857 she exhibited several paintings in the First Pre-Raphaelite Exhibition at Russell Place. The last picture Lizzie ever sat for was Rossetti's *St George and the Princess Sabra* where she kneels before St George holding out a helmet filled with water for him to wash his bloody hands. *Regina Cordium* (1860) is one of the finest portraits, though the star must be awarded to the posthumous *Beata Beatrice* (1863, with half a dozen replicas).

Ellen SMITH:

In Rossetti's *The Beloved* (1865–6) she posed for the virgin bridesmaid, foreground left. In this painting the 'black boy', who has intrigued many, was a lad Rossetti says he met by chance 'at the door of an hotel' and who replaced a (less colourful?) mulatto girl he had intended to use.

Christine SPARTALI:

Marie's sister, painted by Whistler as *La Princesse de pays de porcelain*, the painting which formed the centrepiece to Leighton's Peacock Room at 40 Prince's Gate (the room now recreated and displayed at the Freer Gallery of Art in the Smithsonian Institution, Washington).

Marie SPARTALI:

Daughter of Michael Spartali, who became Greek Consul-General after Ionides, and sister to the similarly beautiful Christine. She became Marie Stillman on marriage to the American journalist William J Stillman, though was sometimes still called Spartali. Marie was so lovely that when Swinburne saw her for the first time he said, 'She is so beautiful that I want to sit down and cry.' W Graham Robertson compared her to Janie Morris: 'The two marvels had many points in common: the same lofty stature, the same long sweep of limb, the "neck like a tower," the

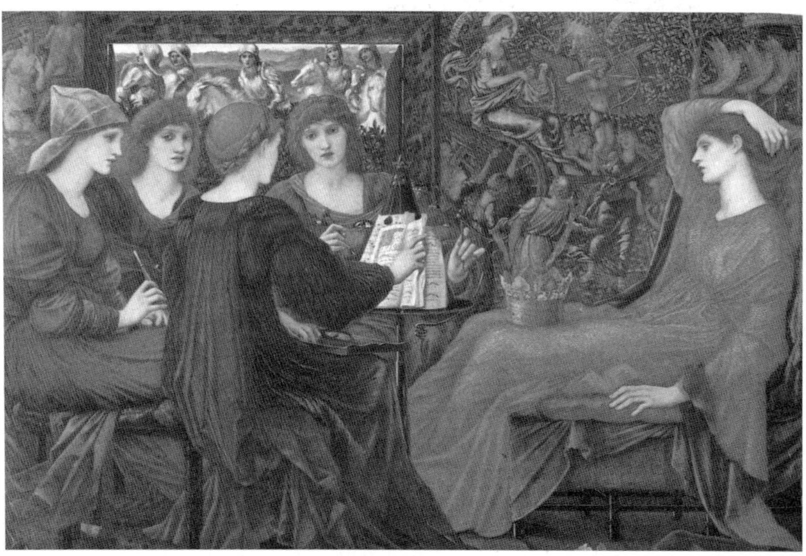

Maria Spartali given the Rossetti treatment in his *A Vision of Fiammetta* (1878)

night-dark tresses and the eyes of mystery, yet Mrs. Stillman's loveliness conformed to the standard of ancient Greece and could at once be appreciated, while study of her trained the eye to understand the more esoteric beauty of Mrs. Morris and "trace in Venus' eyes the gaze of Proserpine".' Rossetti painted her as *A Vision of Fiammetta* in 1878, having earlier teamed her with Alexa Wilding in *The Bower Meadow* of 1871–2. Burne-Jones used her in *The Mill* (1872–80) and *Danae and the Brazen Tower* (1887–8) among other works.

Her Mediterranean hot blood led her, in the 1860s, into a torrid and unfortunate affair with Lord Ranelagh, the man who had earlier been the lover/keeper of Holman Hunt's intended, Annie Miller. Marie became an artist herself, taking lessons from Ford Madox Brown. Barely had she started with Brown when Rossetti snapped her up as a model. Burne-Jones used her too. But her determination paid off and later in life she produced some fine paintings, influenced by Rossetti and Brown but more than mere copies. Gorgeous as artists made her, and gorgeous as by all accounts she was, the photograph of her by Julia Margaret Cameron portrays her as cold and rather plain. Perhaps in this instance the camera lied.

Frederick G STEPHENS:

An original member of the Pre-Raphaelite Brotherhood, he was the model for Ferdinand in Millais's odd but striking *Ferdinand Lured by Ariel* (1849–50).

Marie STILLMAN (*see* Marie Spartali)

William STILLMAN:

He was not a professional model, though he sat for Burne-Jones in *The Beguiling of Merlin* (1874). Stillman was an American journalist, a friend of Rossetti, and was the husband of the artist and model Marie (née Spartali).

Laura TENNANT:

Famed society beauty (wife of Alfred Lyttleton) who is believed to be the model for Burne-Jones's mermaid in *The Depths of the Sea* (1887). A mere pencil study of her head (as used in the painting) sold for £45,000 at Christie's in 2008.

Ellen Terry:

Watts was 46 in 1864 when he married his beautiful young model Ellen Terry. She was a mere 16. Even by the age-tolerant standards of the day their thirty-year difference caused some comment. Men tended not to marry till they'd made their way in the world, so they could lay down some capital and establish a regular and decent income – and while doing

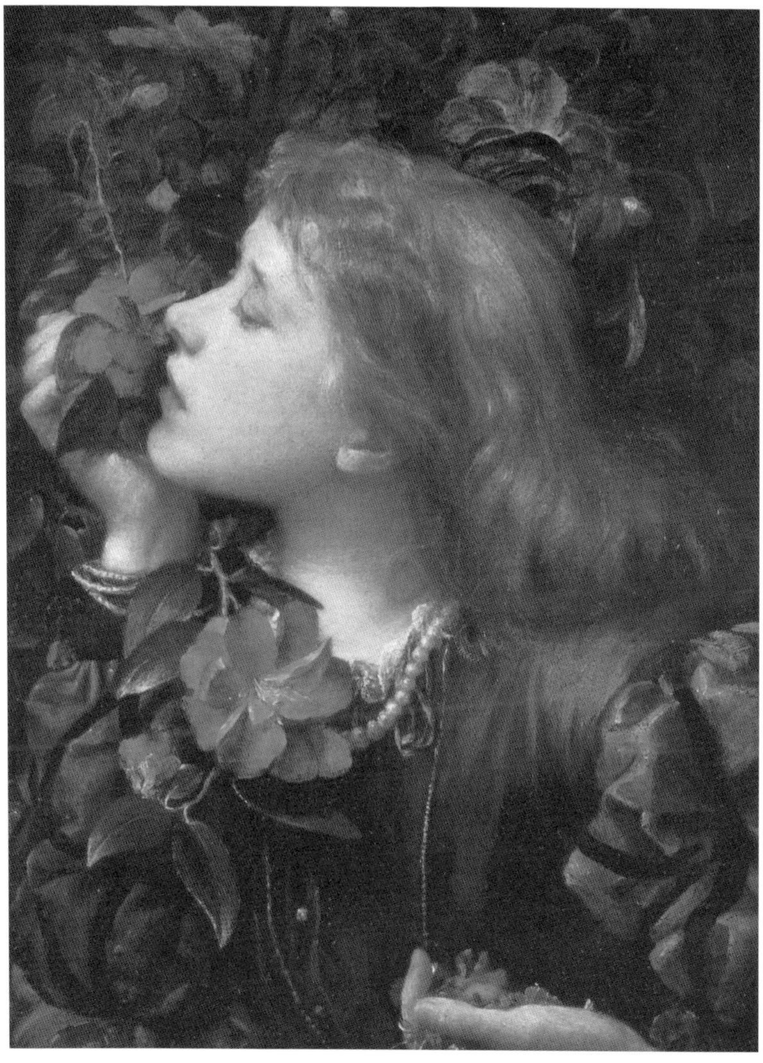

Choosing: the young Ellen Terry painted by Watts

so they were best untrammelled with wife and family. That rule certainly applied to a man hoping to be an artist. A woman, on the other hand, needed to be young – not for the man's sexual gratification (though that helped) but to be strong enough to bear his children: in those days of cruder medical care she needed to be strong. Many a girl saw the older man not as a disappointment, her lot in life, but as an ideal husband, a man who knew the world, who had his place in it, who could provide a safe and secure home – and who might become a second father. Watts, thirty years older, was certainly that. He saw himself as, if not her second father, then at least her benefactor – a not uncommon attitude then, though it may read today as hypocritical. Ellen Terry was on the stage, she came from a theatrical family, and the stage was no place, in Victorian eyes, for a young lady.

'I am going to tell you a thing that will perhaps surprise you,' Watts wrote to Lady Constance Leslie. 'I have determined to remove the youngest [of the Terry daughters] from the temptations and abominations of the Stage, give her an education and if she continues to have the affection she now feels for me, marry her.' He recognised the difference in their ages: 'but I think whatever the future brings, I can hardly regret taking the poor child out of her present life and fitting her for a better.'

It is a powerful stimulus to a man to pluck a young girl from a wretched life and have her eternally grateful to him, even if, as he wrote in that same letter: 'the expense will be considerable, for I shall have to compensate her family for the loss of her services.' The marriage was a famous disaster, lasting less than a year before Miss Terry fled (or according to some accounts, Watts sent her) back to her parents and a far more successful life on the stage. (Before treading the boards again she moved in with the architect Edward Godwin and bore him two children. Once Watts had divorced her she married again – an actor this time, not Godwin – and after that marriage failed she spent many years unmarried before finally marrying a much younger actor when she herself was 60.)

The young Ellen Terry was a beauty; some say she never lost her beauty; she was

> *'the Painter's Actress'*, said Graham Robertson. *'Pale eyes, rather small and narrow, a broad nose tilted at the tip, a wide mouth, a firm, large chin, pale hair, not decidedly golden, yet not brown – by no means a dazzling inventory of charms, yet out of these was evolved Ellen Terry, the most beautiful woman of her time.'*

James William WALLACK:

A leading actor of early Victorian times, who sat as Pizarro in Millais's pre-Pre-Raphaelite painting *Pizarro Seizing the Inca of Peru* (1846). He had played Pizarro in Sheridan's play of that name.

Emma WATKINS:

The country girl temptress in Holman Hunt's *The Hireling Shepherd*. While Hunt and Millais sat in a Surrey field – Hunt painting the background to that picture while Millais did the same for his *Ophelia* – the buxom servant girl would pass the time of day with them. Hunt asked her to model and, although she refused at first, he persuaded her mother to let her come to London to pose in his studio. (She was given her own room.) Hunt became infatuated with her, to the delight of his teasing friends (Rossetti nicknamed her 'The Coptic', for reasons lost in time), but once the painting was completed Emma went back to the country to marry her sailor boyfriend. Years later, in 1858, *Household Words* printed a thinly-veiled account of their relationship in a story by Robert Brough in which an artist not unlike Hunt fell for a country wench model known as 'Calmuck'. The story caused ructions within Hunt's family; Dickens (editor of *Household Words*) apologised, but the affair only inflamed Hunt's incipient paranoia.

WESTALL:

This male model might well hide his face in Millais's *The Order of Release* as he was at the time a deserter from a regiment of dragoons. Later he was arrested in an artist's studio. On his release he became a successful artist's model.

Julia WILD:

Professional model. She is picked out in sunlight as Catherine Roet in Madox Brown's *Chaucer* and portrays 'Protestant Faith' in his *Wycliffe*.

Alexa WILDING:

Possibly Rossetti's most beautiful model, she was the daughter of a piano-maker, and a more respectable young lady than some he used – 'the most retiring and least self-asserting of creatures', was how he described her to his mother. Alexa began sitting for Rossetti in 1865, and the first portrait he made of her was the wonderful *Monna Vanna* (completed in 1866 and later renamed *Belcolore* by Rossetti, though that name has not stuck). *Regina Cordium*, also 1866, was less successful. She was his beautiful *Veronica Veronese*, dressed in sumptuous green and seated at a dressing table while listening to a canary, and was the right-hand figure in *The Bower Meadow* (1870–3). She became the subject of *Dis Manibus* and *The Blessed Damozel* and was 'the lady of the garlands' in *La Ghirlandata* (1873).

MARIA (sometimes **MARIE,** occasionally **MARY**) **ZAMBACO:** Niece to Alexander Ionides, Maria was daughter to Demetrius Cassavetti and his wife Euphrosyne. While very young she married a Greek doctor named Demetrius Zambaco and had two children by him, though the

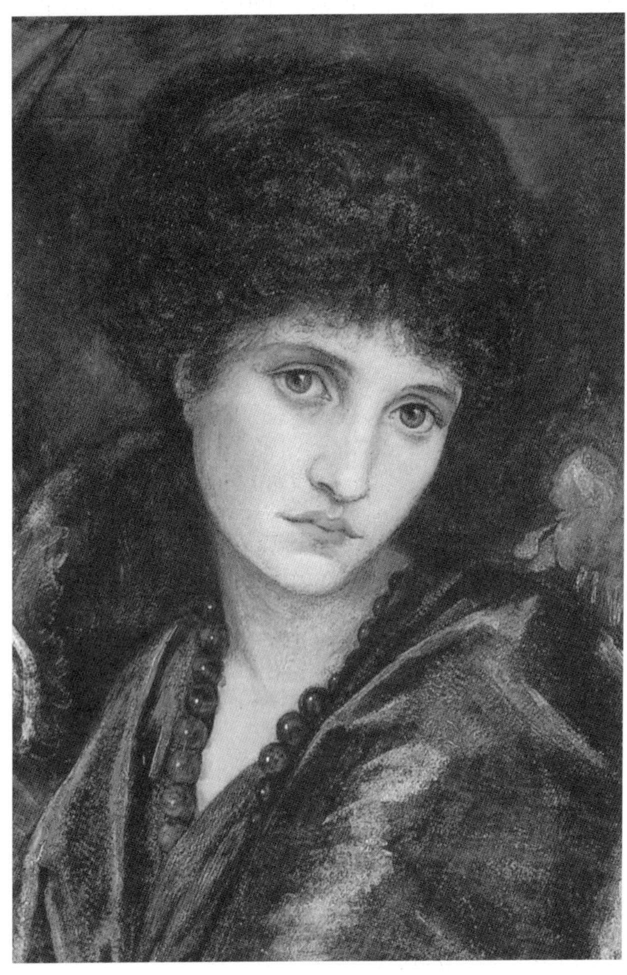

Portrait of Maria Zambaco (1870, detail) by Burne-Jones

marriage was short-lived. Stunningly beautiful, rich and passionately Greek, the young Maria Cassavetti Zambaco won the hearts of many, and in the late 1860s became the mistress of Burne-Jones. She was his model in several famous pictures, firstly as Psyche rescued by Cupid, and notably in *The Mill*, *Chant d'amour*, *The Beguiling of Merlin*, *Phyllis and Demophoon* and *Pygmalion and Galatea*. That she was passionately Greek, as Burne-Jones found to his cost when he tried to end the affair and found himself confronted by his histrionic mistress on the banks of the Regent's Canal, on the path outside Robert Browning's house. In her hand was a bottle containing enough laudanum to kill the pair of them. When Burne-Jones said that not only would he not join her in a double suicide but that their affair must end, she tried to throw herself in the water. Burne-Jones wrestled her to the ground, she fought, she screamed – and Mr Browning called a constable. It was a climactic night, she had played her strongest card, but Burne-Jones came to his senses and a few days later set off with his wife for France. But his nerves were shattered; he collapsed at Dover and had to be brought back home. Georgie wrote to her friend Rosalind Howard: 'For two or three days he was so ill that we kept his being at home a secret, that the house might be quite quiet. The irritation of the brain however has decreased so very much that he is up and in his studio . . .' Work, the soundest medicine.

Maria Zambaco, meanwhile, stormed around London trying to find where her lover was. No one would tell her. During a few days when Georgie, unwisely, took the children off for a holiday, Burne-Jones hid in his house and studio: 'I did not sleep at all in the night and tremble if a ring comes at the bell,' he wrote to George Howard. (There is a portrait of Maria by George Howard also.) Still the sparky Zambaco tried to track him down and, when Georgie returned, Burne-Jones confessed that he could not choose between them: he wanted to stay married to Georgie – whom he loved – but to continue seeing Maria, whom he also loved. What could Georgie do? It was no use telling him to pull himself together – the man was a wreck – and she daren't risk insisting he choose between them. In the end, broken but of stronger stuff than he, Georgie agreed to preserve the marriage. Burne-Jones continued his affair for at least another three years, and he continued to paint Maria. Sometime in the mid-70s she drifted away. Later she trained as a sculptor under Alphonse Legros, exhibiting in London from 1886 and in Paris from 1888.

WHERE TO SEE THE PICTURES

Many of the pictures in this book can be seen in public galleries, as shown below. Those not listed may be in private collections, including the author's own, or have not been traced. Any omissions or amendments should be notified to the publisher for correction in future editions.

Alma-Tadema: *In The Tepidarium*, LAG; **G P Boyce**: *The Mill on the Thames at Mapledurham*, FM; **John Brett**: *The Stonebreaker*, WAG; **Ford Madox Brown**: *The Last of England*, BMAG; *The Pretty Baa-Lambs*, BMAG; *Take Your Son*, Tate; **E C Burne-Jones**: *The Annunciation*, Lady Lever Art Gallery; *Portrait of Maria Zambaco*, Clemens-Sels-Museum, Neuss; *Laus Veneris*, Laing Art Gallery, Newcastle; **Leopold Egg**: *The Travelling Companions*, BMAG; **G Frampton**: *Mysteriarch*, WAG; **W P Frith**: *Annie Gambart*, Mercer Art Gallery; **Sir James Guthrie**: *Miss Sowerby*, NGS; **H von Herkomer**: *portrait of his wife*, Bushey Museum; **George Howard**: *sketch of Burne-Jones*, NPG; *Georgiana Burne-Jones* (drawing), Castle Howard; **W H Hunt**: *Primroses with Bird's Nest*, V&A; **C H Lear**: *Maclise*, NPG; **F Leighton**: *Bath of Psyche*, Tate; **G F Lewis**: *Life in the Hhareem*, V&A; **J E Millais**: *self-portrait 1880*, *My First & Second Sermons*, GAG; Uffizi, Florence; *The Blind Girl*, BMAG; **Albert Moore**: *A Summer Night*, WAG; *Azaleas*, Hugh Lane Gallery; **Richard Redgrave**: *The Poor Teacher*, Shipley Art Gallery, Gateshead; **D G Rossetti**: *The Day Dream*, V&A; *Helen of Troy*, Kunsthalle, Hamburg; *Astarte Syriaca*, CAGM; **J Singer Sargent**: *The Misses Vickers*, Sheffield Galleries & Museum; *self-portrait*, Kepplestone collection; **J J Shannon**: *The Purple Stocking*, National Gallery of S Africa; **Simeon Solomon**: *The Sleepers and the One that Watcheth*, Leamington Spa Art Gallery; **JMW Turner**: *self-portrait aged 23*, Tate; **Queen Victoria**: *self-portrait* (sketch), TRC; **Henry Wallis**: *Mary Ellen Meredith*, Ashmolean; **J W Waterhouse**: *Hylas and the Nymphs*, CAGM; **G F Watts**: *Lady Holland*, TWG; *Mammon*, Tate; *The Dean's Daughter*, TWG; *Choosing*, NPG; **Whistler**: *Little Rose of Lyme Regis*, Museum of Fine Arts, Boston; *The White Girl*, National Gallery of Art, Washington; **Winterhalter**: *The Young Queen*, TRC

BMAG = Birmingham Museum and Art Gallery
CAGM = City Art Gallery, Manchester
FM = Fitzwilliam Museum
GAG = Guildhall Art Gallery
LAG = Lady Lever Art Gallery, Port Sunlight
MOL = Museum of London
NGS = National Galleries of Scotland
NPG = National Portrait Gallery
NT = National Trust
TRC = The Royal Collection
TWG = The Watts Gallery
V&A = Victoria and Albert Museum
WAG = Walker Art Gallery

INDEX OF ARTISTS & MODELS

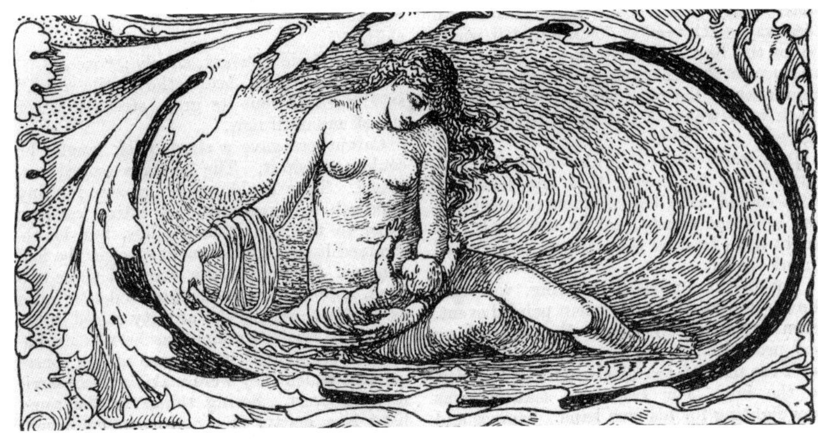

Part of a Walter Crane page design